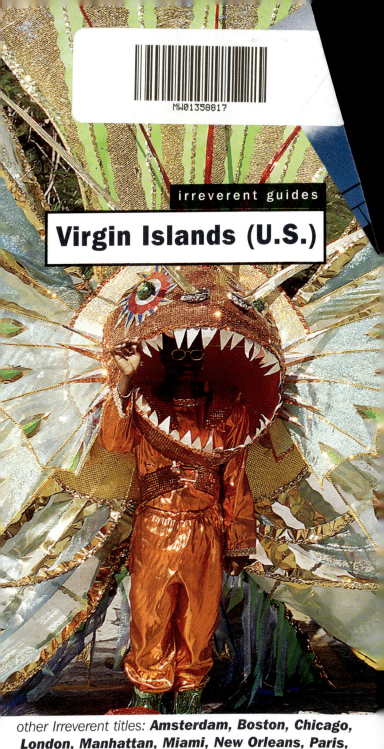

irreverent guides

Virgin Islands (U.S.)

other Irreverent titles: **Amsterdam, Boston, Chicago, London, Manhattan, Miami, New Orleans, Paris, San Francisco, Sante Fe, Washington, D.C.**

irreverent guides

Virgin Islands (U.S.)

BY

JORDAN SIMON

A BALLIETT & FITZGERALD BOOK
MACMILLAN • USA

Where to spot a boatload of tourists...

Cruise ship in Charlotte Amalie, see Diversions

Hobnob with the bigwigs...

Virgilio's, see Dining

Dine in a cliffside dollhouse...

Chateau Bordeaux, see Dining

Take a dip in a homemade ocean...

Pool at St. Croix by the Sea Hotel, see Accommodations

Be served by a beautiful waitstaff...

Asolare, see Dining

Take a hike (with your snorkel)...

Leinster Bay, see Getting Outside

See a castle built of sugar...

Annaberg Plantation, see Diversions

Maroon yourself offshore...

Hotel on the Cay, see Accommodations

Go Cruzan for crafts...

St. Croix LEAP, see Diversions

Tan, eat grapes, and conference call.

Hotel Grand Palazzo, see Accommodations

what's so irreverent?

It's up to you.

You can buy a traditional guidebook with its fluff, its promotional hype, its let's-find-something-nice-to-say-about-everything point of view. Or you can buy an Irreverent guide.

What the Irreverents give you is the lowdown, the inside story. They have nothing to sell but the truth, which includes a balance of good and bad. They praise, they trash, they weigh, and leave the final decisions up to you. No tourist board, no chamber of commerce will ever recommend them.

Our writers are insiders, who feel passionate about the cities they live in, and have strong opinions they want to share with you. They take a special pleasure leading you where other guides fear to tread.

How irreverent are they? One of our authors insisted on writing under a pseudonym. "I couldn't show my face in town again if I used my own name," she told me. "My friends would never speak to me." Such is the price of honesty. She, like you, should know she'll always have a friend at Frommer's.

Warm regards,

Michael Spring

Michael Spring
Publisher

a disclaimer

Prices fluctuate in the course of time, and travel information changes under the impact of the varied and volatile factors that influence the travel industry. Neither the author nor the publisher can be held responsible for the experiences of readers while traveling. Readers are invited to write to the publisher with ideas, comments, and suggestions for future editions.

about the author

Jordan Simon is the author of several guidebooks, as well as co-author of the *Celestial Seasonings Cookbook: Cooking With Tea*. The former contributing editor of *Taxi* and *Hamptons International* writes regularly for *Modern Bride*, *Physicians Travel & Meeting Guide*, *USAir Magazine* and *Caribbean Travel & Life*. He has written on various topics for *Elle*, *Travel & Leisure*, *Town & Country*, *Los Angeles*, *Diversion*, *Ski*, *Snow Country*, *Food Arts*, and *Wine Country International*.

photo credits

Page i: by William "Champagne" Chandler; Page ii: by Jordan Simon; Page iv, top and bottom by Jordan Simon; Page v, top: courtesy of Chateau Bordeaux, bottom: by Jordan Simon; Page vi, top: courtesy of Asolare, bottom: by Jordan Simon; Page vii, top, middle and bottom by Jordan Simon; Page viii: by Jordan Simon.

Balliett & Fitzgerald, Inc.
Series editor: Holly Hughes / Executive editor: Tom Dyja / Managing editor: Duncan Bock / Production editor: Howard Slatkin / Photo editor: Rachel Florman / Editorial assistants: Jennifer Leben, Maria Fernandez, Iain McDonald
Macmillan Travel art director: Michele Laseau

Design by Tsang Seymour Design Studio

All maps © Simon & Schuster, Inc.

Air travel assistance courtesy of Continental Airlines

MACMILLAN TRAVEL
A Simon & Schuster Macmillan Company
1633 Broadway
New York, NY 10019

Copyright © 1996 by Simon and Schuster, Inc.

All rights reserved. No part of this book may be reproduced or transmitted in any form or by an means, electronic or mechanical, including photocopying, recording, or by any information storage and retrieval system, without permission in writing from the Publisher.

Macmillan is a registered trademark of Macmillan, Inc.

ISBN 0-02-860688-4
ISSN 1087-0431

special sales

Bulk purchases (10+ copies) of Frommer's Travel Guides are available to corporations at special discounts. The Special Sales Department can produce custom editions to be used as premiums and/or for sales promotions to suit individual needs. Existing editions can be produced with custom cover imprints such as corporate logos. For more information write to: Special Sales, Simon & Schuster, 1633 Broadway, New York, NY 10019.

Manufactured in the United States of America

contents

INTRODUCTION   1

U.S. VIRGIN ISLANDS MAP   4

YOU PROBABLY DIDN'T KNOW   5

ACCOMMODATIONS   10
    Winning the Reservations Game (13)
    Is There a Right Address? (13)
    THE LOWDOWN   14
        Least bang for your buck (14)
        Best beach for your buck (14)
        Where to find a swimsuit model (14)
        For travelers who can't sit still (15)
        Honeymoon havens (15)
        For singles who would rather not be (15)
        Funky but fun (16)
        Rooms with a view (16)
        Friendliest staff (16)
        Rudest staff (17)
        May I get that for you, sir? (17)
        Wet dreams for water sports (17)
        Cool pools (18)
        Family values (18)

Our hearts were young and gay (18)
For "green" travelers with lots of green (19)
For "green" travelers without much green (20)
Luscious love nests (20)
For travelers with old money (20)
For travelers who confuse cash with class (21)
Liveliest clientele (21)
Where the power brokers stay (22)
Historic surroundings (22)
Cheap sleeps (23)
Condo-mania and suite stuff (24)
Least offensive of the chains (25)
Most elegant ambience (26)
When everything else is filled (27)

THE INDEX 27
A to Z lists of places to stay, with vital statistics
St. Thomas 28
St. Croix 34
St. John 39
MAPS 43

DINING 48
Only in the U.S. Virgin Islands (50)
How to Dress (51)
When to Eat (52)
Getting the Right Table (52)
Where the Chefs Are (52)
THE LOWDOWN 53
Overrated (53)
Truly elegant (53)
Institutions (54)
Where the locals go (55)
Something fishy (55)
Real island cuisine, mon (56)
Best breakfasts (57)
Best brunch (57)
Best lunch (58)
Ringside seats for people-watching (58)
Where the buffet tables groan (59)
The French connection (59)
Around the Mediterranean (60)
Alla Italia (60)
Asian delights (61)
For those who only wear black (61)

Swoony harbor views (62)
Power spots (62)
Best place to seal a deal (62)
See-and-be-scenes (63)
Where the yachties hang (63)
Most beautiful waitstaff (63)
Friendliest waitstaff (64)
Rudest waitstaff (64)
Isn't it romantic? (65)
For single women who want to be left alone (65)
For singles who don't want to be left alone (65)
Best burgers (66)
Best wine list (66)
Caffeine scenes (67)
On the beach (casual) (67)
On the beach (elegant) (67)
Sunset views to choose (67)
Most creative kitchen (68)
Historic settings (69)
For committed carnivores (69)
Pizzas with pizzazz (69)
Best food for the money (70)
Cheap eats (70)
Most sinful desserts (70)
Kid pleasers (71)
Only on Mondays (71)

THE INDEX 72
A to Z lists of restaurants, with vital statistics
St. Thomas 72
St. Croix 82
St. John 90
MAPS 95

DIVERSIONS 100
Getting Your Bearings (102)
THE LOWDOWN 103
Overrated (103)
Tourist traps you won't mind getting caught in (104)
Fortifying yourself (104)
When sugar was king (106)
Gimme that old-time religion (107)
Only in the Cruzan rain forest (107)
Museums without walls (108)
Do-it-yourself museums (110)

Save it for a rainy day (111)
Local color (111)
Bird's-eye views (112)
Fish-eye views (113)
Great walks (113)
A walk on the wild side (115)
Kid stuff (115)
Where to escape the crowds (116)
Green spaces (116)

THE INDEX   **117**
A to Z lists of diversions, with vital statistics
- **St. Thomas**   **117**
- **St. Croix**   **121**
- **St. John**   **123**

MAPS   **125**

GETTING OUTSIDE   130
THE LOWDOWN   132

Hitting the beach (132)
Windsurfing and other macho stuff (136)
With a tube in your face (137)
Par for the course (139)
The tennis racket (139)
With the wind at your back (140)
Ahoy there, matey (141)
Island-hopping, the easy way (142)
Something's fishy (143)
Stretching your legs (143)
Back in the saddle (145)

SHOPPING   146

Target Zones (148)
Bargain Hunting (149)
Trading with the Natives (150)
Hours of Business (150)

THE LOWDOWN   150

If you want to attract attention on the beach (150)
Fashion forward (150)
Natty threads for him (151)
Tackiest tchotchkes (151)
Tchotchkes with cachet (152)
Where money talks (152)
Wacky and one-of-a-kind (152)

Precious old stuff (153)
Fake old stuff (153)
Unusual book nooks (154)
The island beat (154)
Incredible edibles (154)
Putting your two scents in (154)
Diamonds are a girl's best friend (155)
For those born with silver spoons in their mouths (155)
Clothes to make you look grown up (156)
Clothes to make you look young (156)
Objets for the home (157)
The art bug (158)
Ethnic goodies (159)
Leather trade (160)
Kid stuff (161)
How much can I bring back duty-free? (161)

THE INDEX — 161

A to Z lists of shops, with vital statistics

St. Thomas — 161
St. Croix — 169
St. John — 174

NIGHTLIFE AND ENTERTAINMENT — 178

Sources (180)

Liquor Laws and Drinking Hours (180)

THE LOWDOWN — 180

Best happy-hour munchies (180)
Liveliest happy hours (181)
Most outrageous bars (182)
Coziest bars (182)
Where the locals go (182)
Where the labels go (183)
For yachties (184)
For the brunch crowd (184)
Dance fever (184)
If you haven't gotten sick of karaoke (184)
The big game (185)
For drinks that come with those little umbrellas (185)
Best for one-night stands (185)
Best for one-night bands (185)
Safe after-hours walks (186)
Best beach bars—nocturnal variety (186)
Painting the town pink (186)

    The college scene (187)
    For twentysomethings (187)
    For thirtysomethings (187)
    For fortysomethings (188)
    For fiftysomethings (188)
    For a little bit o' sleaze (188)
    On the kinky side (189)
    All that jazz (189)
    Tickling the ivories (189)
    Classical sounds (190)
    The play's the thing (190)
    Concerts and dance performances (190)
    The sporting life (191)

THE INDEX — 191

A to Z lists of nightspots, with vital statistics

St. Thomas — **191**
St. Croix — **197**
St. John — **201**

HOTLINES & OTHER BASICS — 204

    Airports (205)
    Buses (206)
    Car rentals (206)
    Dentists (207)
    Doctors (207)
    Driving around (207)
    Drugstores (207)
    Emergencies (207)
    Ferries (208)
    Festivals and special events (208)
    Guided tours (208)
    Newspapers (209)
    Opening and closing times (210)
    Parking (210)
    Radio stations (210)
    Restrooms (210)
    Smoking (210)
    Taxes (210)
    Taxis (210)
    Telephones (211)
    Tipping (211)
    Travel documents (211)
    Visitor information (211)

introduction

A fellow travel writer once described the U.S. Virgin Islands as Cleveland with palm trees... her husband quickly retorted that Cleveland had cleaned up its act.

Okay, so the U.S.V.I. haven't been one of the more fashionable Caribbean destinations of late. And St. Thomas is admittedly the most developed island in the Caribbean, with its strip malls and ubiquitous satellite dishes (now jokingly referred to as the "local flower").

But then most tourists think St. Thomas *is* the U.S.V.I. Meanwhile St. Croix has some of the most perfectly preserved forts and sugar plantations in the Caribbean. And St. John, more than two thirds of which is protected National Park, is in the forefront of eco-tourism. Both islands are lined with alluring, uncrowded beaches that range from idyllic, palm-lined stretches to secluded, rocky coves accessible only to those with hiking shoes or a boat (see Getting Outside).

In fact, the islands offer different faces to a surprisingly wide range of travelers. For the ecologically minded, St. John and St. Croix are ideal vacation spots. For those who crave colonial atmosphere, the main towns Christiansted, Frederiksted, and even parts of Charlotte Amalie ooze Old World charm. And if you're seeking non-stop action (whether shopping, drinking, or parasailing), St. Thomas fits the bill for fewer bills than most Caribbean destinations. That island's overdevelopment (although even St. Thomas has its pastoral pockets), and the resulting competition between hotels *has* led to some of the Caribbean's best buys. Add to that a range of lodging and dining options unrivaled elsewhere in the Caribbean and you have some of the reasons several million folks visit this unfashionable destination annually.

"So what about the crime problem?" ask confused travelers. Well, for the most part, the problem has been exaggerated by the media. (Yes, three American tourists were shot outside a bar—not listed in this guidebook—on the remote East End of St. Thomas in early 1996. But that incident, the first of its kind in a decade, involved no robbery, and at press time the police were reportedly exploring other motives.)

Media reports suggesting unrest in the wake of Hurricane Marilyn were especially misleading. Cameras from one major network zoomed in on locals carting boxes of fruits and vegetables from big supermarkets, as the reporter discussed generally chaotic conditions. What the report didn't say was that the supermarkets had offered greengrocer's and other perishable items for free, before they rotted. When Governor Roy Thompson himself got wind of this and asked the network to recant its story, the official reply reportedly was, "We'll screen the videotape, but won't mention looting." But looting was precisely what those images conveyed.

In fact, after Hurricane Marilyn, both locals and expatriates rallied together much as they had after Hugo, helping one another rebuild their lives. This doesn't mean you shouldn't exercise the same caution going out in Charlotte Amalie as you would in any other good-sized American town. But let's be direct: Much of this scaremongering reportage smacks of racism—those "gangs on the streets" aren't vicious hoodlums. They're usually locals out liming (partying) on a Friday night.

My introduction to this sort of cultural misunderstanding came during my very first trip to the U.S.V.I. My mother had chosen St. John's Caneel Bay (then as now one of the hoity-toitiest properties in the Caribbean, where children were to be seen but not heard; indeed I believe my mere presence required a special dispensation). I was 12, forced to wear a blue blazer, rep tie, and unmercifully itchy grey flannel pants to dinner. One day, I was bored silly lying on one of the exquisite beaches ringing the resort. An old man, his face as creased as a crumpled paper bag, motioned me over as two hotel guards bore down on him: guests were never to be disturbed.

The fellow winked at me conspiratorially, then placed a little piece of driftwood he had whittled into a fanciful seahorse in my hand before they hustled him off.

Nearly a quarter century later, that memory lingers. What did those guards think? That anyone who could afford to stay at Caneel Bay wanted little or no interaction with the locals? Truth is, there are many Caribbean islands whose service economy barely conceals the residents' contempt for their guests. Although I've never had that experience here, U.S. Virgin Islanders *are* Americans. Which means they're direct, sometimes to the point of brashness, and just as curious about you as you are about them. This is not "Fantasy Island," and the residents aren't going to pretend otherwise. That's part of their charm. And yet, while islanders freely enjoy the trappings and traps of American consumerism, they're also enormously proud of their culture and traditions. That's also part of their charm.

Which brings us back to Cleveland and palm trees. The fact is, St. Thomas, St. Croix, and St. John feel both familiar *and* foreign. English is spoken, but with a graceful tropic lilt. And the islands' African roots emerge in the snatch of a racy reggae ditty along a Charlotte Amalie street; in the spices that heat up the local cuisine; in the jambalaya of sights, sounds and smells of a Carnival that rivals those of Rio, Trinidad, and The Big Easy for sheer flamboyance.

Maybe its just that seductive combination of real-world edge and unexpected exoticism—Cleveland and palm trees— that keeps pulling me back to this corner of the Caribbean.

Recently, I found myself walking down a Charlotte Amalie street, frankly tired of the hucksterism, the obsequious salesladies in the tonier shops, the aggressive vendors in the streets. A woman was selling homemade "bush teas," shouting "cure anyt'ing what ails ya" like any snake-oil salesman hawking his elixirs. I stopped to examine her mixtures, and we animatedly discussed local folklore, interrrupted by several local ladies who purchased the blends of herbs, roots, and flowers designed to combat anything from impotence to impetigo. I turned to leave. "You ain't buying nuttin', mon?" she asked. "Nah, just browsing, thanks," I replied. She eyed me shrewdly. "You worry too much, don't you; probably don't get enough sleep." She reached down for a bunch of soursop leaves and handed them to me. "Brew some tea, mon, it'll help you relax. Don't you forget, dat's why you're here."

Indeed.

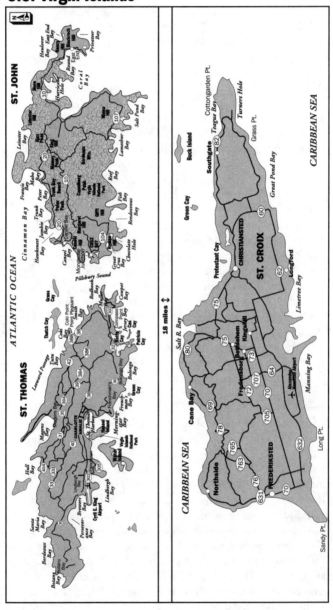

you probably didn't know

How to go about island-hopping by yacht... Determining their own itinerary, sailing from one cay to another in search of the dream beach (and beach bar), yachties feel like the whole Caribbean is their oyster. Bareboating and crewed yacht charters are becoming increasingly popular, and they actually cost less than a landlocked deluxe vacation, without the "if it's Tuesday, this must be Barbados" hysteria of cruises (see p. 132 for more details). That said, there is restricted access to many beaches, especially on St. John. And you must call ahead to reserve a slip in Charlotte Amalie with all the requisite facilities, especially since anchoring stern-to in the harbor is treacherous, thanks to the combination of fierce undertow and heavy wake from all the yachts, fishing boats, commercial ships, and cruise liners.

Where to hide when the cruise ships come in... You can't—not entirely. A plague of shoppers descends daily on St. Thomas, giving Charlotte Amalie the air of a Macy's sale plonked down in the middle of a flea market. The lightest traffic days tend to be Monday and Saturday. Consult the cruise ship listings in the local papers or at the Tourist Office. And even if you hit town on the same day as the "Love Boat," remember: the crowds are here to shop, pausing only maybe to gawk at Magens Bay, the picture-postcard beach on the north shore of St. Thomas. So head for the quieter East End, check out museums like Seven Arches and the historic papers collection of the Enid M. Baa Public Library, stick to your hotel beach, or repair to a local hangout in the Frenchtown quarter. After the swarms leave (around 4pm) the island will be yours again.

How to find a beach to yourself... You won't if you stick to the Magen's Bay/Trunk Bay circuit (though these are often deserted by late afternoon). There are numerous crescents on the northern side of St. Thomas (such as Hull Bay and West and East Carot) that are gorgeous, but not as popular because of the rough Atlantic currents. Four-wheel-drive brings you to the alluring, empty beaches of St. Croix's arid East End. And if you have a boat, the scalloped coves of St. John, like Lameshur and Salt Pond bays, are often yours for the day (see Getting Outside, for more details on all of the above).

Where the best scuba diving is... The denizens of the deep parade in all their finery at Buck Island off St. Croix and Trunk Bay off St. John, both protected reserves. You'll even find a few dramatic caves, drops, and multi-hued walls. The U.S.V.I. offer easy access, with most anchorages close to live reefs and superb conditions for beginning divers.

Is there anything left after all the hurricanes?... No question about it, it took a long time for St. Croix to recover from Hugo, and the one-two punch of Luis and Marilyn knocked off a few more roofs. But signs of devastation are few and far between. As usual, the first media reports were greatly exaggerated, claiming a whopping 80 percent of the buildings on St. Thomas were damaged. It might have been 80 percent, *only* if you count every building that lost so much as a pane of glass or one roof tile. And the most severe damage was to private residences. As of January 1996 the island was still blanketed with "blue roofing"—the Caribbean term for tarp stretched over the building in place of a roof, usually in a fetching shade of teal blue. It can't be stressed strongly enough: tourism is so vital for St. Thomas that whatever it took, things got fixed. By the time this is published, the island will look better than ever. (Locals joke that the hurricanes just give them an excuse to make long-needed repairs.) Most major hotels were up and running (albeit with renovations continuing—a wing here, a pool bar there) by mid to late December 1995. And hotel rates plummeted as much as 60 percent into February 1996 to help drum up business. Vegetation throughout the U.S.V.I. is lusher than it was pre-Marilyn; resort grounds have been lovingly tended. Beaches that had eroded were already returning by December, and many hotels dredged up or imported additional sand. In fact, the hurricane actually expanded some lucky beaches, such as the Hyatt's on St. John and the Grand Palazzo's on St. Thomas. Disregard reports that some hotels have become virtual dive sites; those rooms that were underwater and filled with sand have new paint, carpets, tiles, and furnishings. In some cases, the refurbishment is vastly more tasteful than what was there before.

How addresses work (not)

You know those old comedy routines. A stranger arrives in town, asks for directions, and the reply goes something like: "Well, turn left at the Shell station, go down the road a piece until you see an old woman knitting on her porch—that's Hester Collins—turn right at her chicken coop, and when you get to her former sister-in-law's house (you can't miss it), take a sharp left—then ask the first person you see...." It's no joke in the Virgin Islands. Street addresses plum don't make sense sometimes. Many Christiansted buildings have two street numbers; in St. John's Cruz Bay there's no street name but the building may have a number; and Charlotte Amalie's Main Street has both numbered and unnumbered sections. So, the bottom line is that when there is no formal physical address—just a town or estate name—call or ask someone. Just think of it as a quick introduction to island folklore. And when you get lost, ponder the fact that Columbus never would have found this paradise at all, if he'd known where he was.

Which side of the road to drive on...

The roads are among the best in the Caribbean, although they corkscrew precipitously on mountainous St. Thomas and St. John. The drivers are another matter. Driving is technically on the left, one of the carryovers from the days of Danish rule. Locals tend to drive slowly on flat stretches, stopping frequently in the middle of the road, holding up traffic while they gossip with friends going in the opposite direction. But they delight in taking curves and steeps at breakneck speeds that would make a Grand Prix racer blanch. Neither honking nor the evil eye seem to help; patience and a sense of humor do.

Whether or not the fish is frozen... Sad to say, most fish down here is frozen—and be thankful that it is, because the coral reefs surrounding most Caribbean islands are infested with microscopic parasites called ciguatera. They don't harm the fish that feed on coral, but they just love to attack the central nervous systems of human beings who eat those fish. That doesn't mean you're reduced to eating Mrs. Paul's fish cakes slathered with a tartar sauce that tastes like zinc oxide. Top hotels and restaurants buy from fishermen who trawl several miles out in open water, where the little ciguatera beasties can't thrive. Or they serve fresh-frozen fish; it's a safe bet that your salmon wasn't caught locally, but the kingfish, wahoo, snapper, and tuna probably were.

What the deal is with Charlotte Amalie's cabbies... Early in the morning you'll see them lined up in ranks at Emancipation Square, patient as vultures. Once the cruise ships dock, they keep an eagle-eye out for shopping bags. Be as inconspicuous as possible. Dress downmarket and carry your purchases in a big shoulder bag—without designer labels. A small duffel or backpack is even better. A crazy gleam in the eye, like that of a hardened New York subway rider, wouldn't hurt either. Anywhere outside of Charlotte Amalie, forget about getting a cab until a ferry docks at Red Hook or Cruz Bay. These cabbies are more interested in playing dominoes and gossiping; they're there to corral fares from the ferries, and won't budge between arrivals.

Where to get back to nature... St. John is the obvious choice. It's two-thirds protected national park, with park rangers leading frequent guided walks. But so-called "ecotourism" is generally pretty big on all the islands: there are "green" or eco-friendly resorts on each island, "ecowalks" on the East End of St. Croix, and EarthWatch moonlight expeditions to study gargantuan leatherback turtles laying their eggs during the spring.

How to bone up on local politics... St. Thomas is home to two of the Caribbean's spikiest publications,

Pride and the *V.I. Voice*, which offer everything from scathing indictments of the current administrations to salacious local gossip. And St. Croix's *Island Melee* is a delightfully scurrilous little rag that acts as the proverbial thorn in the side of government.

Where not to watch crab races with drunken yachties... True, just like a Monty Python routine, scads of European tourists love the manufactured limbo contests and booze cruises, thinking they're getting the true Caribbean experience. But it's not all rum and reggae down here. You can also take in the quite civilized classical concert series at St. Thomas's Tillett Gardens (in a beautiful outdoor setting) and St. Croix's Estate Whim Plantation Museum (in a restored 18th-century great house), which are the best places to meet the islands' movers and shakers. Jazz aficionados have their pick of several clubs, from smoky and subdued to bright and loud. There are even several piano bars where straights and gays alike knock down a few and belt out show tunes for all they're worth (see Nightlife and Entertainment).

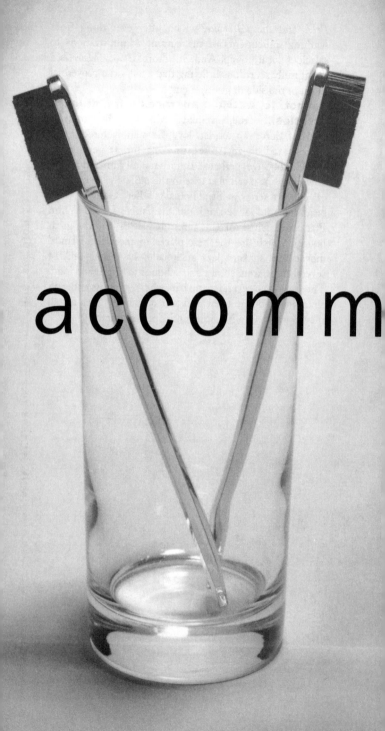
accomm

1
odations

Okay, here are your choices. There are glitzy beachfront resorts, self-contained compounds that are usually stratospherically priced and devoid of island flavor. Then there are the funky little inns. These are usually described as "quaint" in guidebooks, but, depending on what you're willing to pay, the quaintness can extend to leaky plumbing and no air-conditioning. The cheapest accommodations are the ecologically sound campgrounds, like the National Park Service's campgrounds on St. John, an impossibly lush isle where everyone from Rockefellers to rock stars has escaped back to nature.

The only wild card in the offing is an overwhelmingly popular bill passed in 1994 legalizing gambling on St. Croix; the arrival of casinos is contingent on the construction of three humongous hotels (presently no property in St. Croix has more than 150 rooms). The first casinos will be built at the earliest in 1998. In 1989 Hurricane Hugo singlehandedly decimated St. Croix's tourism industry; even after the contractors and repair crews left, hotel occupancy plummeted to below 50 percent, leaving locals desperate to find alternate sources of revenue. Politicos are hoping the new legislation will attract major chains and players to St. Croix. More likely, the complexion of the island will change drastically, with gamblers who never budge from their hotels to add to the coffers of local businesses. If you want a taste of the more bucolic destination St. Croix still is, visit now.

And what of the effects of hurricanes Luis and Marilyn in 1995? St. Croix's hotels suffered almost no damage, and St. John's accommodations were likewise unharmed—with two big exceptions: Caneel Bay and the Hyatt Regency, both as luxe as resorts get. The Hyatt looked fine in January '96; plans were to reopen March 1. Caneel Bay sustained more serious damage to several beachfront rooms, but Rosewood Hotels has vowed to restore everything—including the decor—to its former lavishness. The resort is scheduled to reopen by October 1996.

St. Thomas's major hotels didn't wait for the insurance checks to arrive; all but two reopened by March 1996. (During reconstruction, most stayed open, offering incredible 50-to 80-percent-off deals for December 1995–February 1996.) Grand Palazzo and Stouffer's are not scheduled to be back in business until June 1996; certain properties like Wyndham Sugar Bay will continue refurbishment of some public spaces into October, but they will return—and in pre-hurricane form. In fact, it's safe to say that by the time this book hits the stores, everything will be pretty much back to normal.

The biggest unknown is such condominium properties as Pavilions and Pools, and Point Pleasant. The primary problem here is that the units are individually owned and, of course, it's taking forever for the condo boards to decide how best to proceed. (About the only thing the Point Pleasant board agrees upon is their fury with *Condé Nast Traveler*, which reported in November 1995 that the resort had slid down the hill into the ocean. It hadn't, and gossips are mongering that the board is contemplating suing the magazine, whose motto is "Truth in Travel.") They, too, will return, but opening dates have not yet been set.

Winning the Reservations Game

There is conceivably nothing more annoying than waiting to check in at a hotel's front desk, chatting casually with one of 173 Elks milling about the lobby, and learning that they're paying half what you are. What can you do about it? Unfortunately, not much. (You can always threaten your travel agent that you'll take your business elsewhere, but that's another holiday entirely.) To avoid this vacation-buster, simply ask about package rates when you book. Every resort in the U.S. Virgin Islands, even such snooty properties as Caneel Bay and Grand Palazzo, offers deals. There's a special price break for everyone under the sun: honeymooners, tennis players, golfers, scuba divers, and more. It never hurts to ask for extras anyway; are breakfast, airport transfers, cocktail parties, or beach shuttles (for accommodations in town) included? If you're trying to save money, ask yourself if you really need that ocean view; pool- or garden-view rooms at leading resorts usually have the same configuration and amenities at a far lower rate, and it's not as if you have a view of a brick wall or parking lot. Moreover, if you wait until the snowbirds fly home, you'll receive as much as a 50 percent discount for visiting between April 15 and December 15.

Is There a Right Address?

Needless to say, resorts right on the water are the most expensive, desirable accommodations. In general, the best beaches (and top resorts) are clustered on the western half of St. John, the eastern half of St. Thomas, and the north coast of St. Croix. But if you're looking to save a few bucks (or shopping and nightlife are the main draws for you), consider staying in town. Both Charlotte Amalie and Christiansted offer reasonable lodging in delightful colonial inns, where the ambience is charmingly old-fashioned and the plumbing thankfully newfangled.

The Lowdown

Least bang for your buck... Emerald Beach Resort (St. Thomas) is a perfectly fine property, but woefully overpriced for a glorified motel. So is its St. Croix counterpart the **Tamarind Reef Hotel**: it does offer kitchenettes and far more spacious quarters for lower prices than the larger resorts, but for value it pales in comparison to the condos and Christiansted hotels.

Best beach for your buck... Laurance Rockefeller created **Caneel Bay Resort** as his hideaway because it has what just might be the most fabulous location in the Caribbean: its rooms are sprawled along seven glittering beaches of powdered ivory. On St. Thomas, **Marriott's Morningstar Resort** sits amid extravagant greenery on a beach that stretches out like a cat basking in the sun. It's a favorite with the pretty young things of both genders who work the cruise ships, all tanned, toned, and wearing skimpy bathing suits. The long, lavish strand of **Sapphire Beach** fronts many leading resorts, including the one of the same name. St. Croix's **Buccaneer Hotel** offers a choice of three pristine crescents, including the relatively secluded Whistle Beach, where you never know what romantic doings might be going on. **On the Beach Resort** commands a long, tawny stretch of sand that is one of the Caribbean's classics.

Where to find a swimsuit model... You know that scene in *Ten*, Blake Edwards's middle-aged wet dream, where the camera lovingly pans Bo Derek as she emerges sleek and shining from the sea, water droplets flying off her braided mane? It's a scene that could be replayed daily at the ritzier-than-thou **Grand Palazzo** (St. Thomas), **Carambola Beach Resort** (St. Croix), and **Hyatt Regency** (St. John), all of which have hosted numerous photo shoots. Actually, it isn't much fun when the crews are in town: pony-tailed shutterbugs with phony Euro-accents force management to close off your favorite section of beach for the day, and whale-bellied, cigar chomping, tonsorially challenged men shackled in gold chains make nuisances of themselves, staring at the cheesecake like deer caught in headlights. But hey, it happens at every Caribbean resort currently in vogue.

For travelers who can't sit still... St. John's posh **Hyatt Regency** hums with a topnotch tennis program, a dazzling array of water sports options, two hotel rooms converted into cardiovascular and weight-training rooms, all sorts of regularly scheduled hikes, and much more. St. Croix's **Buccaneer Hotel** has a world-renowned tennis program, a championship 18-hole golf course (with some thrilling Caribbean views), a fully equipped spa and health center, and water sports and nature hikes galore, not to mention a list of weekly activities that runs several pages long—movie screenings, tennis tournaments, and on and on. On St. Thomas, the **Stouffer Renaissance** and **Marriott's Frenchman's Reef/Morningstar Beach Resorts** keep guests occupied with a similar list of frantic activities. But the king, not surprisingly, is the all-inclusive **Bolongo Bay Beach and Tennis Club**, along with its more upmarket sibling, **Bolongo Elysian Beach Resort**. Packages include not one but three sailing trips, tons of recreational options, a state-of-the-art fitness center, and nonstop frenzy by the pools and in the lounges.

Honeymoon havens... St. Croix's **Villa Madeleine** is posh, secluded, and elegant; the staff excels at knowing their business but not yours. If you want a wedding trip loaded with activity in tony surroundings, you won't do much better than the **Buccaneer Hotel** (St. Croix) or St. John's **Hyatt Regency**, both of which provide that honeymoon essential, room service. Although the villas are not on the beaches, the privacy of the individual villas (pools discreetly hidden behind walls and hedges for nude sunbathing and other activities) and super-friendly staff make **Pavilions and Pools** a perennial St. Thomas favorite. If your idea of romance is stone walls, tile floors, antique beds swathed in mosquito netting—and air-conditioning and cable TV—book at **Hotel 1829**.

For singles who would rather not be... No hotels in the U.S.V.I. are particularly noted for their swinging singles scene; **Marriott's Frenchman's Reef** on St. Thomas probably comes closest, if for no other reason than there's so much to do (and so many people of all persuasions to do it with).

Funky but fun... The rooms at both **Club Comanche** (St. Croix) and **Heritage Manor** (St. Thomas) look like they were furnished from garage sales, with an eclectic mix of brass beds, tattered rugs, antiques, dusty prints, and worn Naugahyde or chintz sofas. The former has more of an air of faded, slightly seedy gentility befitting a Graham Greene short story; the latter has a homier, backpacker, pack-rat feel.

Rooms with a view... It's a given that hotels sitting right smack dab on the beach will boast glorious water views. But once you've looked at the beach, what then? And what can you see at night? The real winners are hilltop hotels that give you panoramas of harbor and town. Rooms with higher numbers (30 and above) at **Marriott's Frenchman's Reef Resort** get the prize, opening onto fab vistas of Charlotte Amalie's lights. Although technically in Charlotte Amalie itself, **Bluebeard's Castle** is the runner-up when it comes to views of the cruise ships steaming into port. Also in Charlotte Amalie, **Hotel Mafolie** surveys an idyllic jumble of colorful rooftops and drying wash spilling down emerald hills to the sea.

Four Christiansted hotels are situated right on the wharf, with memorable vistas. **Hotel Caravelle** offers the largest number of rooms with a view, but the choicest rooms at boat-themed **Anchor Inn** and the **King's Alley Hotel** jut right out over the harbor, within peeping-Tom range of the yacht cabins. The hulking modern **Hotel on the Cay** sits on an island in Christiansted harbor, with many rooms looking onto the delightful mustard-colored Danish colonial Fort Christian.

Friendliest staff... Staffers at **Hotel 1829** (St. Thomas), led by general manager Michael Ball, often invite guests to party with them after hours, in wonderful contrast to the proper atmosphere that otherwise prevails. The remarkably warm ambience at the tidy little **Hotel Caravelle** (St. Croix) starts when the front desk manager, Mrs. Beasley, enfolds return guests in a bear hug as they check in; owners Sid and Amy Kalmans and all their staff go out of their way to make your stay memorable. The staff at St. Croix's **Tamarind Reef Hotel** immediately adopts guests as family, whether they like it or not, and are a wonderful source of information about the island.

Rudest staff... Maybe they're just showing disdain for the day-trippers now allowed on the grounds at St. John's **Caneel Bay Resort** (admittedly, it's jarring to see over-muscled, hirsute, tattooed young men in tank tops here), but the waitstaff at the casual beachfront restaurant can be shockingly indifferent, if not downright surly. Or maybe they figure you're just going to the buffet (they don't even bother to shoo the ravenous birds from the table). Those who order à la carte occasionally are served the wrong dish, while a glowering waiter stands there for an eternity, hoping the spineless diner will be cowed into accepting it anyway.

May I get that for you, sir?... Needless to say, whenever a staff excels at snobbishness, it also knows how to bow and scrape, and the folks at the **Caneel Bay Resort** are deliciously obsequious when the occasion warrants. Most of the time, though, the Caneel staffers (many of them old family retainers who have been here as long as the old-money clientele) equal their counterparts at the St. Thomas **Grand Palazzo**, in the kind of dignity practiced by actors in historical miniseries.

Wet dreams for water sports... St. John's **Hyatt Regency** has a lobby devoted almost entirely to all manner of water sports concessionaires, from scuba diving to parasailing outfitters. On St. Croix, the **Buccaneer** resort offers everything from flyfishing to sunset sails, courtesy of Cutlass Cove Watersports, on the lovely beach of the same name. The **Waves at Cane Bay** caters to divers, who adore the spectacular 300-foot walls in Cane Bay; free snorkeling gear is provided to guests, who can view a virtual underwater Main Street—an astonishing parade of the denizens of the deep—just offshore. **Chenay Bay Beach Resort**, which sits on a lovely beach with sterling views of Buck Island and Thatch Cay, has obtained the services of Lisa Neuberger, a windsurfing world champion. **Tamarind Reef Hotel** and St. Thomas's **Sapphire**

Beach Resort both benefit from on-site marinas, with sailing and deep-sea fishing available in addition to the usual windsurfing, snorkeling, kayaking, etcetera.

Cool pools... **St. Croix by the Sea Hotel** claims to have the world's largest saltwater pool, but the dramatic ocean pool of **Waves at Cane Bay**, also on St. Croix, is carved from the rock, the crashing surf forming a foamy, natural whirlpool tub. The pool at St. John's **Hyatt Regency** imitates a lake, all the way down to lapping waves and miniature islands for lounging. On St. Thomas, the **Bolongo Elysian Beach Resort**'s classic Hollywood kidney-shaped pool boasts a waterfall and thatched-roof pool bar. Each mini-villa at **Pavilions and Pools**, as the name suggests, is equipped with its own lap pool, and what could be more spectacular than that?

Family values... The white-and-gray wooden bungalows of St. Croix's **Chenay Bay Beach Resort** are staggered throughout 30 acres blooming with palms, genips, hibiscus, and bougainvillea. Kids love the long ribbon of beige sand, snorkeling trails right off the beach, and the fact that they're allowed to roam at will (as do the three children of owners Richard and Vicki Locke). Water sports are complimentary (except windsurfing), and the family plans, which allow children under 18 to stay and eat free, are a sensational value. Children under 12 stay for free at St. Croix's **Buccaneer** resort, where the "Pirate's Playhouse" program entertains kids 5–12 with arts and crafts, nature walks, pool games, remote-control car races, and the like. **Sapphire Beach Resort** is the top family pick on St. Thomas, in good measure because kids under 13 stay and eat free with their parents, a remarkable deal. Throw in scads of activities, a gorgeous beach, and sleek units (all with kitchenette, terrace or balcony, and sofa bed), and you have a top-notch family resort. On St. John, the **Hyatt Regency**'s super Camp Hyatt program keeps kids busy all day—and what's more, it strives to give a true island experience, with instruction in native crafts, lessons on local flora and fauna, Caribbean-tinged lunches, and even reggae jump-ups.

Our hearts were young and gay... Three historic St. Thomas properties cater discreetly to same-sex couples (and cast a blind eye if singles don't end up sleeping alone). The gay-owned and operated **Blackbeard's Castle** has become *the* place to stay in the Caribbean for soigné gay couples (and the occasional flirtatious single); curiously, it also seems to be where they send their retired parents from the Midwest. **Bluebeard's Castle** is the largest resort of choice for gay men and lesbians, maybe because so many harried clients (and even travel agents) confuse it with Blackbeard's. **Hotel 1829** corrals many fashionable gays, who appreciate its refined Old World atmosphere. St. Croix's **On the Beach Resort** had become terribly rundown (and lured an increasingly seedy clientele) before the original owner, Bill Owens, took it over again in 1994. He has spruced up the joint, which now attracts very married, middle-class gays and lesbians looking for a relaxing holiday (straight couples *are* welcome as well, Bill stresses). Note: this is not a place for cruising; even your maiden Aunt Agatha would feel at home. The **Pink Fancy** hosted Noel Coward several times in the 1930s and '40s; need we say more?

For "green" travelers with lots of green... All 16 units at **Harmony** (St. John) are solar- or wind-powered, and recycled materials crop up even where you'd least expect them (like the bathroom tiles made from crushed lightbulbs). The handsome bungalows are decorated with such p.c. artwork as Andean shawls and woodcarvings from the Brazilian rain forest. Each contains a kitchenette, private bath, computer (to gauge energy use), and terrace with sweeping views of Maho Bay. Susan Ivey, the aptly named manager of St. Croix's **Colony Cove**, takes guests on enthusiastic tours of her extensive herb garden, giving lessons in the medicinal properties of each plant (her grandfather was a botanist). If you have a cold she'll pluck some eucalyptus for you, for insomnia some soursop leaves, aloe for sunburn—Susan even has something for menstrual cramps and depression, and it's not Motrin or Prozac. The **Buccaneer** has created "ecopackages" that include rain-forest walks with local botanists, hikes through the Salt River Preserve with naturalists, and participation in a sea turtle research project during the summer (egg-laying season). The deluxe oceanview **Point Pleasant Resort** condominiums on St. Thomas seem hacked from the lush surrounding undergrowth.

Management leads nature walks through the grounds, and iguanas sun themselves by the pool—they're partial to hibiscus, and so tame they'll nibble from your hand.

For "green" travelers without much green... On St. John, the "tent-cottages" at **Maho Bay Camp**, all with linens, utensils, fan, and propane stove, careen drunkenly up the hill overlooking the pristine beach of the same name. The tentsites and cottages at **Cinnamon Bay Campground** are spartan and ground-level without sea view, but neat, cheap, and particularly popular with families. Coolest of all are the space-age **Estate Concordia Villas and Eco-tents**, which combine the high-tech appurtenances of Harmony with the open-air camping experience of Maho Bay. (The resemblance is more than coincidence—all three of these environmentally aware properties are run by the same visionary entrepreneur, Stanley Selengut.) Everything is solar or propane-powered; there are composting toilets; handrails are made from 50 percent plastic and 50 percent sawdust; slashed rubber tires serve as welcome mats; and nails are fashioned from remelted steel.

Luscious love nests... Maintaining guests' privacy has always been a fetish at St. John's **Caneel Bay**, making it a perfect place to get away from prying eyes. No one's saying, of course, but some of the rooms have probably hosted bigwigs with their wives one week, and their girlfriends the next. Whatever your reason for getting away from it all, you'll have no difficulty at **Estate Concordia**, stunning villas on a remote eastern part of St. John, or snazzy **Villa Madeleine**, which crowns a rocky promontory at the extreme eastern end of St. Croix. On St. Thomas, the choice is the aptly named **Tranquility Villa**, a small lodging with three master suites, perched precariously on a cliff overlooking the Caribbean (and spectacularly set just off the 18th hole of the Mahogany Run Golf Course, if you want to tee off).

For travelers with old money... Since Rosewood Hotels took over St. John's fabled **Caneel Bay Resort** (founded by Laurance Rockefeller as a back-to-nature retreat for the rich and famous in the 1960s), this former Rockresort has slipped a rung or two on the social ladder. Devotees worried that Rosewood would repeat the same "mistakes" they made when they renovated sister resort Little Dix Bay (air-conditioning and phones in half the rooms, gasp!). Fears that they cashed in its cachet are unfounded, however. True, they added the ultrachic Equator restaurant, day trippers are now allowed on the grounds, men no longer have to wear jackets while dining in low season, and fewer of the beautiful if decaying clientele (median age in season, 55) seem to have been deeded their rooms and chaise longues. But the new decor is lush without being louche, and the service impeccable, if haughty.

If you think the Kennedys now qualify as "old money," try the **Buccaneer** resort (St. Croix), where Ted used to bunk regularly (and where he still plays tennis). If nothing else, the fact that the Armstrong family has owned the estate since the 18th century (nine generations—not quite the Mayflower, but as venerable as the U.S.V.I. gets) gives it a certain cachet that even tour groups and conventioneers can't erase. Also on St. Croix, the sedate **Cormorant Beach Club** (where staffers have actually shushed rambunctious guests as if it were the Society Library) has always appealed to wives who "lunch" and husbands who power-breakfast. It's tempting to call the arcaded faux-Renaissance **Grand Palazzo** (St. Thomas) ostentatious and nouveau riche—except that everything is so damn well done. Besides gardens fragrant with frangipani, oleander, and jasmine, there's a large freshwater pond filled with Bahamian ducks, and a genuine mangrove swamp.

For travelers who confuse cash with class... The **Hyatt Regency** (St. John) is unabashed, unapologetic glitz, right down to its theme gourmet restaurant, Ciao Mein (yes, we know, but other Hyatts have Chow Bellas...). On any given day, a quarter of the beachcombers seem to carry cellular phones, honeymooners included. So much about St. Croix's convention-oriented **Carambola Beach Resort** impresses, but some might be disconcerted when the bellboy politely inquires, "Are you with the proctologists' convention, sir?"

Liveliest clientele... Marriott's **Frenchman's Reef** is the busiest, most bustling resort on St. Thomas, and that's saying plenty. It caters mostly to honeymooners, tour groups, and conventioneers, with a mind-boggling assortment of restaurants, nightspots, activities, and shopping. Also on St. Thomas, the all-inclusive **Bolongo Bay Beach and Tennis Club** offers everything lower-rent singles and honeymooners could want in a hassle-free vacation: a wildly popular karaoke/live music beach bar, booze cruises, limbo shows, and a pulsating disco reminiscent of a tropical Studio 54 well after its heyday. For whatever reason, the undistinguished **Windward Passage Hotel** (St. Thomas) is always filled to the rafters with yachties in town for the latest regatta, or Europeans on a shopping spree. The interior atrium is always jammin' and there's a greenhouse you can visit on the second floor. Though comparatively small, St. Croix's **Hibiscus Beach Hotel** compensates with a hopping bar scene, staff so enthusiastic they should be G.O.s at Club Med, and the best, cheapest theme-buffet evenings on island.

Where the power brokers stay... **Grand Palazzo** (St. Thomas) and **Caneel Bay** (St. John) both cater to CEOs (nothing lower than a VP of Product Development). If you're looking for a place to play the real-life *How To Succeed...*, you've found it.

Historic surroundings... On St. Thomas, **Hotel 1829** is a lovingly restored burgher's residence, decked out in period splendor. **Galleon House Hotel** is another early-19th-century mansion right next door, but the property is in such sad disrepair that you'll swear it hasn't been refurbished since it was built. The rooms at **Blackbeard's Castle** are forgettably modern-motel, but the site is on the National Register of Historic Places for its 1679 lookout tower, said to be the headquarters for the infamous Edward Teach himself. **Bluebeard's Castle** counters with its own 18th-century pirate's lookout tower on the premises, although it too has forgettably contemporary rooms. **Villa Santana** was the residence of General Santa Anna (of Alamo fame). The lovely buildings have whitewashed adobe or rough-hewn stone walls and cathedral ceilings; the units are filled with superb mahogany and antique rattan furnishings, and there are several tempting mango trees on the grounds.

Although most of the buildings and accommodations at St. Croix's **Buccaneer** are contemporary, the resort is located on the grounds of an 18th-century sugar plantation that has remained in the same hands for nine generations. The **King Christian Hotel** occupies a beautiful mustard-colored 17th-century brick-and-stone warehouse; at press time, though, the place was in the midst of extensive renovations and negotiating with its potential third owner in just over a year (red flag). **Club Comanche** is an odd hodgepodge, a rambling 18th-century stone edifice with nooks and crannies galore and rooms with an air of slightly decaying gentility. The most notable regular was probably J. Robert Oppenheimer (you know, the guy who built The Bomb), who stayed here in the 1940s and '50s and helped construct the fake sugar mill that shadows the small pool. **Sprat Hall Plantation**, which dates back to 1670, is the only authentic great house operating as a hostelry in the U.S.V.I., and it looks the part, with burnished hardwood floors, wrought iron spiral staircases, crystal chandeliers, lace curtains, and antiques and family heirlooms, including carved mahogany armoires and four-poster canopy beds. Three sometimes-quibbling sisters share the property and stables.

Cheap sleeps... **Bayside Inn and Fitness Center** offers one of the most extraordinary values on St. Thomas, with extremely comfortable contemporary rooms, free use of the extensive spa/health club, and the Bolongo Bay beach just across the street. **Admiral's Inn** is a shipshape little motel convenient to the marvelous restaurants in Frenchtown. **Galleon House** has the advantage of being dirt cheap—emphasis on both adjectives—but many backpacking young Europeans like its elegant flophouse aura, the non-stop antics and stand-up spiels of the owner, and central Charlotte Amalie location. Although the rooms at **Blackbeard's Castle** are nothing special, they're reasonably priced, well outfitted, and the relaxed ambience is special indeed. At inexpensive **Heritage Manor**, each room, though hardly an *HG* fashion plate, is warm and distinctive; each is named for a different city, with travel posters and other thematic paraphernalia, and there are 12-foot ceilings and huge picture windows. **Carib Beach Hotel** is a two-minute walk from the beach at Lindbergh Bay, making its smallish, fussily tropical rooms a better buy than many beachfront properties. **Island Beachcomber Hotel** is barely half the price of its vaunted neighbor, Emerald Beach and, though a little dowdier, perfectly satisfactory for fun in the sun.

On St. Croix, the **Danish Manor** occupies a beautifully restored 18th-century mansion, but the somewhat cramped rooms are strictly from a Miami motel of the Eisenhower era; the unrenovated budget units are literally bargain basement. **The Frederiksted**'s rooms are musty, though the hotel was built only a few years ago, but each has a kitchenette, the rates are right, and the Frederiksted beach is just a two-minute stroll down the street. **Holger Danske** is the local Best Western chain motel; the decor, including seasick-green carpeting and floral bedspreads with way too much pink, is enough to give nondrinkers a hangover. But each room has a TV, fridge, air-conditioning, and full bath, and most have at least a sliver of ocean view.

The Inn at Tamarind Court is the best cheap choice on St. John, offering both efficiencies and cleverly decorated "jungle cabins." The rooms at **Raintree Inn** are basic, but clean and brightened with colorful local artworks. For camping, see "For 'green' travelers without much green."

Condo-mania and sweet suites... All of the accommodations in this category come with a fully equipped kitchen, TV, VCR, and air-conditioning (except as noted), and many are individually owned and decorated. The fully equipped two-bedroom units at St. Croix's **Villa Madeleine** strike a perfect blend of old-fashioned (four-poster beds) and contemporary (glass-topped coffee tables). **Club St. Croix's** units are immaculate in white wicker, with mirrored closets and glass tables; nicest are the duplexes, while the still-sizable studios feature Murphy beds. There are several condominium complexes on the same beach, but these offer the best ocean views throughout. **Colony Cove** is as notable for friendly manager Susan Ivey as it is for the spotless, ultramodern facilities. **Schooner Bay**, in the Gallows Bay neighborhood, is convenient to Christiansted shopping, dining, and nightlife. The units tend toward very contemporary furnishings, and all have—*quel miracle*—a washer and dryer. Those at the top of the hill (in the group called the Freedom block) have magnificent views of the Christiansted harbor, but the Courageous and Vigilant blocks get the most refreshing breezes. On St. Thomas, the condos at **Point Pleasant Resort** all have balconies that open onto fabulous water views. The individually owned and decorated units at **Pavilions and Pools** have a welcoming lived-in feel, and the atmosphere is one of the warmest on the island. Sophisticated **Secret Harbour Beach Resort** appeals to lots of Europeans and suits; there are always several cellular phones in use on the nearly empty beach, which is slung conveniently with hammocks. **Crystal Cove Condominiums** occupies the choicest location on spectacular Sapphire Beach, though the apartments, while perfectly serviceable, can be a little worn. On St. John, the brand-new villas of **Estate Concordia**, on the wilder eastern half of the island, are for those who truly want to be out in the boonies; the remote location pays extra dividends in suprisingly low prices. **Gallows Point Suite Resort** is for those who want the amenities of their own home, with the conveniences of a hotel. Its situation on one end of Cruz Bay is another plus if you don't want total isolation, and the suites are charmingly old-fashioned with lots of rattan and ceiling fans (but no air-conditioning). The top units at **Battery Hill**— a collection of coral-, turquoise-, and eggshell-colored condo buildings, the decor all rattan and pastels—have breathtaking 360-degree views of St. John. The nicely appointed condos of **Lavender Hill Estates**, with their unparalleled view of the Cruz Bay harbor, represent one of the best values on-island. Whitewashed **Villas Caribe** is a near-luxury development just outside downtown Cruz Bay, with wrought-iron gates and a riot of gardens reminiscent of the Côte d'Azure. Celebrity alert: Jane Pauley and Garry Trudeau own one of the units.

Least offensive of the chains... The **Hyatt Regency** (St. John) may be flashy, but it's also deluxe and ultracomfortable. The rooms at **Wyndham Sugar Bay Plantation Resort** (St. Thomas) betray its origins as a Holiday Inn, but the reception area does a decent job of imitating genteel plantation living: gleaming marble floors, crystal chandeliers, a glorious staircase, and towering potted palms dwarfed by the cathedral ceiling. A cabaret singer holds court in the lobby lounge, the gourmet restaurant is one of the island's classiest hotel dining rooms, and the nightclub is a smashing replica of an Art Deco ocean liner (though, unfortunately, at press time management was considering converting it into a meeting space.) Blond wood furnishings, ceramic lamps, throw rugs, and immaculate tile floors give the **Marriott's Morningstar Beach Resort** a posher air than most chain hotels, and the beach alone is a sybaritic delight. Laura Ashley meets the Caribbean at the luxurious Westin **Carambola Beach Resort** (St. Croix), where the cultured room decor runs toward terra-cotta floors, mahogany ceilings, paneling, and furniture (including rocking chairs and overstuffed sofas), frilly floral fabrics, and ceramic lamps.

Most elegant ambience... The sunkissed ochre-and-white **Grand Palazzo** (St. Thomas) tumbles lavishly through virtual botanical gardens to the Caribbean, with fabulous views of St. John through endless stuccoed arches—all very Mediterranean. The doge himself would approve of this palazzo, which even features Roman lion fountains and a classic Italian Renaissance campanile. **Hotel 1829** is a treasure trove of Spanish tile, Danish brickwork, heavy Dutch hardwood doors, and French iron grillwork, attesting to the original owners' prosperity. The rooms, furnished in period style, are equally exceptional.

On St. Croix, the **Villa Madeleine** resembles a society matron's estate. Its public spaces—with exquisite driftwood sculpture and Haitian artworks, rattan furniture, stone tiles, leather-bound books, Japanese prints, and accents of peacock blue and maroon—were profiled in *Architectural Digest,* for what that's worth. The reception area of **Hilty House** is elegant without being ostentatious, with its wood beams, crystal chandeliers, handpainted Florentine tilework, and an enormous fireplace. The individually decorated rooms, each named for its predominant color scheme and bursting with white wicker, rattan, and lace, help make this a dollhouse B&B. How ritzy is the **Cormorant Beach Club**? Well, a cart carrying coffee and tea is placed discreetly outside your door first thing every morning, and a mood of genteel leisure prevails throughout the day, with a croquet lawn to distract the well-heeled (and docksidered) guests, in addition to a restaurant, bar, pool, snorkeling, and two tennis courts. Red tile roofs and white stucco arches suggests the ambience of the Italian Riviera.

The grounds alone at St. John's exclusive **Caneel Bay Resort** (all 170 splendiferous acres) set an elegant tone, lavishly landscaped in the best English romantic tradition, an atmosphere reinforced by the aging preppy clientele. Rosewood Hotels has done an admirable job of refurbishing this classic, with bright fabrics in mango and mint complementing the stone walls, tile floors, and natural wicker furnishings. But they didn't install TV or air-conditioning—the regulars would have had a fit, and anyway, the breezes from the beaches and ceiling fans usually suffice.

When everything else is filled... Ramada Yacht Haven (St. Thomas) is, in the opinion of some guests, a tacky, peeling pink eyesore nicknamed by some locals Ramada Yucch Haven. But yes, you can usually get a room and it does come with all the expected amenities.

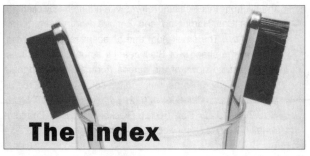

The Index

$$$$$	over $325
$$$$	$250–$325
$$$	$175–$250
$$	$100–$175
$	under $100

Price is for a standard double room in high season, exclusive of 7.5 percent tax and service charge—up to 10 percent, if any. All are air-conditioned with private bath and TV, unless otherwise noted.

Abbreviations: EP=European Plan (no meals); CP=Continental Plan (Continental breakfast included); BP=Breakfast Plan (full breakfast included); MAP=Modified American Plan (breakfast and dinner included).

St. Thomas

Admiral's Inn. This ultratidy glorified motel in a less-traveled part of Charlotte Amalie offers a pool, bar, fine views of town, and complimentary Continental breakfast. The rooms, completely refurbed after Marilyn, boast blond wood, rattan, and terra-cotta floors.... *Tel 809/774–1376, 800/544–0493, fax 809/774–8010. Villa Olga, Frenchtown 00802. DC not accepted. 16 rms. $$–$$$*

Bayside Inn and Fitness Center. This restored 19th-century manor now houses a complete health club, including swimming pool, and four bedrooms that truly are furnished like someone's private home. The beach is right across the street, and guests have privileges at megaresort Bolongo Club Everything.... *Tel 809/777–3300, fax 809/775–3208. 7140 Estate Bolongo 00802. DC not accepted. EP. 4 rms. $–$$*

Blackbeard's Castle. Charlotte Amalie is a short walk down the hill from this pleasant retreat with a largely gay clientele (owners Bob Harrington and Enrique Konzen are themselves gay). The small pool and adjacent restaurant's terrace, in the shadow of Blackbeard's actual lookout tower, have splendid views of the harbor. Rooms are comfortable if a tad dowdy. Only the junior suites could be called rooms with a view.... *Tel 809/776–1234, 800/344–5771, fax 809/776–4321. Box 6041, Blackbeard's Hill, Charlotte Amalie 00801. D not accepted. CP. 25 units. $$*

Bluebeard's Castle. Another "historic" property with disappointingly modern, pedestrian rooms in the usual bright Caribbean colors. The most expensive boast harbor views; other units compensate with extras like kitchenettes. The three on-site restaurants (Entre Nous, Guava Grille, and A Room With a View—see Dining) are uniformly top-notch, and the small pool (with waterfall) has smashing views of cruise ships pulling in.... *Tel 809/774–1600, 800/524–6599, fax 809/774–5134. Box 7480, Bluebeard's Hill, Charlotte Amalie 00801. D not accepted. 170 rms. $$$*

Bolongo Bay Beach and Tennis Club and **Limetree Beach Resort.** Formerly soldered together into one giant all-inclusive playground, these now operate separately. Limetree remains all-inclusive, while Bolongo Bay is being marketed as a more affordable alternative. Guests can use facilities at both, and technically you can do European plan at Limetree and all-inclusive at Bolongo Bay; there's a shuttle between the two on call. All villas have full kitchens, and many rooms have kitchenettes; extras include VCRs and safes. Complimentary sports include use of tennis courts, snorkel gear, canoes, Sunfish sailboats, and paddleboats. The Caribbean Lobster House is a surprisingly good restaurant, worth a visit even if you're not staying.... *Tel 809/779–2844, 800/524–4746, 800/524–4746, fax 809/775–3208. Estate Bolongo 00802. EP/all-inclusive. 225 units. $$–$$$ (Bolongo Bay); $$$$$ (all-inclusive at Limetree)*

Bolongo Elysian Beach Resort. The sunny, well-equipped units, many with large balconies, are as stylish as time-share units get, with tile floors and rattan and bamboo furnishings. They can be broken down into one-bedroom suites, studios, and standard hotel rooms.... *Tel 809/775–1000, 800/343–4079, fax 809/776–0910. 6800 Estate Nazareth, 00802. DC not accepted. CP/all-inclusive. 175 rms. $$$$$*

Carib Beach Hotel. A much better bargain than its sister resort, Emerald Beach (both Best Western outposts) just because it's a two-minute walk to Lindbergh Bay. All rooms boast sea views as well as a great prospect on the airport runways. Rooms are smallish and feature gaudy tropical prints. Use of the Emerald Beach facilities is included.... *Tel 809/774–2525, 800/79–CARIB, fax 809/777–4131. Box 340, Lindbergh Bay 00801. DC not accepted. 80 rms. $$$*

Crystal Cove Condominiums. The main attraction of these comfortable, individually decorated, fully equipped units is the alluring Sapphire Beach virtually at your doorstep.... *Tel 809/775–6660 or 800/524–2037, fax 809/775–4202. 6222 Estate Nazareth 00802; Sapphire Beach. DC not accepted. 20 villas. $$$$*

Emerald Beach Resort. Although the Emerald Beach is a model development in many respects, it's no longer a better bargain than its larger brethren; the rooms are Best Western-standard in jungle colors, and the air traffic in and out of the nearby airport is distracting to say the least.... *Tel 809/777–8800, 800/233–4936, fax 809/776–3426. 8070 Lindbergh Bay 00802. 90 rms. $$$$*

Galleon House Hotel. The rooms are rather dreary and threadbare, but they're cheap and air-conditioned, the owners are quite charming, and the hotel is centrally located.... *Tel/fax 809/774–6952, 800/524–2052. Box 6577, Government Hill, Charlotte Amalie, 00804. D, DC not accepted. 14 rms, 2 with shared bath. $–$$*

Grand Palazzo. Six three-story, arcaded, Mediterranean-style ochre and sienna villas surround formal gardens, all spilling down to a champagne-colored beach. Rooms are on the small side, but luxuriously appointed in rich Italian fabrics. Four tennis courts, two swimming pools, two superlative restaurants (Palm Terrace and Cafe Vecchio, see Dining), a beach grill, glitzy boutiques, catamaran, water sports center, and fitness room.... *Tel 809/775–3333, 800/545–0509, fax 809/775–4444. 6900 Great Bay Nazareth 00802. 152 units. $$$$$*

Heritage Manor. Pretty in pink describes this charming guest house with rooms around an interior courtyard, including a tiny, cleverly designed pool. Eclectic room furnishings include brass beds; suites have refrigerators, and two rooms have kitchens. Continental breakfast is complimentary during the winter season.... *Tel 809/774–3003, 800/828–0757, fax 809/776–9585. 1A Snegle Gade, Box 90, Charlotte Amalie 00804. D, DC not accepted. CP. 8 rms, 4 with shared bath. $–$$*

Hotel 1829. One of the most delightful small inns in the Caribbean. Rooms, mostly in handsome faux period decor, overlook either the town or the interior courtyard; all have TV and air-conditioning. There's a postage-stamp-sized pool, renowned restaurant (see Dining), and wonderfully intimate bar.... *Tel 809/776–1829, 800/524–2002, fax 809/776–4313. Box 1567, Government Hill, Charlotte Amalie 00801. D not accepted. EP. 15 rms. $$*

Hotel Mafolie. Extraordinary views and superobliging staff make this glorified, rambling guesthouse popular with Europeans and honeymooners on a budget. Decor is nothing special, but the pool and restaurant have extraordinary views of St. Thomas. Continental breakfast and beach shuttle are included. But, unfortunately, Mafolie may end up a casualty of Marilyn; its status was uncertain at press time.... *Tel 809/ 774–2790 or 800/225–7035, fax 809/774–4091. Box 1506, Mafolie Hill, Charlotte Amalie 00804. D, DC not accepted. CP, MAP. 23 rms. $$*

Island Beachcomber Hotel. The rooms here are pleasant, if a little frayed around the edges; they include the usual amenities, plus minifridges. The property has a South Seas feel, with thatched umbrellas, bridges, birdcages, and tropical foliage. Guests receive complimentary snorkel gear; there's a free shuttle to town, and a beachfront restaurant and bar.... *Tel 809/774–5250, 800/982–9898, fax 809/774–5615. Box 2579, Lindbergh Bay 00803. D not accepted. 48 rms. $$*

Limetree Beach Resort. See **Bolongo Bay Beach and Tennis Club**.

Marriott's Frenchman's Reef and Morningstar Beach Resorts. These twin resorts are a short walk (or shuttle) away from each other; guests at either have full use of the facilities at both, which include everything from restaurants and bars to helicopter tours. Morningstar's rooms have either ocean or garden view (the latter much cheaper), and a classier feel. The rooms at Frenchman's are more chain-hotel-like, though spacious; those with higher numbers (30 and above) have views of the Charlotte Amalie harbor.... *Tel 809/776–8500, 800/524–2000, fax 809/776–6249. Box 7100, Morningstar Beach 00801. EP, MAP. 420 rms (Frenchman's Reef), 96 rms (Morningstar). $$$$–$$$$$ (Frenchman's), $$$$$ (Morningstar).*

Pavilions and Pools. Each of these unassuming homes-away-from-home has its own small lap pool. A nice extra is the VCR in each unit. Water sports are available at adjacent Sapphire Beach. Continental breakfast, a weekly cocktail party, and a barbecue are included in the rate.... *Tel 809/775–6110, 800/524–2001, fax 809/775–6110. 6400 Estate Smith Bay 00802. D, DC not accepted. CP. 25 units. $$$$*

Point Pleasant Resort. Several buildings cling to a jungle-carpeted hill above Smith Bay, each unit boasting vistas of St. John and Drake Passage. Studios and one- and two-bedroom units feature wood ceilings, white tile floors, pastel colors, and blond woods, as well as full kitchen and balcony. Every guest gets four hours' free use of a car daily; there are three pools, a lighted tennis court, and a water sports center. Big bonus: children under 21 (that's not a misprint) stay free.... *Tel 809/775–7200, 800/524–2300, fax 809/776–5694. 6600 Estate Smith Bay 00802. D, DC not accepted. EP, MAP. 135 units.* $$$$

Ramada Yacht Haven Hotel and Marina. The rooms, all garish salmon and teal, are in dire need of refurbishment (or at least redecorating), which they may finally get with post-hurricane repairs. Most rooms have fine harbor views, and there's plenty of activity around the full-service marina.... *Tel 809/774–9700, 800/228–9898, fax 809/776–3410. 5400 Long Bay Rd., Charlotte Amalie 00802. EP. 151 rms., 2 suites.* $$$–$$$$

Sapphire Beach Resort and Marina. Two sensuous strands of beach separated by a small peninsula are ringed with reefs that explode with color—a treat for snorkelers. Each unit has a fully equipped kitchen, gigantic balcony, and sofa bed; first-floor units open right onto the beach. The Little Gems Kids Klub is a model program.... *Tel 809/775–6100, 800/524–2090, fax 809/775–4024. Box 8088, Red Hook 00802. D not accepted. EP, MAP. 171 rms.* $$$$–$$$$$

Secret Harbour Beach Resort. Each attractive unit (from studios to two-bedroom apartments) qualifies as oceanfront or ocean view; all feature huge balconies, full kitchen, and TV/VCR. There's a water-sports center/dive shop, two tennis courts, pool, restaurant, and two bars. A favored retreat for corporate types.... *Tel 809/775–6550, 800/524–2250, fax 809/775–1501. 6280 Estate Nazareth 00802. DC not accepted. EP. 48 units.* $$$$

Stouffer Renaissance Grand Beach Resort. This megaresort with a marble atrium lobby does a brisk convention trade; the wide range of facilities includes fitness room, full water sports center, lovely beach, two giant pools, six tennis courts, and two fine restaurants. Kids can knock themselves out with iguana hunts, T-shirt painting, and sand-castle building.... *Tel 809/775–1510, 800/233–4935, fax 809/775–2185. Smith Bay Rd., Box 8267, 00801. D not accepted. EP, MAP. 297 rms. $$$$*

Tranquility Villa. This luxurious villa set by the Mahogany Run Golf Course has three master suites, each with its own Jacuzzi, steam room, full kitchen, and pool.... *Tel 809/774–6462, fax 809/774–3028. Box 4123 Mahagony Run 00803. DC, D not accepted. $$$$$*

Villa Santana. These whitewashed 19th-century buildings overlook Charlotte Amalie and the harbor. Units are mostly furnished with antique rattan and mahogany; each has a distinctive touch, like handcrafted cradle beds from Puerto Rico, spiral staircase, or rattan four-poster. Some have superb views; all have at least a kitchenette, though no air-conditioning or TV. Small pool.... *Tel 809/776–1311, fax 809/777–8009. Denmark Hill, Charlotte Amalie 00802. D, DC not accepted. 8 units. $–$$*

Windward Passage Hotel. Very typical stateside-type hotel in a fairly central Charlotte Amalie location. All units feature fridge, TV, safe, air-conditioning, and balcony (except the largest suites, which at least have wraparound views). Otherwise, it's standard tropical fabrics, pastel walls, and palm-tree prints. Pool, restaurant, bar, and complimentary buffet breakfast and beach shuttle.... *Tel 809/774–5200, 800/524–7389, fax 809/774–1231. Box 640, Veterans Drive, Charlotte Amalie 00804. EP. 151 units. $$$*

Wyndham Sugar Bay Plantation Resort. Behind the grandiose southern-mansion facade and public rooms, expect standard mid-range chain decor, and you'll have to take a shuttle to the beach, pool, and restaurant—a major annoyance. The rooms in the block closest to the ocean have extraordinary vistas; all rooms have a balcony, most with a view of the ocean. Children under 19 stay free when sharing a room with parents.... *Tel 809/777–7100, 800/927–7100, fax 809/777–7200. 6500 Estate Smith Bay 00802. BP, MAP. 300 rms. $$$$*

St. Croix

Anchor Inn. This pretty seafoam-green and white wooden structure looks like it might topple into the harbor at any moment but is suprisingly yar, as the yachties who sometimes frequent the place might say (It's yachtie for "comfortable"). Cutesy touches include little anchor knockers on the doors. Small pool, popular restaurant and bar.... *Tel 809/773–4000, 800/524–2030, fax 809/773–4408. 58 King St., Christiansted 00820. EP, MAP. 31 rms. $$*

The Buccaneer Hotel. This flamingo-pink beauty on a former sugar plantation has many devoted repeat guests. About half of the rooms are in the main house, with other accommodations scattered throughout the manicured 300 acres in guest cottages. Deluxe rooms are enormous, with four-poster beds; several oceanfront rooms are receiving the Laura Ashley treatment. Three gorgeous beaches and many facilities.... *Tel 809/773–2100, 800/255–3881, fax 809/773–0010. Box 25200, Gallows Bay 00824; Cutlass Cove. EP, MAP. 150 units. $$$$*

Carambola Beach Resort. Each room is identical in layout and decor, making those with a garden view a much better bargain; all boast a private patio and enormous marble bathroom (shower only). The decor is extra-tasteful (mahogany furnishings, terra-cotta floors, floral and paisley fabrics), as is the Mediterranean-style architecture, with graceful arcaded walkways snaking through manicured gardens; Independent travelers may rue the upscale tour groups.... *Tel 809/778-3800, fax 809/778-1682. Box 3031, Kingshill 00851; Davis Bay. 151 rms. $$$$$*

Chenay Bay Beach Resort. Kids happily crawl all over this resort, its soft gray bungalows topped with gleaming white roofs; inside are terra-cotta floors, tropical floral fabrics, and dark rattan. Only the view (of the ocean or the lovely, tangled gardens) determines the difference in prices—all units have kitchenette, minibar, and cable TV. The water-sports facilities are among the best on island.... *Tel/fax 809/773–2918, 800/548–4457. Box 24600, Christiansted 00824; Chenay Bay. D not accepted. EP, MAP. 50 units. $$$*

Club Comanche. Stylish restaurant, dowdy but somehow charming rooms, like something from a Graham Greene novella. The owners have just received their insurance money from Hugo (don't ask) and want to lighten up some of the rooms; it would actually be rather a pity. There is a small shabby pool as well.... *Tel/fax 809/773–0210. 1 Strand St., Christiansted 00820. D, DC not accepted. EP, MAP. $*

Club St. Croix. Each sunny condo looks out onto Christiansted harbor and Buck Island. Bamboo furniture, white tile floors, glass tables, colorful throw rugs, and mirrors everywhere give them a chic feel.... *Tel 809/773–4800, 800/635–1533, fax 809/773–4805. 3820 Estate Golden Rock 00820. D, DC not accepted. EP. 54 suites. $$$*

Colony Cove Condominiums. Amateur naturalist and ultraprofessional manager Susan Ivey and her eco-garden are what really distinguish this superlative condo property, but the glossy contemporary units in stark monochromes are a refreshing change from the pastels and gaudy tropical prints of most Caribbean accommodations. The kitchens are especially modern.... *Tel 809/773–1965, 800/828–0746, fax 809/773–5397. 3221 Estate Golden Rock 00820. D, DC not accepted. EP. $$$*

Cormorant Beach Club. At this upscale Riviera-esque resort, the beachfront rooms are especially delightful, with dark wicker furniture, pale apricot walls, white tile floors, and unique coral-and-rock-walled showers. The public spaces are cool oases with stone walls and overstuffed wicker armchairs and sofas.... *Tel 809/778–8920, 800/344–5770, fax 809/778–9218. 4126 La Grande Princesse, Christiansted 00820. D not accepted. EP, MAP. 34 rms., 4 suites. $$$$$*

Danish Manor. This charming stone-and-brick building dates back a good 150 years, yet the rooms are straight from a drab fifties motel, with imperial purple and coral accents. The small interior courtyard includes a tiny pool; complimentary Continental breakfast is usually served.... *Tel 809/773–1377, 800/524–2069, fax 809/773–1913. 2 Company St., Christiansted 00820. D, DC not accepted. EP. 34 rms. $*

The Frederiksted. The inviting tile courtyard, with its elaborate green hedge and striped yellow-and-white awnings, has a small pool and restaurant/bar. Alas, the guest rooms are already becoming rather shabby, with worn print linens and chipped rattan furniture. For only a few bucks more, opt for an ocean view, despite the street noise.... *Tel 809/773–9150, 800/524–2025, fax 809/778–4009. 20 Strand St., Frederiksted 00840. D not accepted. EP. 40 rms. $$*

Hibiscus Beach Hotel. The immaculate coral buildings of this excellent buy are staggered to ensure ocean views from every room; the Hibiscus building—each is named for a different tropical flower—is closest to the water (for the same price). Blood-red hibiscus flowers strewn everywhere contrast with the stark white tile floors and walls. Enthusiastic staff, festive theme nights, as well as a pool and complimentary snorkeling equipment.... *Tel 809/773–4042, 800/442–0121, fax 809/773–7668. Box 4131, La Grande Princesse 00820. EP. 38 rms. $$$*

Hilty House. Warm hosts Jacquie and Hugh Hoare-Ward have opened their captivating home to guests. It's in the middle of nowhere, so a car is a must, but many guests spend the day lying by the pool, reading a book from the extensive library, or strolling the lovingly tended garden.... *Tel/fax 809/773–2594. 2 Herman Hill, Box 26077, Gallows Bay 00824. 4 rms., 2 cottages. No D, DC. CP. $–$$*

Holger Danske. The fake whitewashed stucco buildings with their slatted, dirt-colored wooden balconies are actually the most attractive aspect of this Best Western hotel. The rooms are fair-sized and well equipped, but the bright decor would startle even the color-blind (though refurbishment is in the works). The best water views are from the third floor units; the higher the number, the better the harbor vista. Indifferent restaurant, bar, pool.... *Tel 809/773–3600, or 800/528–1234. 1100 King's Alley, Christiansted. EP. 30 rms. $$*

Hotel Caravelle. Probably the best buy in Christiansted, the large rooms are attractively decorated in blues; all have at least partial water view, and you can fling open the windows in the "superior" rooms and gaze onto the harbor. The restaurant is a popular local hangout; there's also a small pool and water-sports concession.... *Tel 809/773–0687, 800/524–0410, fax 809/778–7004. 44A Queen Cross St., Christiansted 00820. EP. 43 rms. $$*

Hotel on the Cay. The ugly modern buildings on this cay in the middle of Christiansted harbor resemble a Miami beehive, but the marvelous views and the lushly overgrown grounds (complete with man-made waterfalls) compensate.... *Tel 809/773–2035, 800/524–2035. Box 4020, Christiansted 00822; Christiansted Harbor. D, DC not accepted. EP, MAP. 55 rms., 2 suites w/ kitchenette. $$*

King Christian Hotel. In its magnificent 17th-century warehouse on the wharf, this has always been a well-run family-owned hostelry, even if the rooms had no period touches. Under new owners, however, it's undergoing extensive renovations.... *Tel 809/773–2285, 800/524–2012, fax 809/773–9411. 59 King's Wharf, Christiansted 00820. D, DC not accepted. EP. 39 rms. $$*

King's Alley Hotel. The best rooms are in the "prow" of the hotel, jutting right into the harbor where the seaplanes take off. Decor is indifferent at best (the chartreuse touches have to go, and management promises they will). The owner also plans to add an upscale mini-shopping arcade with two more restaurants, as well two additional buildings containing 12 large deluxe suites, by the end of 1996.... *Tel 809/773–0103, 800/843–3574, fax 809/773–9707. 1000 King's Alley, Christiansted. D, DC not accepted. EP. 23 rms., 12 suites. $$*

On the Beach Resort. Bill Owens has labored mightily to spruce the place up since taking it over again in 1994, but the accommodations are still best described as unpretentious, with lots of mint and ecru. There is a wide range of oddly configured rooms, from claustrophobic to palatial, but nothing is extravagantly priced. The clientele is heavily gay and lesbian, mostly couples. Magnificent beach, small pool, al fresco bar/bistro.... *Tel 809/772–1205, 800/524–2018, fax 809/772–1757. Box 1908 00841; 127 Smithfield, Frederiksted. D, DC not accepted. EP, MAP. 14 rms. $$$*

The Pink Fancy. A 1780 Danish town house is the centerpiece here; the original stone walls and foundations surround the tiny courtyard pool. Rooms are spacious and uncluttered, with polished hardwood floors, tropical-print fabrics, wicker furniture, and boldly colored local art. Complimentary breakfast and cocktails.... *Tel 809/773–8460, 800/524–2045, fax 809/773–6448. 27 Prince St., Christiansted 00820. AE, D, DC not accepted. CP. 13 rms. $$*

Schooner Bay Condominiums. Aside from being furnished attractively, mostly in muted colors, these condos all have a VCR and washing machine and dryer. Units higher up the hill have amazing views of Christiansted. Two pools, Jacuzzi, tennis court.... *Tel 809/778-7670, 800/524-2025, fax 809/778-4009. 5002 Gallows Bay 00820. D, DC not accepted. EP. 64 units. $$*

Sprat Hall Plantation. This sprawling, poorly maintained 20-acre seaside Frederiksted property is a restored 1670 plantation estate, the oldest in the U.S.V.I. The non-air-conditioned rooms in the great house, crammed with antique furniture, are by far the nicest accommodations; the newer family cottages are drab indeed. Complimentary Continental breakfast, dinner upon request (for guests only).... *Tel 809/772-0305, 800/843-3584. Box 695, Frederiksted 00841; Sprat Hall Beach, Rte. 65. D, DC, MC, V not accepted. EP. 9 rms., 8 suites. $$$–$$$$*

St. Croix by the Sea Hotel. The immense saltwater pool and a soaring lobby filled with chic local artworks are the most noteworthy aspects of this rather tired property, whose rooms are standard (not another seashell pattern!) in more ways than one. The fridges are a nice extra, though. Pool, two bars, and a restaurant celebrated for its theme buffets and Sunday brunches.... *Tel 809/778-8600, 800/524-5006, fax 809/773-8002. Estate St. John, Box 248, Christiansted 00821. D, DC not accepted. EP, MAP. 65 rms. $$*

Tamarind Reef Hotel. This friendly, glorified motel enjoys a marvelous setting with tremendous water views of Green Cay and Buck Island from every room. Fittingly, the beach is one of the best on St. Croix for snorkeling—right offshore—though many guests prefer the sizable pool. A marina and lively bar/grill draw scads of yachties. Rooms are spacious, all with kitchenette and terrace or balcony.... *Tel 809/773-4455, 800/619-0014, fax 809/619-0014. 56*

Southgate, 5001 Tamarind Reef 00820. D, DC not accepted. EP. 46 rms. $$–$$$

Villa Madeleine. The main building replicates a turn-of-the-century West Indian plantation great house, with public spaces lavishly decorated with Oriental rugs, artwork, and polished hardwood and rattan furnishings. Relentlessly upscale private guest villas are staggered up a steep hill, guaranteeing fine views; each has a kitchen and private pool.... *Tel 809/778–7377, 800/548–4461, fax 809/773–7518. Box 3109, Christiansted 00822. DC not accepted. EP. 43 villas. $$$$$*

Waves at Cane Bay. The only real drawback to this happily remote hotel is the tiny rocky beach that all but vanishes at high tide, but you can stroll to the more expansive Cane Bay (legendary among divers for its spectacular walls). The hotel's unique pool was actually carved from the coral along the shore. Huge rooms, all with kitchenette, TV, and in-room safe, are outfitted in cool cream and pastels; not all have air-conditioning. Restaurant, bar, complimentary snorkeling gear.... *Tel 809/778–1805, 800/545–0603. Box 1749, Kings Hill 00851. D, DC not accepted. 12 rms, 1 suite. $$*

St. John

Battery Hill. These condos all have full kitchens and balconies with sweeping views. You must request AC and TV, the former being vital in the downstairs units (upstairs units catch strong sea breezes). The decor is standard upscale Caribbean. The rather poky Frank Bay beach is a few minutes' walk, or you can lounge by the pool.... *Tel/fax 809/693–9100, 800/858–7989. Box 618, Battery Hill, Cruz Bay. D, DC not accepted. 8 two-bedroom apts, 1 studio. $$$*

Caneel Bay Resort. This 170-acre resort was originally part of a plantation owned by the Danish West India Company; the 19th-century sugar mill has been converted into the restaurant Equator (see Dining). Opened in 1936, the resort was bought by Laurance Rockefeller in the 1950s; recently, Rosewood Hotels took over and restored it. Sunny, airy rooms each have minibars but no AC, phone, or TV. Eleven tennis courts, three superb restaurants, full water sports facilities, fitness room—and seven out-of-this-world beaches.... *Tel 809/776–6111, 800/928–8889, fax 809/693–8280. Box 720, Cruz Bay 00831. D, DC not accepted. EP, MAP. 171 rms. $$$$$*

Cinnamon Bay Campground. Tents, four-unit cottages, and bare sites are available at this National Park Service location hacked from the undergrowth bordering glorious Cinnamon Bay beach. The 10 x 14-foot tents are equipped with flooring, eating utensils, gas stove, cots, and linens; cottage rooms have twin beds and electricity. Bare sites, which include a picnic table and charcoal grill, must be reserved well in advance (eight months at least).... *Tel 809/776–6330, 800/223–7637, fax 809/776–6458. Box 720, Cruz Bay 00830-0720; Cinnamon Bay. D, DC not accepted. EP. 40 tents, 40 4-rm cottages, 26 bare sites. $*

Estate Concordia Villas and Eco-tents. Stanley Selengut's showcase eco-digs. The fashionable, fully equipped villas aren't all that environmentally friendly, but they were designed according to the sustainable development theory (building a facility with the least negative impact on the surrounding environment). No wonder Baba Ram Dass hosts weekends here.... *Tel 809/693–5855, 800/392–9004, fax 809/776–6504. Box 310, Cruz Bay 00831; Concordia Hill. D, DC not accepted. EP. 12 villas, 5 tents. $$–$$$ (villas), $ (tents)*

Gallows Point Suite Resort. Patterned after Danish Colonial cottages, these light-gray buildings feature the usual terra-cotta floors, rattan, and floral fabrics. Units are individually owned. The ground-level villas have enormous sky-lit showers; top-floor units feature loft bedrooms. There's no air-conditioning, so request a harborside villa (but expect noise floating across from Cruz Bay).... *Tel 809/776–6434, 800/323–7229, fax 809/776–6520. Box 58, Cruz Bay 00831; Gallow Point. D not accepted. EP. 60 rms. $$$$*

Harmony. These space-age villas are state-of-the-art in conservation; thoroughly solar- or wind-powered, each sports a microwave, fridge, ceiling fan, computer (to help guests gauge energy use). Great views of Maho Bay; artwork (on sale) imported from the Amazon Basin.... *Tel 809/776–6226, 800/392–9004, fax 809/776–6504. Box 310, Cruz Bay 00831; Maho Bay. D, DC not accepted. EP. 12 units. $$*

Hyatt Regency St. John. This 34-acre property at Great Cruz Bay is meticulously maintained, with a raft of large, handsomely appointed guest rooms looking onto the beach or pool and formal gardens. Two top restaurants, tennis courts, health club, water sports, catamarans....The only letdown is the rather small man-made beach, but the pool, with waterfalls and islands, more than compensates.... *Tel 809/693–8000, 800/233–1234, fax 809/693–8888. Box 8310, Great Cruz Bay 00830. EP, MAP. 285 rms. $$$$$*

The Inn at Tamarind Court. This is barebones lodging; the only stabs at decor are a few vividly colored tropical prints, and you must request towels and soap at the front desk when you check in. It's fairly clean if dilapidated, management is helpful, and Etta's, the courtyard bar/restaurant, is a popular local hotspot. Continental breakfast is included.... *Tel 809/776–6378, 800/221–1637. Box 350, Cruz Bay 00831; 34E Enighed. D not accepted. CP. 20 rms, some with shared bath. $*

Lavender Hill Estates. Great values and greater views lure repeat guests year after year to these fully equipped condos. A pool and laundry room are the only facilities on-site.... *Tel 809/776–6969. Box 3606, Cruz Bay 00831; Lavender Hill. AE, D, DC not accepted. 8 units. $$$–$$$$*

Maho Bay Camp. These canvas, wood, and oilcloth tent-cottages are connected by a series of wooden boardwalks, staircases, and ramps that lead down to the beach. The best views of Maho Bay are from the "A" and "D" blocks (no extra charge). The 16 x 16 tent cottages are fairly luxurious by campground standards, with beds, dining table and chairs, propane stove, cooler, electric lamps (and outlets), and kitchenware. Advance bookings (up to a year in high season) are vital at this wildly popular, highly congenial spot.... *Tel 212/472–9453, 800/392–9004. Cruz Bay 00830. No credit cards. 113 tent-cottages. $*

Raintree Inn. The appealing efficiencies here feature kitchens and slightly claustrophobic sleeping lofts; they have red tile floors, colorful Indian spreads, incongruous pine paneling, and partially open-air bathrooms with showers surrounded by shell-and-stone gardens. Smallish conventional hotel rooms have wraparound decks. In keeping with the rustic feel, there are no TVs or phones in the rooms. The excellent Fish Trap restaurant is next door.... *Tel/fax 809/693–8590, 800/666–7449. Box 566, 00831;5A Cruz Bay. DC not accepted. EP. 8 rms, 3 efficiencies. $–$$*

Villas Caribe. These units, among the most deluxe on St. John, are within walking distance of Frank Bay beach and Cruz Bay. All have kitchen, TV, VCR, CD player, air-conditioning—the works. The whitewashed multi-level structure has lavish gardens; the separate Orion House has a tiled Jacuzzi, vaulted ceilings, and enormous panoramic windows.... *Tel/fax 809/693–9100, 800/858–7989. Box 618, Cruz Bay 00831. D, DC not accepted. EP. 4 units, 1 house. $$$$*

St. Thomas Accommodations

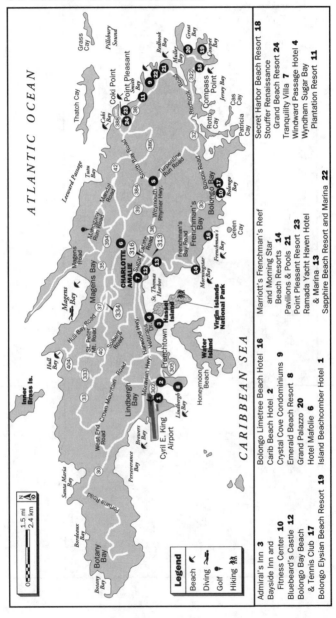

Charlotte Amalie Accommodations

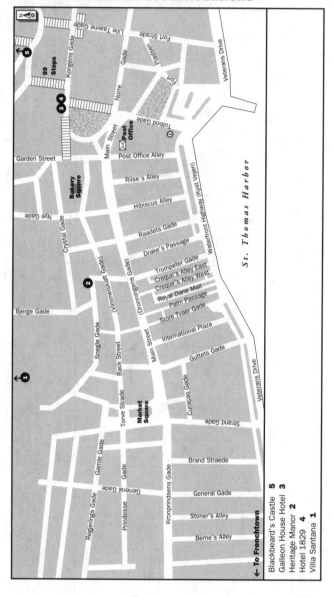

Blackbeard's Castle **5**
Galleon House Hotel **3**
Heritage Manor **2**
Hotel 1829 **4**
Villa Santana **1**

St. Croix Accommodations

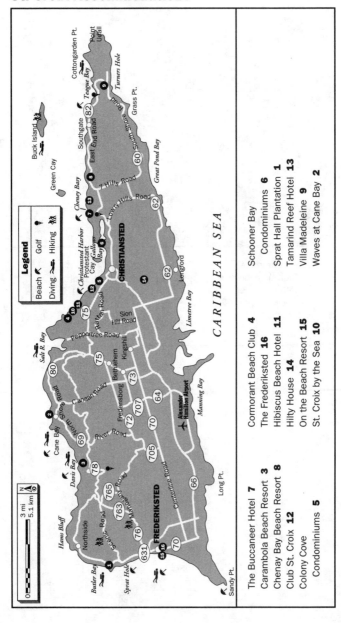

The Buccaneer Hotel **7**
Carambola Beach Resort **3**
Chenay Bay Beach Resort **8**
Club St. Croix **12**
Colony Cove
 Condominiums **5**
Cormorant Beach Club **4**
The Frederiksted **16**
Hibiscus Beach Hotel **11**
Hilty House **14**
On the Beach Resort **15**
St. Croix by the Sea **10**
Schooner Bay
 Condominiums **6**
Sprat Hall Plantation **1**
Tamarind Reef Hotel **13**
Villa Madeleine **9**
Waves at Cane Bay **2**

Christiansted Accommodations

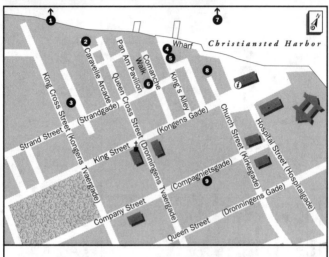

Anchor Inn **4**
Club Comanche **6**
Danish Manor **9**
Holger Danske **3**
Hotel Caravelle **2**
Hotel on the Cay **7**
King Christian Hotel **8**
King's Alley Hotel **5**
The Pink Fancy **1**

St. John Accommodations

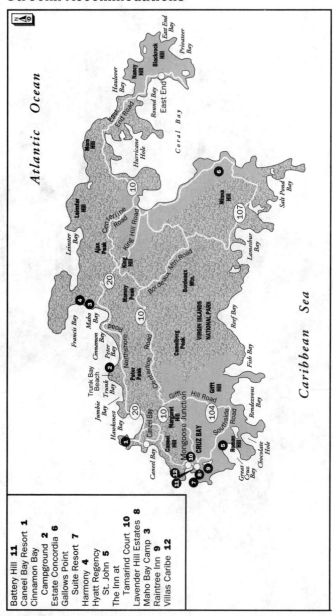

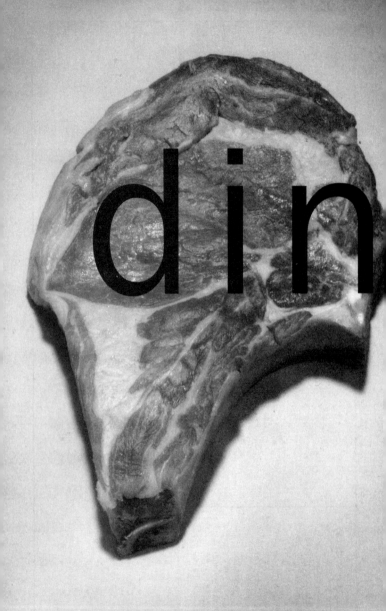

ing 2

For years, dining out in the U.S.V.I. seemed frozen in the Eisenhower era. Even the best restaurants wrote their menus in French for snob appeal, tableside flambés were considered the height of elegance, and a chef's idea of innovation was to garnish a dish with fresh herbs. You can still find such nostalgic dining experiences, especially on St. Thomas and St. Croix, but most restaurants entered the '90s with gastronomic abandon, importing whatever they couldn't grow, raise, or catch locally. The price for this new-found creativity can be stratospheric. The cheapest choices remain local restaurants, burger joints, and fast-food franchises (every chain is represented down here—just one more way in which these islands prove their American-ness).

Ethnic food is still essentially confined to French, Italian, Chinese, and Mexican. But "fusion" cuisine—one of the latest foodie trends, borrowing elements of southwestern, Pacific Rim, and Caribbean cooking—is the current rage, even on St. John, which used to be such a culinary backwater. An otherwise by-the-book bouillabaisse might be accented by Thai lemon grass, or a stolid smoked salmon juiced with juniper. Many visitors take advantage of hotel meal plans—FAP (Full American Plan, all three meals) or MAP (Modified American Plan, breakfast and dinner)—which is a decent money-saving alternative, now that the quality of hotel dining is higher than it once was (you'll also save cab fare). Restaurants such as the Marriott's **Tavern on the Beach** and **Caesar's,** the Grand Palazzo's **Palm Terrace,** and **Entre Nous** in Bluebeard's Castle are so good, labeling them hotel restaurants almost seems an insult. On the other hand, what you often get is absurdly lavish buffet spreads, like something out of a Vegas casino, with food that sometimes sits in its warming pans for hours. And if you opt for the hotel's "gourmet" restaurant, there may be sneaky hidden costs like surcharges for the more expensive or elaborate dishes.

Only in the U.S. Virgin Islands

Local cuisine is primarily a savvy blend of Arawak (the indigenous people) and African influences. The Arawaks contributed native tubers like yuca (also known as cassava) and dasheen (a type of taro root), as well as cilantro, allspice, and achiote for flavoring. The slave ships introduced plantains, sweet potatoes, pigeon peas, and assorted peppers. Various European colonizers brought in fresh garden staples like onions and tomatoes. Shellfish such as conch and whelks are popular, usually stewed creole-style (onions and peppers) or in butter; conch fritters head up many a menu, along with a fiery dipping sauce.

The chefs down here aren't generally big on presentation. Some dishes, especially the stews, look downright unappetizing: dark and lusty, they seem to have been bubbling for days, the meat falling off the bones. But who cares what they look like—they make up for it in flavor. Portions tend to be big, with ample side helpings of rice and peas, sweet potatoes, and the original Caribbean comfort food, fungi (cornmeal boiled with okra). Many folks wash it all down with local juices: mango, guava, papaya, and less-familiar flavors like tart tamarind; milky, mouth-puckering soursop; pulpy passion fruit; bitter yet refreshing maubey (made from tree bark); and thick, milk-shakey sea moss (yes, made from sea moss), which is reputed to have aphrodisiacal powers (as locals say, "Puts lead in your pencil, man"). The local Cruzan rum packs quite a punch; its aged Diamond Estate is as smooth and rich as a fine cognac.

Tables for tunes

Most of the restaurants on the islands pride themselves on providing some form of entertainment; here is a list—by no means a complete one—of restaurants where live music is on the menu. **Barnacle Bill's** *serves up an eclectic menu of music, spotlighting folk or Irish one night, zydeco or jazz the next; the open mike Monday is a St. Thomian tradition. True to its Hispanic roots,* **Cafesito** *presents sizzling flamenco music several nights weekly.* **Tavern on the Beach, The Old Stone Farm House,** *and* **Blackbeard's Castle** *will appeal to those who enjoy a pianist tickling the ivories, with a sophisticated repertoire leaning more toward "My Funny Valentine" than "Melancholy Baby."* **Etta's** *is the best place to mingle with locals while listening to reggae, calypso, and soca.* **Eeez's Specialty Cafe** *cooks with Power Surge, a high-voltage reggae band, weekend nights. And a great mix of locals and tourists parties to live blues, rock, or reggae on the sands at* **La Grange Beach Club** *weekend nights.*

How to Dress

Dress is usually informal, though long pants and collared shirts are preferred in the better restaurants at night, especially in high season. Even the formerly stuffy Caneel Bay resort on St. John has relaxed its standards: jacket and tie are no longer required (which doesn't mean you shouldn't wear one; some of the more elderly old boys, not to mention the snootier waiters, can wither you with a glance). Women can get away with almost anything, as long as it covers the bare necessities. Bathing suits are generally frowned upon at lunch, except in the most casual beach restaurants. That Carolina Herrera or DKNY number you just bought in Charlotte Amalie? Wear it if you want, but only to impress your date: the locals don't care, and nine out of ten cruise passengers won't know what it is.

When to Eat

For most people it's early to bed, early to rise on the islands. Dinner is rarely served past 10. (The bars are something else entirely, often staying open past the official closing time of 2am.) Breakfast, for that matter, is usually cleared by 10 in the hotels. The dining hours (and habits) are very middle-American: breakfast 7–10, lunch 12–3, dinner 6–10.

Getting the Right Table

Forget the old adage, "Money talks." Greasing palms never did work in the Virgin Islands. Believe it or not, the truth (or an expedient fib) does—but keep the whining and wheedling to a minimum. In other words, tell them it's your honeymoon if you want a table with a harbor view. Confide that your husband or wife just found out about your affair and you want to make it up. Say your kids are well-behaved. Whatever you do, don't waltz into the fancier restaurants expecting to be seated without a reservation—they're imperative, especially in winter. (That also goes for lunch in Charlotte Amalie and Christiansted when cruise traffic is heavy.) Even hotel guests risk being turned away at the on-site restaurant if their name isn't in the maitre d's big black book. This doesn't mean you have to reserve a table weeks—or even a week—in advance, even at the hottest current bistro; two or three nights' notice should do it.

Where the Chefs Are

Thanks to fierce competition, the bigger hotels often have very innovative dining rooms—you won't find stars from the Michelin galaxy, but you'll often run into recent graduates from the C.I.A. (that's Culinary Institute of America—a hotbed of gastronomic subversiveness these days). These operatives generally hang around for a season or two, honing their skills and catching some rays before they open their own restaurants stateside; no matter how good they are, they're eventually replaced with somebody just as good and quality stays high. The real stars of the restaurants are the owners, many of whom still lend a hand in the kitchen. Among those who've established an enviable track record are **Christopher Rosbrook** (Chateau Bordeaux and the new Asolare in St. John), **Virgilio** (the eponymous restaurant in St. Thomas), and **David Kendrick** (Kendrick's on St. Croix).

The Lowdown

Overrated... Everything about **Hotel 1829** (St. Thomas) is as advertised—except the vaunted views. The terrace itself is lovely, and there is a view of the harbor—unfortunately, it's obscured by a jungle of telephone wires. The food at St. Thomas's **Il Cardinale** has been wildly inconsistent ever since the former managers left—and on a sunny day, who wants to sit inside this somber dining room, which needs only cobwebs to duplicate Miss Havisham's moldy digs in *Great Expectations*? **Morgan's Mango** (St. John) is too cute for words, from the name (Morgan is the owner's pet iguana) to the overly ambitious pan-Caribbean menu. What else can you expect from a restaurant whose drinks list is a page long? Everyone raves about **Top Hat** (St. Croix), but despite its refined ambience, congenial proprietors, and unusual menu (running toward Danish specialties), nothing can disguise the all-too-often pedestrian, unimaginative cooking.

Truly elegant... Distinguished silver-haired CEOs and their third wives or husbands mingle with young guppies resplendent in blue blazers and white ducks at the bar of St. Thomas's **Blackbeard's Castle.** Gershwin and Porter melodies float on the balmy breeze, courtesy of a pianist or jazz combo; the terrace opens onto the hotel pool and smashing views of the harbor. Add waiters in tails bearing silver trays and it could be one of Gatsby's parties. **The Old Stone Farm House** is perhaps the apotheosis of fine dining on St. Thomas, a near-perfect blend of Old World architecture and antiques and stylishly modern food; the clientele ranges from starry-eyed honeymooners to retirees who don't depend on Social Security. **Entre Nous** (also on St. Thomas, this time in

Bluebeard's Castle), is a throwback to glamorous 1960s hotel dining, with crisp napery, candlelight, fine china and crystal, and baskets overflowing with dried-flower arrangements. **Palm Terrace** occupies a sweeping, cathedralesque space overlooking Pillsbury Sound on St. Thomas; tinkling gin-fed laughter and piano music float out toward St. John. **Villa Madeleine Greathouse** seeks to re-create the days before tour groups descended on St. Croix, when the only people who vacationed here had trust funds. The decor is so patrician, it's been profiled in *Architectural Digest*. Also on St. Croix, **Kendrick's** is the dining equivalent of a *Vogue* fashion shot: boldly chic and intelligently laid out. Starched white linens, bone china, and bow-tied waiters complete the look. St. Croix's **Picnic in Paradise** is the kind of place where you ask for water and they immediately serve the designer variety; the delightful interior features whimsical historic prints, an aquarium, a fireplace, and rattan furniture. Sit on the terrace for the full stars-and-surf effect. **Asolare** (St. John) means the "purposeless, agreeable, and leisurely passing of time," and monied diners do just that all evening in this tastefully decorated converted private home, with several British Virgin Islands moodily silhouetted across the bay.

Institutions... **Hotel 1829** (St. Thomas) seems frozen in the 1950s—and that's meant as a compliment. Tableside pyrotechnics—filet mignon au poivre, warm spinach salad—and those famous dessert soufflés still dominate the menu. Many of the waitstaff have been here for years (one started at age 14 in 1967; his father had tended bar for 45 years). Also on St. Thomas is **Virgilio's**, whose popularity hasn't waned since it opened, thanks to consistently top-notch Italian fare, the slightly fussy Rococo decor, and, most of all, owner Virgilio del Mare's caring service. **Top Hat** has long been the choice for a fancy evening out on St. Croix; the elegant, congenial Hanne Rasmussen at the door, and her husband Bent in the Danish-influenced kitchen, have been pampering diners for a couple of decades. **Club Comanche**, also on St. Croix, feels like a tropical colonial movie set from the 1940s—you half expect to find Noel Coward, Graham Greene, or Somerset Maugham holding court at the bar (reputedly, they all have), and the doggedly Continental menu has probably changed little from those days. The combination of stunning sunset views, chic rustic decor, and sterling French cuisine has made **Chateau Bordeaux** (St. John) a must on every serious foodie's list.

Where the locals go... On St. Thomas, those in the know head for Frenchtown, just outside downtown Charlotte Amalie; **Alexander's** and **Craig and Sally's** seem to cater exclusively to a local crowd, which prefers it that way. Only locals seem to know about St. Croix's cute bistro **South Shore Cafe**, too, and the charming seaside **No Name Bar and Grill**. The cab fare and long ride to **Miss Lucy's** (St. John) guarantee that day-trippers will stay away in droves, but they'll miss out on some of the best Creole food anywhere.

Something fishy... Seafood paintings, crustacean napkin holders, wooden fish, and shakers of sea salt attest to the fact that they take fish *seriously* at **Agavé Terrace** (St. Thomas). The catch of the day can be grilled, panfried, blackened, poached, baked, or batter-fried with one of nine sauces (hollandaise, lemon butter, lobster-cream, teriyaki-mango, etc.); also try the cracked conch or coconut–fried shrimp with banana fritters. Also on St. Thomas, at Bolongo Bay, the **Caribbean Lobster House** states clearly what its specialty is, and you can order it several ways. Casual, New England-y **Hook, Line and Sinker**, which sits dockside in Frenchtown, offers a virtual seafood smorgasbord, from shrimp Bahia (fragrant with coconut milk) to bouillabaisse. On St. Croix, **Antoine's** stands out for the mind-boggling variety of seafood on its aquarium-like menu (with explanations of the sea critters thoughtfully provided): alligator to abalone, skate to shad roe, all panfried, poached, sautéed, blackened, or creamed. While nothing is truly memorable at St. Croix's **Banana Bay Club**, it's got a dynamite setting on the water, the staff is personable, and the seafood is always reliable. With so many trendy new restaurants on St. John, **Ellington's** is often unjustifiably forgotten. The chefs here whip up a smashing, steamy fish chowder, swimming with enormous chunks of whatever's fresh; specials might include three fish (catch of the day like wahoo, grouper, and kingfish) sautéed with tomato, basil, and cucumber over tortellini. Don't expect anything fancy at St. John's **The Fish Trap**: they just broil, grill, and sauté everything perfectly.

Real island cuisine, mon... A large jar of "roots" (a swampy blend of cane rum, cashews, peanuts, seagrapes, and tania that seems to have been steeping forever) greets you at the bar of **Eunice's Terrace** (St. Thomas), a giveaway that they take their traditions seriously. The first shot is complimentary; any more and you might not be able to taste the conch fritters, honey-dipped chicken, and herb-stuffed lobster for which Eunice is famous. **Victor's New Hideout** is the local St. Thomas restaurant every tourist has heard of, but it lives up to its billing, with succulent ginger pork chops and triggerfish creole among the better offerings. Also on St. Thomas, **Diamond Barrel** attracts locals with such rotating specials as bullfoot stew or pigtail dumplings. **Gladys' Cafe** wisely appeals to all tastes and pocketbooks, so along with all-American sandwiches and burgers you'll find more exotic fare like mutton stew and saltfish and dumplings. **Cuzzin's** serves the same kind of fare (in a more upscale space) to the St. Thomian upper crust, for which they and you pay a couple of bucks more. **Le Petite Pump Room** also seduces island power-brokers, with its sublime callaloo soup and conch in butter sauce as well as its fine harbor views.

Anabelle's Tea Room (St. Croix) specializes in Puerto Rican dishes like the thick, sultry rice stew (*asopao*) and pork or chicken slow-roasted with garlic. **Villa Morales,** a good choice for those sightseeing on St. Croix's West End, near Estate Whim Plantation Museum and the St. George Botanical Gardens, offers a hybrid Latino/West Indian menu. **Harvey's** presents heaping helpings of the best fungi, whelks in butter, and conch creole on St. Croix, while the specialty at **Eeez's Specialty Cafe** is authentic Antiguan fare—classics like bull's foot soup, souse, and salt fish—cooked the traditional way on coalpots. People certainly don't come for the decor at **Kim's,** another St. Croix spot that practically defines hole-in-the-wall, but the baked chicken and stewed fish are sublime; homey **Vel's** is beloved for its robust, aggressively seasoned food (they often run out of specials early). **The Purple Door** (St.

John) serves up a savory blend of traditional hearty West Indian food and lighter, healthful Ital fare. Everything tastes so fresh at **Miss Lucy's**, also on St. John, that you can't help wondering if the goats and chickens ambling in the yard are on the menu. The spicy sauces at St. John's **Etta's** will bring tears to the bravest diner's eyes, and well they should.

Best breakfasts... **Tavern on the Beach** (St. Thomas) makes the fluffiest, richest, eggiest French toast, soaked in Frangelico, you may ever have eaten. Elsewhere on St. Thomas, **Guava Grille** offers up huge stacks of banana pancakes, and **Bumpa's** does good, oozy omelets and great griddle grub like waffles with bacon; it's also one of the few restaurants down here where you can get a bagel and lox. Nearly every major hotel in the U.S.V.I. prides itself on the length of its breakfast buffet, playing "can you top this?" like giggling, hormonal teenage boys. St. Croix's Carambola Beach Resort's **The Saman Room** has them all beat, with a spread guaranteed to raise your cholesterol level just by looking, though health fanatics will find fresh fruits, nuts, and yogurts, and can even order egg-white omelets. Over in Frederiksted, the **Market Street Cafe** markets a delectable seafood omelet (and you can also get filling lunches for under $5), though remember, it closes by 2pm—the owner has to pick up her kids at school. If you like your huevos really rancheros, with kick-ass salsa, head for **JJ's Texas Coast Cafe** on St. John, where they'll garnish everything with jalapeños if you let them.

Best brunch... A large, jovial man in a Hawaiian shirt surveys the scene at **The Saman Room** (in the Carambola Beach Resort, St. Croix), patting his belly with Buddha-like serenity. Everywhere he looks there are gleaming chafing dishes and carving stations for roast beef, smoked salmon, turkey, not to mention sublime sushi, pasta primavera, schools of leviathan shrimp on ice. The scene is played out at nearly every major resort hotel in the U.S.V.I., but The Saman Room still sets the standard. If you'd rather order à la carte, try **Villa Madeleine Greathouse, Picnic in Paradise,** and **On the Beach**, all on St. Croix; and **Blackbeard's Castle** and **Cafe Vecchio** on St. Thomas. All of these at least venture beyond eggs

Benedict, offering some more imaginative breakfast choices like shrimp and salmon on English muffins with red pepper coulis.

Best lunch... Ardent shoppers can't do any better than the great grilled sandwiches at **Cafe Amici**, which occupies a prime location smack in the middle of St. Thomas's Royal Dane Mall, where the labels go to be outfitted. Also on St. Thomas, **Cafesito**'s varied selection of tapas makes for a perfect light bite in the sultry climate. If they can stuff it in pita, they serve it at **Cafe Sagapo**, from swordfish pockets to standard gyros; this neat little Greek place in Charlotte Amalie also serves fantastic pizzas and salads. If you're in the mood for a more refined setting and you find yourself on St. Thomas's East End, **Cafe Vecchio** in the sumptuous Grand Palazzo Hotel fits the (pricy) bill. Locals love **Anabelle's Tea Room** (St. Croix), set in a funky courtyard overgrown with hanging plants. The thick conch chowder or black bean soup make meals in themselves. **Tommy and Susan's Taverna**, also on St. Croix, is literally a Greek diner, Caribbean-style, where locals go for chef/owner Tommy Borodemos' souvlaki, broiled chicken with feta, and zesty salads. If you're on St. Croix and want to linger over a rarefied lunch, stop by the **Cormorant Beach Club**, a lovely hotel dining room that's most tranquil at lunchtime, or **Picnic in Paradise**, whose creative sandwiches are the best thing they serve. On St. John, **The Purple Door** whips up thirst-slaking iced bush teas (made from the leaves or seeds of local plants like mango, soursop, and guava), aromatic with lemon grass and mint; hearty veggie soups brimming with pigeon peas, okra, corn, carrots, and whole-wheat dumplings; grilled catch of the day; and wonderful salads.

Ringside seats for people-watching... This category comes with a proviso: it's applicable only during the winter. (In summer, there aren't enough people around to watch.) You never know who's going to walk into **Paradiso** or **Saychelles**, both on St. John. On the best nights, their bars alone are wonderful living theater: sun-streaked blond(e)s, lobster-hued men in loud Hawaiian shirts, Rastafarians in drag, waif-like models so thin it hurts. And there's no cover. If your idea of beautiful is lacquered hair, perfect posture, and surgically enhanced cheekbones, you'll enjoy gazing at the dollar signs at creative, urbane **Equator**, the "new" restaurant in St. John's old-money Caneel Bay resort (habitués frankly prefer the resort's stuffy Turtle Bay restaurant, open only to guests, with a menu carved in stone). If you prefer rubbing elbows with rich yuppies on their honeymoons, try St. John's sister restaurants **Chateau Bordeaux** and **Asolare.** On St. Thomas, the crowd at **Hotel 1829** is a melange of society matrons, corporate honchos, Wall Street youngbloods, and their respective mates dressed to the hilt. You'll find the same mix over at **Blackbeard's Castle,** with a few soigné gay couples thrown in. The scene is less frenzied on St. Croix, but **Tutto Bene** and **Indies** corral more than their share of young, trust-funded preening pretties.

Where the buffet tables groan... Remember the French film *La Grande Bouffe*, where the main characters gorged themselves to death, or the classic, lusty eating scene in *Tom Jones*? The extravagant buffets at Carambola's **Saman Room** (St. Croix) are in the same vein, catered as if for tempermental stars. There are theme buffets several evenings a week; West Indian night, for example, offers scrumptious barbecue, various fishes in creole sauce, and mounds of side dishes, plus fire-eaters, glass-walkers, and mocko jumbies (spirits) on stilts. **The Hideaway,** on a breezy terrace, offers economical West Indian, Texas BBQ, Oriental, Mexican, and Italian nights, not to mention an evening devoted to seafood. Toney St. John isn't a buffet kind of isle, so the Hyatt Regency's **Cafe Grand** has little competition, with a huge array of dishes on its theme nights (all-you-can-eat Cajun shrimp Tuesdays are a particular draw).

The French connection... The finest French restaurants in the U.S.V.I. make a brilliant marriage between classic French preparations and indigenous ingredients (though you can always rely on such standards as foie gras). **Entre Nous** (St. Thomas) fits this description to a T, not to mention a drinks list that specializes in champagne cocktails, rather than tired rum concoctions. Also on St. Thomas, **Café Normandie** serves traditional haute cuisine—none of that casual bistro/brasserie stuff. **The Old Stone Farm House,** one of St. Thomas's best restaurants, gives French food a clever Asian spin, ingeniously incorporating curry, chutney, and ginger into its dishes. **Le St. Tropez** is the best on St. Croix, practically by default, though the Provençal cuisine is comme il faut. For the best French restaurant in the U.S.V.I., however, head for St. John and **Chateau Bordeaux**; the food here isn't classic French, having a decidedly Asian twist, but it's fabulous, and the cliffside setting is breathtaking.

Around the Mediterranean... Caesar's on St. Thomas would get a thumbs-up from any emperor with its dazzling Tuscan-style grilled items and chef Ron Balldaseseroni's earthy approach. The menu at St. Thomas's **Cafesito** blends several Spanish culinary traditions, from Catalan to Andalucian, with loads of garlic. The seafood is particularly sublime, as though it has sprung straight from the sea to your plate. The emphasis, predictably, is on Greek fare at St. Thomas's **Cafe Sagapo/Zorba's** with everything from phyllo to pita. The chef at **Saychelles**, on St. John, hails from Texas, yet he juggles several culinary traditions—Greek, Italian, Catalan, Andalucian, Provençal—with aplomb.

Alla Italia... Listen to the owner's accent and you'll realize that **Virgilio's** has to be authentic—it has long set the standard for Northern Italian cuisine on St. Thomas. Also on St. Thomas, **Romano's,** under simpatico chef/owner Tony Romano, concentrates on old family recipes and classics given an inventive twist. If you're looking for a homey mom-and-pop place where the aroma of garlic meets the St. Thomas sea breeze, **Ferrari's** is the spot. On St. Croix, **Dino's** offers the most original Italian food on the islands, deftly incorporating indigenous ingredients in traditional recipes; **Tutto Bene** counters with classic, almost stereotypical fare from veal piccata to fettuccini primavera. On St. John, **Paradiso**'s new owners have ditched the menu's staid standbys in favor of such innovative dishes as herb-crusted calamari with sun-dried tomato aioli or seared yellowfin tuna with braised fennel and citrus sauce. These certainly have the edge over the "transcultural" offerings at **Ciao Mein,** which consist mostly of deftly prepared standards like chicken parmigiana and fettucine alfredo (though new chef Steven Carl may prove more adventurous).

Asian delights... On St. Thomas, fresh fish is a highly prized commodity; great quantities of it are sliced and diced Japanese-style at **Beni Iguana's Sushi Bar**. The owners call sushi "edible art," and their presentation bears them out; try the Texas roll ("same as a California roll, only bigger"), Philly roll (smoked salmon and cream cheese), specials like "surf and surf" (eel and shrimp roll), or whatever's fresh that day. Robert Smith, the supremely talented young chef at St. John's **Asolare,** proudly admits he hates Thai food but was looking for a challenge. You wouldn't know it from his expert preparations, a symphony of textures and flavors culled from the Pacific Rim. The unfortunately named **Ciao Mein**, also on St. John, is only half Italian; the other half of its menu offers some of the best Asian food in the islands, like crispy duck salad with wonton croutons and honey ginger vinaigrette or Mongolian beef with scallions, bamboo shoots, ginger, and hoisin sauce.

For those who only wear black... **Pangaea** (St. Croix) means "all earth," and its decor certainly resembles an international garage sale: coconut husk masks from Hawaii, Japanese kimonos, African gourd instruments, Moroccan beads, and the like. Curlicues of incense waft through the room, windchimes provide background music, and the multicultural menu offers robust, marvelous food. In fine contempt for more orthodox couplings, the chef at Pangaea whips up such concoctions as Kashmiri tuna with soursop or mahi mahi with mangoes and sun-dried tomato pesto. If you like Rasta Ital (vegan) fare, stop in at the barebones **UCA Vegetarian Restaurant,** also on St. Croix, whose food is so good, filling, and cheap it could convert any carnivore (they do wondrous, meat-like things with tofu).

Seabreeze Cafe (St. John) is a laid-back gathering spot, serving an eclectic menu of basic dishes to artists of all mediums—there are rotating art exhibits on the walls, weekly poetry readings, occasional jam sessions, and even performance art on the postage stamp–sized stage. Other St. John hot spots: **Luscious Licks**, which started out serving "all natural" Ben & Jerry's ice cream, then expanded to heavenly, healthful, vegetarian dishes; and **The Purple Door**, which pays tribute to St. John's African heritage, with King Sunny Ade on the sound system, various tribal art and artifacts, and such reading material as *International Hot Spice* ("The Metaphysical Co-op, Love Inc. Educational Monthly").

Swoony harbor views... Several restaurants rival **Blackbeard's Castle** (St. Thomas) in the views department, but the real reason it heads every list is the atmosphere. The terrace abuts the hotel pool, making you feel like you're dining at the estate of your college roommate's rich uncle Ned. The huge picture windows of the aptly named **A Room with a View** look directly onto the lights of Charlotte Amalie and its convoy of cruise ships. The more down-to-earth **Frigate** (the one in the Hotel Mafolie, *not* its sister branch in Red Hook) may have the most spectacular, sweeping views on St. Thomas: a nearly 360-degree panorama of town and harbor. On St. John, casual/chic **Ellington's** isn't as upscale as more recent arrivals **Asolare** and **Saychelles** (which also have great views), but its appealing terrace lets you sit outside and gaze out over Cruz Bay, with technicolor sunsets as a bonus.

Power spots... On St. Thomas, local politicians, writers, and anyone who's anyone hobnob at **Virgilio's** at lunch, **Alexander's Cafe** at dinner. **Le Petite Pump Room** is run by Michael Watson, the brother of the Assistant Commissioner of Tourism, and the current governor's wife used to cook there—need we say more? On St. Croix, power brokers congregate at **Bombay Club** and **Camille's,** where they can sequester themselves in private booths for lunch. **Indies** is St. Croix's current fashionable spot to see and be seen at dinner, followed by **Tutto Bene,** where island bigwigs entertain money people who can help finance their pet projects. When the local senators and their aides want to hunker over a plentiful, cheap lunch away from prying eyes, they make a beeline to **Vel's** in Frederiksted.

Best place to seal a deal... Many of the "power" hangouts listed above, ironically, have cramped tables that practically encourage eavesdropping. That's why St.

Thomas's **Hotel 1829** should be your choice for a small, important business function; its two intimate inside rooms can be closed off completely, with heavy wood doors ensuring no one will hear even the most heated arguments. The stolid Continental menu and extensive wine list will command respect, too.

See-and-be-scenes... **Blue Marlin** (St. Thomas), a casual Red Hook dive just down the harbor from the marina, reels in big fish off the yachts like Whitney Houston, John Travolta, and Martin Lawrence. Down the street, the **East Coast Bar and Grill** hooks the rest, especially athletes like Charles Barkley, Jose Canseco, and Mark McGwire (they do a particularly brisk trade in Bay Area celebs, since the owners hail from San Francisco); it's also a favorite watering hole for America's Cup veterans like Dennis Conner and Peter Hamburg. **Paradiso** (St. John) attracts the Martha's Vineyard set; there have even been unsubstantiated Kennedy sightings in season.

Where the yachties hang... Yachties usually want a minimum of fuss—just a slip, cold draft beer, cheap fresh seafood, and maybe a little live music (or at least a good jukebox). The al fresco deck of **Latitude 18** (St. Thomas), right on the Vessup Marina, delivers on all counts; the **East Coast Bar and Grill** is the indoor version—a classic sports bar, raucous, dimly lit, and woody. **Columbus Cove** sits among the palms and mangroves of St Croix's Salt River National Park (the reputed site of Columbus' landing here in 1493), with assorted yachts and dinghies bobbing in the marina; casual atmosphere, not the steak-and-seafood menu, is the main thing here. On St. John, most of the chi-chi yachties (almost no bareboaters here) hang at **Paradiso** in Cruz Bay's ultra-chic shopping mall, Mongoose Junction. The rest of them head for **Skinny Legs** at Coral Bay, on the other side of the island both geographically and spiritually.

Most beautiful waitstaff... **Chateau Bordeaux** and **Asolare**, both on St. John and under the same dynamic ownership, seem to import their waitstaff straight from Soho (New York or London) and Melrose Avenue—they look like would-be actors and models, all wearing the appropriate gear (including hoops in one ear and/or ponytails for the men). Despite that, they're surprisingly friendly. If you agree with the Beach Boys about California girls, head for **Tutto Bene** (St. Croix), where the waitresses look like they wandered in from a UCLA frat party, nearly each and every one blonde, lithe, and tanned. On St. Thomas, the occasionally indifferent staffers at the Marriott Morningstar's ultra-trendy **Caesar's** and **Tavern on the Beach** are so pretty they can't help but pose, especially the men. Straight or gay, they all seem quite willing to flirt, and they expect to be tipped accordingly.

Friendliest waitstaff... Hands down, it's the crowd at **Hotel 1829** (St. Thomas), led by maitre d'/general manager Michael Ball. The atmosphere is cultured, the Continental food refined, and the service impeccable—but once the dining room closes, local characters and foodies cluster around the bar, Ball reappears in his T-shirt and jeans, and the carousing begins as they sample new wines, old rums, and cigars. Any guest who keeps up may just end up drinking free. At **Eeez's Specialty Cafe** (St. Croix), Eeez himself (a.k.a. Everette Parker) is the main attraction. He'll regale you with his life story (he's been a fashion model, dancer, and sous chef at the Waldorf Astoria), then take you through the family photos that cover every inch of wall space. There are hundreds of snapshots of all seven daughters and four sons, as well as their mothers. (No grandchildren as yet: "The girls ain't giving up nothing and the guys ain't getting nothing.")

Rudest waitstaff... **Le St. Tropez** (St. Croix) is the kind of place that continues to give the French a bad name. The Gallic staff roll their eyes if you order by the English translation—or, *quelle horreur*, mangle the French pronunciation. Then, if you don't tip well, they'll rush out to scold you. They've imported some American waitresses, so service might improve. The maitre d' at **The Old Stone Farm House** (St. Thomas) also treats diners with French indifference bordering on contempt. Even when he smiles, you can't help but wonder if it's because a piece of entrecôte has stuck in your teeth. This attitude fortunately doesn't infect the attractive young servers here.

Isn't it romantic?... St. Thomas has three restaurants perfect for proposals of any sort: the exquisite **Old Stone Farm House** (no 18th-century farmhouse would have been outfitted so opulently); **Virgilio's**, where candlelight flickers off fine china and crystal, the waiters approve your choice no matter what, and superlative Italian food is served (the only thing missing is a strolling violinist); and **Blackbeard's Castle**, where the lights of Charlotte Amalie sparkle like diamonds on black velvet below you. On St. Croix, it's a toss-up between **Villa Madeleine Greathouse** and **Picnic in Paradise**: the patio of the former is more stylishly decorated, with bricks, tiles, and wrought-iron tables; the terrace of the latter has a great nighttime panorama of sky and sea. **Chateau Bordeaux** remains St. John's top fairy-tale dining experience, a tiny house clinging precariously to Bordeaux Mountain, with picture-postcard views and dollhouse decor.

For single women who want to be left alone... On St. Thomas, the folks at **Alexander's Cafe** are way too refined to bother you, the clientele at **Blackbeard's Castle** will be either gay or married, and the watchful, protective owner at **Virgilio's** keeps things on the up and up. Stick to the fancier, pricier restaurants on any of the islands, and your only hassle will be an overattentive waiter.

For singles who don't want to be left alone... Those seeking romance of a more transient nature flock to St. Thomas. The local **Hard Rock Cafe** franchise takes the virgin out of the islands: you'd swear you were back in the '70s when singles were lined up Friday nights at the bar two or three deep. (Live music nightly in season also packs them in.) The bar section of **Sib's Mountain Bar and Restaurant** is a magnet for every college kid on St. Thomas, whether they're looking for action or not. **The Greenhouse** occupies an enviable position on Charlotte Amalie's waterfront, smack in the middle of the downtown shopping district. During the day it's mostly cruise shippies; at night it's more cruisers and chippies. (They're not looking for their first mate, that's for sure.) Just from the name, you could guess that **Tickles Dockside Pub** (with two locations, in Red Hook and Charlotte Amalie) is not a place where people come for the food; it's strictly brews, burgers, and "Hey, baby, what's happening?"

Best burgers... All those **Hard Rock Cafes** must be good for something other than T-shirts and sex, drugs, and rock 'n roll; the one here on St. Thomas excels at burgers. These are hefty and dripping with juice, with just the right amount of charcoal coating. And the fries are crisp on the outside, almost raw on the inside, a paean to Idaho produce. **Pusser's** (St. John) is the Brit version of Hard Rock, including the same assortment of name-brand merchandise, but the beefy burgers at least do the English love of meat proud. The twenty-somethings who gather at **Cheeseburgers in Paradise** (St. Croix), where the mood is as festive as the bright yellow exterior, could honestly not care less about the quality of the food. But this roadside diner flings a mean (and big) burger, stomach-crunching chili dogs, and greasy, gooey nachos. If you prefer ambience with your burger, check out snug **Camille's,** also on St. Croix, with its beamed ceilings, brick walls, and local artwork displays.

Best wine list... Marston Winkles, the savvy general manager of the Grand Palazzo on St. Thomas, loves his wine, and the hotel's **Palm Terrace** list offers ample proof—over 7,500 bottles' worth. Winkles takes such pride in his cellar that if a hotel guest casually mentions that his favorite wine isn't listed, it will be quietly offered (subject to availability) within the next few nights. The price for this impeccable service is outrageous (typically running $5–$10 more per bottle than competitors), but then the clientele here can well afford it. Until the Palazzo opened, **Hotel 1829**, also on St. Thomas, had bragging rights to the best, most comprehensive list in the U.S.V.I.; it's still admirably balanced, with decent buys in South American, Australian, and Iberian wines. While its cellar ranks a couple of notches below, St. Thomas's **Virgilio's** does offer the best selection of Italian wines, including such high-priced, high-profile labels as Gaja Barbaresco, Biondi Santi Brunello, Sassicaia, and Solaia; Virgilio himself keeps some special bottles in reserve—ask nicely for your favorite, and it just might turn up.

Caffeine scenes... Alexander's Coffee House (St. Thomas) seems straight from Vienna (or at least Salzburg, Alexander's hometown), with newspapers and tempting tortes in addition to the array of international brews. If you prefer Italian roast (or at least espresso), try **I Cappuccini**, which also serves light lunch fare in Charlotte Amalie's pretty Taste of Italy courtyard mall. The place to get jump-started on St. Croix is the **Morning Glory Coffee House**, which imports beignets from Cafe du Monde in New Orleans (no chicory coffee, though) and bakes its own terrific muffins and biscotti.

On the beach (casual)... St. Croix's **Duggan's Reef** is a breezy, congenial eatery with fine fresh seafood and a spirited clientele. The umbrellas of **On the Beach** are parked right on St. Croix's finest beach, just outside downtown Frederiksted; on the other side of town, **La Grange Beach Club** is a popular spot for locals and tourists alike to get their feet wet, watch the ships cruise in, then munch on burgers and simple grilled seafood. On St. John, **Miss Lucy's** has only a tiny patch of beach, but chaise longues are available for those who want to sip a killer passionfruit daiquiri (mango and guava are other good choices) before adjourning inside for the main event.

On the beach (elegant)... The St. Thomas choice is **Caesar's**, which leads right to the hedonistic Morningstar Beach, one of the most perfect crescents in the Virgin Islands. (The Marriott's other restaurant, **Tavern on the Beach**, cheats: it only overlooks the sand and surf.) On St. John, **Saychelles'** terrace opens onto a beach on the Cruz Bay harbor; you wouldn't necessarily take a dip here, but the moon reflecting on the water more than makes up for this.

Sunset views to choose... Restaurants with phenomenal views rarely offer food to match, and **Café du Soleil** (St. Croix) is no exception. Stick to appetizers like the charcuterie plate or simple grilled items like beef tenderloin; accompany them with a few sunset-colored house special drinks as the sun fireballs across the sky. **The Bar at Paradise Point** (St. Thomas) cooks nothing more strenuous than a cheeseburger, but no one cares, thanks to sensational live music, knockout rum punches, and sunsets so magnificent they can make you giddy. **Chateau Bordeaux** (St. John) sits atop the highest point on St. John, with jaw-dropping views of several British Virgin Islands silhouetted against the twilit sky.

Most creative kitchen... The "New World" creations—carryovers from famed start-up chef Eddie Hale's menu—at **Tavern on the Beach** on St. Thomas appeal equally to the taste and to the eyes, with sculpted entrees set amid abstract swirls of sauce. The presentation is no less elaborate at **Entre Nous,** also on St. Thomas, where garnishing has achieved levels of extraordinary artistry—dishes are not so much cooked as they are constructed, such as a towering vegetable napoleon sitting in two concentric puddles of tomato and basil coulis. **The Old Stone Farm House** also excels at presentation; witness one of the signature dishes, roasted red snapper in a crispy potato crust that duplicates fish scales, gliding through caramelized shallots in Zinfandel sauce. Sally Darash, the inspired amateur in the kitchen at St. Thomas's **Craig and Sally's,** merrily synthesizes various traditions from Cajun to Provençal. St. Croix's **The Mahogany Room** is a throwback to the nouvelle days when a slice of fruit here, a lattice of vegetables there, three shrimp or a rectangle of wahoo are exquisitely arranged in appetizing pools of delicate sauce. Also on St. Croix, **Pangaea**'s radical menu fuses African, Caribbean, and Asian cuisines without pretension, while at **Dino's,** Dino Natale and Dwight DeLude continually experiment with new items, giving their Italian fare a welcome Caribbean gloss.

On St. John, **Equator**'s presentations verge on the pretentious; the gimmick here is to use ingredients and preparations from various countries bordering the equator. At **Asolare,** chef Robert Smith paints the plate like a canvas, bright colors complementing his bright, bold flavors; Asolare's sister **Chateau Bordeaux** takes French standards and slyly reinvents them with a Pacific Rim flair, such as house-smoked, char-grilled pork loin in kiln-dried cherry and shiitake *demi glace,* or Peking duck breast pan-seared in cilantro marinade with pear-tomato-saffron coulis. At **Saychelles,** also on St. John, the hip, young, C.I.A.-trained chef Chris Coble doesn't seem to take himself—or his food—too seriously, and the sense of fun translates to the plate in such dishes as grilled pork tenderloin with sweet potato puree and black bean salsa, zucchini charlotte, or mako escabeche.

Historic settings... On St. Thomas, **The Old Stone Farm House** is just that, the hub of a late-17th-century sugar plantation called Estate Loveland; **Hotel 1829** does indeed date from 1829, and has the heavy carved wooden doors with iron bolts to prove it, in addition to original brick walls; and the entrance to **Blackbeard's Castle** is guarded by a 17th-century stone tower (on the National Register of Historic Places) built by that infamous pirate, though the restaurant structure itself dates from the 1970s. On St. Croix, most of Christiansted's restaurants occupy gorgeous 18th-century stone buildings, notably **Kendrick's, Tutto Bene, Top Hat,** and **Bombay Club**; **Indies** is actually built over a cemetery—no, there haven't been poltergeist sightings, but the owners will gladly show you the sole remaining gravestone right there in the interior courtyard. **Equator,** the only truly historic restaurant on St. John, is housed in a converted sugar mill on the Caneel Bay resort.

For committed carnivores... Despite the marina setting, wood-and-brass shipboard look, and nautical name, seafood is not the reason St. Croix locals flock to **The Galleon**: they come here for some of the tenderest, most flavorful beef on the island, including classic chateaubriand and prime rib. **Lime Inn** (St. John) is like an al fresco Sizzler with trellises and tropical plants (but without the salad bar) and utterly dependable steaks and shrimp. Though they are chain restaurants, the two Virgin Islands outposts of **The Chart House** (St. Croix and St. Thomas) are surprisingly decent, with thick, juicy cuts of steak charbroiled to perfection.

Pizzas with pizzazz... The twin eatery **Cafe Sagapo/ Zorba's** (St. Thomas) makes some fairly outrageous pizzas in a wood-burning oven, with standouts including Greek (lamb, olives, peppers, feta), tropical (tamarind sauce and chicken), Mediterranean (shrimp, squid, grouper, feta), and Santorini (spinach, onion, feta) pies. The profusion of "gourmet" pizzas has gotten out of hand worldwide, but the grilled duck version at St. Thomas's

Guava Grille is an unexpected delight, like crispy Peking duck on an even crispier crust. If all you want is a crunchy crust topped with fresh tomatoes, basil, oregano, and mozzarella, race over to **Ferrari's.**

Best food for the money... As if the incredible prices for wine at **Randy's** (St. Thomas) weren't enough, the simple but lovingly prepared food is a great deal. Try appetizers like potato rosti with smoked salmon and onion cream sauce, or shells stuffed with sun-dried tomatoes, pine nuts, potato, and squash in an herb-tomato sauce (both $4.95), then segue into an unimpeachable duck a l'orange or New York strip in a mushroom Bordelaise (both $14.95). St. Thomas's **Cafesito** is also remarkably priced, given the freshness of its seafood and its perfect waterfront location; make a meal here on tapas plates alone, and it's an astounding bargain. The menu at **Alexander's Bar & Grill** lists many of the same dishes, including the delicious wiener schnitzel, as **Alexander's Cafe**, minus a few dollars and a little ambience. The best buy on St. Croix is the bountiful Friday night barbecue at **Serendipity Inn**, priced at only $10 (return trips to the buffet encouraged).

Cheap eats... It doesn't come any cheaper than **Chef Romeo's** and the **Texas Pit BBQ**, two barbeque stands on the Charlotte Amalie waterfront on St. Thomas. Five bucks buys you a half chicken or slab of ribs with heaping helpings of cole slaw, potato salad, and tossed greens. On St. Croix, mountains of nachos are served at low-priced **Luncheria**, where you can also scarf down surprisingly good tacos, burritos, and enchiladas; **Secret Garden**, a pleasant hole-in-the-wall smack in the middle of Christiansted, offers free rum and cokes with dinner and $1 beers at happy hour. **Woody's Seafood Saloon** is where the overgrown hippies and sailors on shore leave hang out on St. John, guzzling beer and munching on grouper fingers, conch fritters, and clam strips.

Most sinful desserts... Hotel 1829 (St. Thomas) is justly legendary for its soufflés—airy, light, and just a little runny, decorated with dollops of whipped cream in flavors like amaretto, Grand Marnier, chocolate, passionfruit. (Many locals stop by just for a soufflé and coffee before repairing to the bar for a nightcap and backgammon.) Also on St. Thomas, **Virgilio's** makes a fabulous tiramisu, as well as its famous cappuccino spiked with several Italian liqueurs; **Café Normandie** serves specialty coffee drinks and a chocolate fudge pie immortalized in *Gourmet*; **Entre Nous** seduces with old-fashioned favorites like bananas Foster, cherries jubilee, and baked Alaska; **Palm Terrace** makes divine ice creams and sorbets, paired with desserts like coconut crème fraîche. And at St. Thomas's **The Old Stone Farm House**, one almost expects to be carried out on the dessert tray, a lascivious display of mousses and tortes, all topped with fresh whipped cream, as well as textbook Grand Marnier crème brûlée and profiteroles. On St. John, **Equator** has the most alluring exotic desserts in the U.S.V.I.: cinnamon-honey fry cake with pomegranate syrup and papaya ice milk; lime–lichee nut layer cake with guava sorbet; Thai sweet black rice with tropical fruits and sesame cookies.

Kid pleasers... No one really knows why, but **Barnacle Bill's** on St. Thomas has become a family hangout Friday nights, when you'll find 50 10-year-olds racing about; maybe it's the video games in back that suck them in.

Only on Mondays... Jacqueline Hoare-Ward's guests at the charming **Hilty House** B & B on St. Croix were forever complimenting her on the breakfasts and asking her to prepare dinner; she finally gave in and now throws the best dinner parties on the island every Monday, with an invigorating mix of knowledgeable locals and travelers. Jackie and her husband Hugh set up tables by the pool, prettily illuminated by Japanese lanterns. Fifty lucky people mingle over hors d'oeuvres, then repair to a three-course themed feast—one night it might be Moroccan, another Indian, another Italian—all for only $25. The St. Croix Heritage Dance Theater performs traditional quadrilles in native dress at **Jackie's Courtyard** on Mondays; the audience comes as much for the first-rate West Indian buffet as for the dancing.

The Index

$$$$$	over $45
$$$$	$35–$45
$$$	$25–$35
$$	$15–$25
$	under $15

Per person for three courses, not including drinks, tip, or tax.

St. Thomas

Agavé Terrace. Glorious water views, dark rattan, and salad prepared tableside all contribute to the comfy feel at this superb seafood restaurant. The wine list is one of the island's best.... *Tel 809/775–4142. 4 Smith Bay. Reservations recommended. D, DC not accepted. $$$*

Alexander's Bar & Grill/Alexander's Cafe/Alexander's Coffeehouse. Three side-by-side eateries, under the same ownership. The cafe is discreetly high-tech; the pub dimly lit with sports playing on the bar TV; both serve Austrian specialties like schnitzels and sausage platters, as well as lighter spa fare like turkey burgers, grilled shrimp over spinach, and seafood pasta salad. The sachertorte and Black Forest cake at the coffeehouse will instantly transport you to Vienna.... *Tel 809/776–4211. 24A Honduras, Frenchtown. D, DC not accepted. $ (Coffeehouse), $$ (Bar and Grill), $$$ (Cafe)*

The Bar at Paradise Point. Okay, it's really just a terrace serving drinks, burgers, nachos, and barbecued chicken atop a mountain, but it's an obligatory stop for sunset watchers. You say you're just coming for a drink, then the music starts, you get the munchies, and.... *Tel 809/777–4540. Paradise Point. No reservations. D, DC not accepted. $*

Barnacle Bill's. You can't miss this big barn, with its bright red lobster speared by cactus on the roof (Bill rescued it from a Carnival junk heap). Food plays second fiddle to the large stage, where the likes of Spyro Gyra and Dave Mason have performed; the bar is strung with Christmas lights and strung-out revelers on the rowdier nights, but in general the clientele runs toward young couples and families. Decent burgers, great sandwiches (with potato salad and cole slaw), and grilled fish.... *Tel 809/744–7444. 16 Sub Base, Charlotte Amalie. D, DC not accepted. $–$$*

Beni Iguana's Sushi Bar. This delightful oddity occupies a scrubbed-out old cistern. The decor is smart without being smart-ass: lacquered lipstick-red chairs contrast with black banquettes, and kimonos, coolie hats, fans, and wildly colored plastic mugs with goofy sayings complete the decor. (You can also dine in the charming courtyard of the old Grand Hotel.) The gorgeously presented sushi is slightly eccentric.... *Tel 809/779–4068. Grand Hotel Plaza, Charlotte Amalie. DC not accepted. $$$*

Blackbeard's Castle. The glittering panorama of Charlotte Amalie at night goes well with the creative Caribbean-accented Continental fare (pretentiously dubbed "New World cuisine" by foodies), such as mahi mahi in macadamia crust and pompano wrapped in plantains.... *Tel 809/776–1234. Blackbeard's Hill, Charlotte Amalie. Reservations necessary. $$$$–$$$$$*

Blue Marlin. A mix of celebrities and local fishermen appreciate the low-key ambience, fresh sea breezes, and fairly priced seafood on this pleasant wood deck. The fish is excellent, although the regulars never order it (as the manager says, "They're sick of fish"). But the West Indian chefs are amazingly adroit at pastas; try linguini with black beans, tomato salsa, sour cream, and peanuts.... *Tel 809/775–6530. American Yacht Harbor, Red Hook. Reservations recommended. D not accepted. $$–$$$*

Bumpa's. The sun streams through the windows of this second-floor eatery overlooking the Charlotte Amalie harbor, where they stick to eggs and luncheon meats for the shopping crowd.... *Tel 809/776–5674. 38-A Waterfront, Charlotte Amalie. Reservations not accepted. No credit cards. $*

Caesar's. Plaster-of-Paris gods guard this bright, noisy, split-level trattoria sitting on one of St. Thomas's most beautiful beaches. The food is lusty Tuscan—try the meaty, char-grilled portobellos set off by leek and fennel salad; sea scallops with roasted peppers and citrus risotto; or shrimp encrusted in pignoli on a tomato basil salsa…. *Tel 809/776–8500. Marriott Morningstar Beach Resort, Estate Bakkeroe. Reservations necessary. D not accepted. $$$–$$$$*

Cafe Amici. Well-heeled shoppers rest their tired feet in this brick courtyard cafe shaded by towering palms. Lunch highlights include montrachet and mixed green salad in walnut vinaigrette, linguini pesto, and chicken parmigiana…. *Tel 809/774–3719. 36–37 Riise's Alley, Charlotte Amalie. Reservations not accepted. D, DC, MC, V not accepted. $–$$*

Café Normandie. It could be stuffy, dining to the strains of Piaf and Montand in a classic setting gleaming with brass, Lalique, and stained glass. But owner George Johnson adds a playful touch, serving his sumptuous fare on individually painted plates, and jazzing up traditional dishes with regional ingredients (lobster with vanilla bean essence, pan-seared salmon with mango salsa). Still, the menu is mostly for purists—beef Wellington with foie gras mousse, rack of lamb with morels, and duckling with shallot and apple confit…. *Tel 809/774–1622. 70-A Honduras, Frenchtown. Reservations recommended. D, DC not accepted. $$$$*

Cafe Sagapo/Zorba's. The front section, Sagapo (which means "I love" in Greek), has hardwood floors, enormous throw pillows, and ceramic plates, tapestries, and bazoukis dangling from the brick walls; squeeze through a narrow courtyard to Zorba's, with its tile floors, crumbling stone walls crawling with hanging plants, and cramped tables. The menu (the same in both sections) is staunchly Greek: tender roast lamb and artichokes in avgolemono (lemon egg sauce), shrimp with velvety feta and roast garlic encased in phyllo, and flavorful moussaka…. *Tel 809/776–0444. 1854 Hus Government Hill, Charlotte Amalie. D, DC, MC not accepted. $$*

Cafe Vecchio. Coral walls, rattan furnishings, and sea breezes make this a delightful spot, especially at lunch, when you can cut the bill in half by ordering marvelous salads and sandwiches. But even at dinner, you can find relative bargains like grilled pompano with roast garlic and tomato coulis or pan-roasted sesame-crusted free-range chicken breast with orange mint sauce.... *Tel 809/775–3333. Grand Palazzo Hotel, Great Bay Estate, Nazareth. Reservations necessary. $$$–$$$$*

Cafesito. Sit either in the Moorish-style dining room or in the airy courtyard under bamboo umbrellas. The food explodes with color and flavor (chef Findlay apprenticed at New York's Palio and Union Square Café)—try pan-seared, praline-glazed salmon in mango compote or grilled N.Y. strip with wild mushrooms and feta.... *Tel 809/774–9574. 21 Dronnigens Gade, Charlotte Amalie. D, DC not accepted. $$*

Caribbean Lobster House. This satisfying beachside eatery, part of the island's only all-inclusive resort, is great for people-watching. Order your lobster grilled with drawn butter, sautéed with ginger and scallions over angel-hair pasta, drowned in shellfish cream sauce (Newburg), or swimming in grated cheese (Thermidor). The owners, bemoaning the difficulty of getting fresh lobster, may change the name (though several crustaceans will still grace the menu).... *Tel 809/775–1800. Bolongo Bay Beach Club, 50 Bolongo Estate. D not accepted. $$$–$$$$*

The Chart House. At press time, this restaurant was scheduled to move in March 1996 from its original stunning location in an 18th-century great house on the tip of the Frenchtown peninsula, but the basics are sure not to change: a bountiful salad bar; kebabs; chicken; shrimp and pork with Polynesian sweet-and-sour or teriyaki sauce; and big thick steaks.... *Tel 809/774–4262. Villa Olga, Frenchtown. Reservations accepted for 10 or more. D not accepted. $$$*

Chef Romeo's. Zip ambience (unless you count some of the local characters who hang out here), but this stand serves dirt-cheap, lip-smacking BBQ ribs or chicken and mouth-watering brisket with deli-style sides.... *No telephone. Sub Base, Charlote Amalie. No credit cards. $*

Craig and Sally's. No views here, so the murals on the walls make one up: Sandy Cay, the Frenchtown harbor, and the sunset over Culebra, along with fanciful touches like a billowing sultan's tent. Sally Darash's menu is wildly eclectic: veal chops grilled with smoked ancho chile sauce, roasted corn-cheddar polenta, and sweet peppercorn relish; duck breast and duck sausage with espresso-tangerine sauce, black beans, and potato pancakes. Distinguished wine list.... *Tel 809/777–9949. 22 Honduras, Frenchtown. Reservations recommended. D, DC not accepted.* $$$

Cuzzin's Caribbean Restaurant and Bar. Brent Steele's restaurant has a more upscale decor than other native eateries—wood ceilings, tile floors, and old brick walls hung with colorful art naif. The food alternates dishes like conch in butter sauce and curried mutton with a few bland dishes catering to American tastes. Try the heavy but good coconut or guava tarts for dessert.... *Tel 809/777–4711. 7 Back St., Charlotte Amalie. Reservations recommended. DC not accepted.* $$–$$$

Diamond Barrel. This true local hangout is decorated with murals of marine life, seashell tablecloths, rattan chairs, and colorful prints of daily life in the Caribbean. If you've ever wanted to try souse (stewed pickled pigs' feet) or goatwater stew, here's your chance. Just check the blackboard for daily specials and dig in.... *Tel 809/774–5071. 18 Norre Gade, Charlotte Amalie. No credit cards.* $

East Coast Bar and Grill. Bud Light signs, team pennants, and autographed celebrity photos (Joan Lunden! Loverboy! Kevin Johnson!) provide the decor at this popular rustic joint, founded by the owners of Bay Area jock hangouts Barbary Coast and Shanghai Kelly's. Specials like snapper piccata, chicken parmigiana, and Cajun shrimp are listed on the blackboard. Next door is the Shark Room (see Nightlife) for the coolest music on island.... *Tel 809/775–1919. American Yacht Harbor, Red Hook. D, DC not accepted.* $$

Entre Nous. The epitome of a fancy night out, with flickering candles competing with the lights of cruise ships in the harbor. Chef Richard Brosseau's imaginative dishes include inventions like sliced roast breast of duck over pappardelle with pumpkin sauce, or pepper-crusted venison in lingonberry sauce. (At press time, Entre Nous was set to move to the even more spectacular space occupied by Guava Grille while renovations were completed).... *Tel 809/774–4050. Bluebeard's Castle Hotel, Bluebeard's Hill, Charlotte Amalie. Reservations required. D, DC not accepted. $$$$-$$$$$*

Eunice's Terrace. You don't come here for atmosphere—it overlooks a dump—although lovely antique straw-and-bamboo screens and rattan chairs give the spartan space a colonial feel. You do come for pineapple coconut fried shrimp, herb-stuffed lobster, grilled pork chops Creole, and sweet potato pie. A calypso guitarist sometimes patrols the premises, making up saucy ditties about the diners.... *Tel 809/774–4262. Rte. 38, Smith Bay. D, DC not accepted. $$*

Ferrari's. Out of the way in the middle of a peaceful residential area, this is an unassuming place with stereotypical red-and-white checked tablecloths and chianti flasks. The food is pure Neapolitan—zesty tomato-based sauces, garlic bread, eggplant parmigiana—and addictive.... *Tel 809/774–6800. Crown Mountain Rd. Reservations recommended. D, DC not accepted. $$–$$$*

Frigate. Customers come for the thrilling views from the dark wood terrace; otherwise, it's straightforward cooking and service at straightforward prices. Best items: teriyaki chicken, shrimp kebab, chargrilled swordfish and wahoo, and peanut butter and key lime pies. The chorus of tree frogs makes quite a mellifluous racket.... *Tel 809/774–2790. Mafolie Hotel, Mafolie Hill. D, DC not accepted. $$–$$$*

Gladys' Cafe. When her lovely courtyard cafe was transformed into a fishbowl, Gladys simply moved to even prettier, more elegant quarters. Her new space occupies an 18th-century building with stone walls and hardwood floors, set off by black chairs and blue cushions. Play it safe with omelets, burgers, and warm chicken salad, or opt for flavorful Caribbean lobster rolls or saltfish and dumplings.... *Tel 809/774–6604. 17 Main St., Charlotte Amalie. Reservations not accepted. D, DC, MC, V not accepted. $–$$*

The Greenhouse. Look for fake fish on the walls, wood floors, and lots of grillwork at this basic restaurant, where shoppers take a load off and singles get loaded. Several types of burgers (try the Mexican, with cheddar, bacon, mushrooms, and smoky BBQ sauce) and salads (taco, sesame-chicken, cobb, crab-guacamole), cheap forgettable pastas, and ribs.... *Tel 809/774–7998. Veteran's Dr., Charlotte Amalie. D, DC not accepted. $$*

Guava Grille. Decked out in cheerful pastel colors, set in a grove of banana trees, and open to the sparkling harbor views, Guava Grille is far more casual than its sister restaurant Entre Nous (see above). Stick to the unusual island-themed rotisserie staples (grilled chicken with pineapple salsa, mango jerk pork chops), pizzas, and competent pastas. (At press time, Guava Grill was being occupied by Entre Nous, whose own digs were being renovated; everyone is expected to be back in place by June 1996).... *Tel 809/774–4050. Bluebeard's Castle Hotel, Bluebeard's Hill, Charlotte Amalie. D, DC not accepted. $$–$$$*

Hard Rock Cafe. You've seen one, you've seen 'em all.... *Tel 809/777–5555. International Plaza, Charlotte Amalie. Reservations not accepted. D, DC not accepted. $–$$*

Hook, Line and Sinker. This casual dockside spot has marvelous views of the harbor and downtown. It's appealing if you enjoy fresh seafood (great clams and almond-crusted yellowtail) and can ignore the old codgers sitting at the bar and the families scarfing down buckets of shrimp at the bleached wood tables..... *Tel 809/776–9708. 2 Honduras, Frenchtown. D, DC not accepted. $$–$$$*

Hotel 1829. Brick-and-stone walls, Spanish porcelain, Moroccan tile floors, and authentic Tiffany glass windows create an exquisite backdrop for old-fashioned Continental dining at decidedly '90s prices. Caviar, rack of lamb bearnaise, filet mignon in pepper sauce, lobster with garlic-scallion beurre blanc, and soufflés are fixtures on the menu. The new chef occasionally challenges regulars with free-range chicken over mesclun with berry vinaigrette or grilled swordfish and shrimp with papaya-lime relish. The wine list is extensive and well-considered.... *Tel 809/776–1829. Government Hill, Charlotte Amalie. Reservations necessary. D, DC not accepted. $$$$$*

I Cappuccini. Fancy-schmancy for a coffeehouse, with cushy, patterned banquettes, stone walls, and lots of mirrors. Light lunch specials might include gnocchi al pesto or involtini di melanzane (eggplant stuffed with ricotta and pine nuts).... *Tel 809/775–1090. 4-5 Back St., Taste of Italy Mall, Charlotte Amalie. D, DC not accepted. $–$$*

Il Cardinale. Alas, the sexy mural outside (a white woman and black man bearing the fruits of the earth) promises more than it delivers; inside is dark, woody, and restrained, as is the kitchen. Stick to the pastas.... *Tel 809/775–1090. 4-5 Back St., Taste of Italy Mall, Charlotte Amalie. D, DC not accepted. $$$*

Latitude 18. The access road is memorably bumpy, which may explain why most of the clientele arrive by boat (especially weekends for the live music). A string of Christmas lights, a skull-and-crossbones, and a Confederate flag sum up the decor. The food is similarly no-nonsense—chicken stirfry, blackened snapper, pasta primavera.... *Tel 809/775–9964. Vessup Point. Reservations not accepted. D, DC not accepted. $$*

Le Petite Pump Room. Politics and cuisine may make strange bedfellows, but the marriage works at this two-story deck with cathedral ceilings overlooking the harbor; it's *the* spot for a power lunch among island politicos, with traditional West Indian food lovingly prepared. On Thursday—payday for government employees—there's a wonderful roast pork special. And who would have thought that the cheesecake was among the best in the Caribbean?.... *Tel 809/776–2976. Veterans Dr. at the B.V.I. ferry dock, Charlotte Amalie. Reservations recommended. D, DC not accepted. $$*

The Old Stone Farm House. Two-foot-thick stone walls, hardwood floors, brass sconces, throw rugs, antique credenzas, and rusting farm utensils create a romantic atmosphere, while chef Mark Hanson wows diners with his French/American/Pacific Rim hybrid cuisine. Outstanding choices include homemade ravioli brimming with shiitakes, cepes, and boletus perfumed with basil; and scallion gâteaux layered with red onion, Sevruga, salmon caviar, and crème fraîche.... *Tel 809/775–1377. Mahogany Run. Reservations necessary. D, DC not accepted. $$$$*

Palm Terrace. Highback natural wicker chairs, trees that threaten to burst through the roof, and an intricately hand-carved bar of Filipino mahogany help set the tone. The most pompous menu descriptions in the U.S.V.I.–duck foie gras au natural served with brioche fleurons and a salad of haricots verts and wild mushroom persillade on a white port aspic, anyone? Fortunately, the kitchen is brilliant enough to carry it off, and the wine list is equally fabulous.... *Tel 809/775–3333. Grand Palazzo Hotel, Great Bay Estate, Nazareth. Reservations necessary. D not accepted. $$$$$*

Randy's Wine Bar and Bistro. Racks of wine and still-lifes of wine bottles on the forest-green walls signal the interest here. Sneak into the liquor store next door if the list doesn't satisfy; bring back your selection and pay only a $5 corkage fee. Convivial atmosphere and basic but delicious food, such as pork tenderloin Dijon, baked brie in phyllo, and shrimp scampi over linguini.... *Tel 809/777–3199. 4002 Raphune Hill, Al Cohen's Plaza, Charlotte Amalie. D, DC not accepted. $$*

Romano's. The owner's remarkable collection of museum-quality Haitian and Dominican artwork clutters the track-lit, starkly white stucco walls of this sophisticated hideaway. Tony Romano prepares innovative variations on Italian classics, some subtly seasoned (like veal tongue in red wine or penne in a cream sauce with mushrooms, prosciutto, pine nuts, and Parmesan), others more assertive (like chicken with sundried tomatoes, mushrooms, white wine, and the anise kick of fennel).... *Tel 809/775–0045. 97 Smith Bay. Reservations recommended. D, DC not accepted. $$$–$$$$*

A Room with a View. The views *are* incredible at this plush bistro with soft track lighting and table lamps. (Owner George Hajimhalis likens it to being in the cockpit of a plane.) It's the perfect spot for a glass of wine, specialty coffee, appetizers, simple dinner (like lasagne), or dessert. The food is solid, if uninspired, but who cares, with that panorama?... *Tel 809/774–2377. Bluebeard's Castle Hotel, Bluebeard's Hill, Charlotte Amalie. DC not accepted. $$*

Sib's Mountain Bar and Restaurant. The bar and restaurant are in separate buildings and have completely different clienteles: college kids in the bar, their parents in the pretty dining room with its vine-laden white trellises. Swordfish, salmon, and pasta specials are usually reliable.... *Tel 809/ 774–8967. 33 Estate Elizabeth. D, DC not accepted. $$*

Tavern on the Beach. Twinkling stars and lights of far-off cruise ships, crashing waves, and chic decor (slanted wood beams, black-and-white umbrellas, and potted palms) only partially explain why this is one of the island's hottest restaurants. Although chef Eddie Hale, late of Miami's hip South Beach, has moved on, you can still expect such vibrant dishes as cod fritters with fennel, oranges, and sabayon; tamarind honey-glazed rack of lamb with parsley crust and tabouli mint salad; and chili and tamari seared king salmon with crunchy rice noodles. Sous chef Doug Grant dazzles with desserts.... *Tel 809/776–8500. Marriott Morningstar Resort, Estate Bakkeroe. Reservations necessary. D not accepted. $$$$*

Texas Pit BBQ. A waterfront stand pretty much the same as its next-door neighbor, Chef Romeo's (great ribs, chicken, brisket, deli-style sides, no ambience), but the sauce here is definitely kick-ass.... *Tel 809/776–9579. Sub Base, Charlotte Amalie. No credit cards. $*

Tickles Dockside Pub. A large polished wood bar is the focal point of these two classic meet-markets, with dining relegated to white plastic tables and chairs shaded by Coors Light and Amstel umbrellas. The menu runs toward burgers, fish and chips, and chicken-fried steak, all greasily competent.... *Tel 809/775—9425, American Yacht Harbor, Red Hook; tel 809/776—1595, Crown Bay Marina, Charlotte Amalie. D, DC not accepted. $–$$*

Victor's New Hideout. This wood barn, with tablecloths—and waitresses—in bright island prints, has 360-degree views of Crown Point Marina and the industrial section of Charlotte Amalie. Vernon Sydney has been dishing it out for 20 years; every tourist has heard about this place, but it doesn't disappoint, especially with the lobster Montserrat in a creamy curry sauce, or tender conch.... *Tel 809/776–9379. 103 Sub Base. D, DC not accepted. $$–$$$*

Virgilio's. Once past the crumbling facade, you're overwhelmed by neo-Baroque splendor: stone arches, gilt mirrors, bud vases, walls cluttered with artworks from ersatz to Erté, cabinets filled with ornamental old brandy bottles. *I Pagliacci* seems to play on a loop. Add definitive fried calamari, nearly 20 outstanding homemade pastas, and superior renditions of osso bucco, chicken parmigiana, and sole Florentine.... *Tel 809/776–4920. Dronningens Gade, Charlotte Amalie. Reservations necessary. D, DC not accepted. $$$$–$$$$$*

St. Croix

Anabelle's Tea Room. You'll feel like hacking your way through the jungle of plants leading to this rickety gingerbread terrace overlooking a fountained courtyard. Fine Latino-accented fare—asopaos, spicy pumpkin soup, lobster Louis, and warm roast chicken are among the top choices.... *Tel 809/773–3990. Quin House Courtyard, 51 ABC Company St., Christiansted. Reservations not accepted. No credit cards. $–$$*

Antoine's. Tony Doos whips up great breakfasts, as well as Austrian specialties like tafelspitz, sauerbraten, and wiener schnitzel, but the real curiosity on the menu is the exotic seafood, from barracuda to urchin. The setting overlooks the harbor, with gingerbread trellises, murals of ships, and red tablecloths.... *Tel 809/773–0263. 58A King St., Christiansted. D, DC not accepted. $$–$$$*

Banana Bay Club. Harbor views and potent drinks are the main attraction here. The food is unimaginative, except for particularly good creole or blackened fish. Stay away from pretentious "stuffed" food in heavy sauces, save room for the snickers pie or banana split.... *Tel 809/778–9110. Caravelle Arcade, Queen Cross St., Christiansted. D, DC not accepted. $$–$$$*

Bombay Club. This historic, cozy stone-and-brick pub is hung with striking, even startling local artworks. The food leans toward gussied-up pub grub, like roast garlic with brie, cheddar nachos, pita pizzas, pastas (best is fettucini with broccoli in lemon butter) and gorgeous onion rings.... *Tel 809/773–1838. 5A King St., Christiansted. D, DC not accepted. $$*

Café du Soleil. Pretty in pink (and mauve, lilac, maroon—sunset colors, get it?), this upstairs cafe specializes in sundown views. The food wins no kudos; you're safe ordering appetizers like charcuterie, gravlax, and terrines.... *Tel 809/772–5400. 37 Strand St., Frederiksted. D, DC not accepted. $$–$$$*

Camille's. Brick walls, terra-cotta floors, a restaurant-length polished wood bar strewn with newspapers, and photos of low-wattage sports celebs set the laid-back tone at this local hangout. Deli sandwiches, burgers, and hearty soups, give way to inexpensive, competent prime rib and grilled fish come evening.... *Tel 809/773–2985. 53B Company St., Christiansted. No credit cards. $$*

The Chart House. This franchise has an appealing setting on the harbor, dark wood paneling, marine paintings and photos, terra-cotta floors, wicker furnishings—and a huge saman tree vaulting through the ceiling. The food? A salad bar with over 20 items; kebabs; chicken; shrimp and pork smothered in Polynesian sweet-and-sour or teriyaki sauce; and huge slabs of steak.... *Tel 809/773–7718. Kings Wharf, Christiansted. D not accepted. $$$*

Cheeseburgers in Paradise. Think of this bright yellow shack as the Caribbean answer to those messy, marvelous Fat Burgers in L.A., only with margaritas and live music weekends.... *Tel 809/773–1119. 67 Southgate. Reservations not accepted. MC, V not accepted. $*

Club Comanche. This breezy terrace sports glorious mahogany ceilings, baskets of hanging plants, an outrigger canoe, and wicker peacock chairs. The menu emphasizes Continental stalwarts: shrimp scampi, lobster Louis (glorified Russian dressing), and filet mignon in bearnaise sauce.... *Tel 809/ 773–2665. Strand St., Christiansted. Reservations recommended. D, DC not accepted. $$$*

Columbus Cove. A corrugated tin roof, trellises, fish nets, and boats bobbing in the marina serve as decor; yachties enterprising enough to make the trip to St. Croix pounce on conch fritters, mozzarella and zucchini sticks, and simple broiled steaks and seafood (avoid anything that sounds fancy).... *Tel 809/778–5771. Salt River Marina. D, DC, MC, V not accepted. $$–$$$*

Cormorant Beach Club. Arched picture windows overlooking the surf, bamboo walls, sleek black chairs, tile floors, and floral napery beautify this hotel dining room. Dishes might include sole Veronique (poached with cream and raisins) or roast pork loin with mango-tamarind glaze.... *Tel 908/778-8920. Cormorant Beach Club Hotel, La Grande Princesse. D, DC not accepted. $$$*

Dino's. Chef/owners Dwight DeLude and Dino Natale have moved their original arty boite to a larger, more elegant space in the Buccaneer Hotel, with huge picture windows and jade tile floors, but they still prepare an ingenious cucina rustica with Caribbean accents. Pastas range from sweet potato-and-eggplant ravioli to fettucine glistening with a zingy ginger, cilantro, chicken, rum, black bean, and pepper sauce. There's only 10 tables, but people willingly line up to eat at the bar.... *Tel 809/773-2100. Buccaneer Hotel, Cutlass Cove Shoys. Reservations recommended. $$$*

Duggan's Reef. Rattan and wicker furnishings lend a touch of class to this otherwise casual seaside eatery, plastered with pennants from New England-based sports teams (owner Frank Duggan is a Bostonian). The kitchen scores with surprisingly ambitious specials like lobster-stuffed chiles rellenos, in addition to the usual teriyaki, piccata, Cajun, and Dijonnaise sauces swabbed over fresh fish or steak.... *Tel 809/773-9800. Route 82, Reef Beach. D, DC not accepted. $$-$$$*

Eeez's Specialty Cafe. Essentially a Caribbean cafeteria, with a palm-shadowed interior courtyard, Eeez's serves authentic Antiguan specialties like pumpkin fritters, cod pâté, johnnycakes, salmon balls, and ducana (saltfish scrambled with eggs and spinach).... *Tel 809/773-9765. 8AB Company St., Christiansted. No reservations. No credit cards. $*

The Galleon. The ambiance is restful—sailing prints, terra-cotta floors, candlelight, a paneled wood roof, and a sing-along piano bar, with a backdrop of marina views. Best on the menu: steak au poivre, filet mignon topped with lobster and bearnaise, and chateaubriand.... *Tel 809/773-9949. Green Cay Marina. Reservations recommended. D, DC not accepted. $$-$$$*

Harvey's. Daily specials like conch creole and baked chicken, served with heaping helpings of heavenly fungi and sweet potatoes, are listed on the blackboard at this basic but cheerful restaurant. Owner Sarah Harvey's booming laugh and joy in cooking are infectious.... *Tel 809/773–3343. 11 Company St, Christiansted. No credit cards. $–$$*

The Hideaway. This open-air beach restaurant in the Hibiscus Beach Hotel features lively buffets, notably West Indian night (when the Caribbean Dance Company performs) and vegetarian nights.... *Tel 809/773–4020. Hibiscus Beach Hotel, La Grande Princesse. Reservations recommended. DC not accepted. $–$$*

Hilty House. Every Monday night the engaging Jacqueline and Hugh Hoard-Ward host what amounts to a private dinner party by their pool in this elegant B&B. Jacqueline cooks whatever suits her fancy; rest assured it's estimable and exotic. The $25 prix fixe buys hors d'oeuvres, three courses, and delightful talk.... *Tel 809/773–2594. Reservations necessary. No credit cards. $$*

Indies. Chef Catherine Plav-Driggers was a mainstay at the stodgy Cormorant Beach Club for years before opening her own restaurant in this 250-year-old arched courtyard, cooled by whirring ceiling fans, lit by hurricane lamps, and bursting with bougainvillea. Her food, glowing with fresh indigenous ingredients, is clearly influenced by Alice Waters (of Chez Panisse fame); try the Caribbean Bouillabaisse, spiked by spicy coconut ginger broth, or spice-rubbed chicken in pineapple salsa. She also serves marvelous sushi Wednesdays and Fridays at the bar. Calypso and jazz combos weekends.... *Tel 809/692–9440. 55-56 Company St., Christiansted. Reservations recommended. D, DC not accepted. $$$*

Jackie's Courtyard. Dine either at multicolored plastic tables arranged around a mermaid fountain, or inside the cozy restaurant, its 18th-century brick-and-stone walls dripping with bromeliads and shell art. Bargain $5 lunches, first-rate curries and rotis anytime.... *Tel 809/773–1955. 46 King St., Christiansted. D, DC not accepted. $$*

Kendrick's. This classic recently moved into spacious, contemporary new quarters in Chandler's Wharf, filled with soothing jazz and savory scents. David and Jane Kendrick turn out

Nouvelle American items like chilled tomato, basil, and walnut soup; salmon with pistachio-peanut crust, spinach strudel, and lime-caper cream; and lemon-thyme fettuccine with grilled chicken and sweet corn.... *Tel 809/773–9199. Chandler's Wharf, Christiansted. Reservations recommended. D, DC not accepted. $$$$*

Kim's. The only stab at decor is pink tablecloths, but the island fare more than compensates, especially the kingfish creole. Even the Dominican hookers up the block stop in to fuel up.... *Tel 809/773–3377. King St., Christiansted. Reservations not accepted. D, DC, MC, V not accepted. $–$$*

La Grange Beach Club. Fantastic happy hours and live-music weekends have always been the draw at this casual, lime-green trellised hangout on a burnished beach. New owners threaten to tart up the menu (chicken with garlic and herb fondue, crabcakes with passionfruit vinaigrette); it's anyone's guess whether it will catch on.... *Tel 809/772–5566. 72 Estate La Grange. D, DC not accepted. $$*

Le St. Tropez. The patio, hidden behind banks of bougainvillea, is most charming, as are the mahogany bar and tiny dining room, crammed with bric-a-brac. Very French owners Andre and Danielle Ducrot know their way around a fish soup, salade niçoise, quiche lorraine, ratatouille crepes, and pissaladiere (onion tart), among other tasty items. It's so Gallic, you can even order frogs' legs.... *Tel 809/772–3000. 67 King St., Frederiksted. D, DC not accepted. $$–$$$*

Luncheria. Service is cafeteria-style at this courtyard hangout. The food is an afterthought to the beers and slurpy margaritas, but at least it's el cheapo and the enchiladas and burritos are better than Taco Bell's.... *Tel 809/773–4247. Apothecary Hall Courtyard, Company St., Christiansted. Reservations not accepted. No credit cards. $*

The Mahogany Room. The room gleams with stone walls, wood beams and columns, table lamps, and elegant high-back chairs that aren't as uncomfortable as they look. CIA-trained chef Larry Rampulla dubs his food "Contemporary Classic": crab and scallop cakes with tomato-mango salsa, grilled wahoo with roasted red pepper cous-

cous, scallions, and hoisin-sesame glaze. Meat dishes are far more traditional, favoring wild mushrooms, demi glaces, and the like.... *Tel 809/778–3800. Carambola Beach Resort. Reservations recommended. D, DC not accepted. $$$$–$$$$$*

Market Street Cafe. This sun-filled courtyard is dominated by a huge mural of diners enjoying their food—soothing, runny omelets or fish tacos with rice and refried beans, for $5 or less.... *No telephone. Market St., Frederiksted. Reservations not accepted. No credit cards. $*

Morning Glory Coffee House. It's in a somewhat out-of-the-way neighborhood (Gallows Bay, just outside downtown Christiansted), but the hiss of cappuccino machines and aroma of fresh roasted coffees make this like a little bit of Seattle, where you can nibble on biscotti and read the morning paper.... *Tel 809/773–6620. Gallows Bay. Reservations not accepted. No credit cards. $*

No Name Bar and Grill. Lace curtains, floral tablecloths, and candles—and wacky cloth fish and wooden parrots. Beloved by locals, the No Name doesn't put on airs (the motto of the Cane Bay Reef Club Hotel is "Sun, sand, and personal counseling"), and the food is just as forthright: mussels marinara, blackened mahi mahi in dill sauce, lamb chops flamed in peppermint schnapps.... *Tel 809/778–0035. Cane Bay Reef Club, Route 80. D, DC not accepted. $$–$$$*

On the Beach Bar and Cafe. Just what it sounds like: a few umbrellas and tables on the sand, where attractive young gays and lesbians, mostly coupled, enjoy the sunsets along with mahi mahi in white wine sauce or chicken veronique. Brunch is also quite good.... *Tel 809/772–4242. On the Beach Resort, Frederiksted. $$*

Pangaea. Like the coolest college dorm imaginable. David Hurst's robust, rough-textured Euro-Afro-Asian-Caribbean fare moves to the same reggae beat as the sound system—kashmiri seared tuna with fresh soursop and toasted ginger crisps; mahi mahi with sliced mangoes and sun-dried tomato pesto; baked molasses chicken breast with onion-rum relish. Absolutely stunning.... *Tel 809/773–7743. 2203 Queen Cross St., Christiansted. No credit cards. $$$*

Picnic in Paradise. Sit on the dreamy terrace for the full effect of the star-filled sky and violent surf. The Continental-Caribbean fare—drowned in butter, vegetables woefully overcooked—doesn't quite match the setting but sometimes the kitchen delights, as with Thai shrimp and vegetable spring rolls in peanut-passionfruit sauce or puff pastry salmon with lobster shrimp mousse in lemon-cream sauce. Best for lunch or brunch.... *Tel 809/778-1212. 6 Northstar. Reservations necessary. D, DC not accepted. $$$–$$$$*

The Saman Room. A luxurious open-air space with vaulting ceilings and pastel linens, the Saman Room is recommended for its eye-popping buffets, though the à la carte menu's very old-fashioned, moderately priced food (chicken Oscar—with crabmeat, asparagus, and bearnaise sauce, for goodness' sake) more than satisfies.... *Tel 809/778-3800. Carambola Beach Resort. Reservations recommended. D, DC not accepted. $$$–$$$$*

Secret Garden. Don't be put off if there's no one else eating at this little-known spot. The space is quite pretty, with tropical murals in arched walls, floral tablecloths, and sprays of wilting flowers everywhere, and you won't mind the adequate chicken teriyaki, shrimp curry, and ribs, all priced to move.... *Tel 809/692-9331. King Cross St., Christiansted. No credit cards. $$*

Serendipity Inn. This informal spot, overlooking both the beach and a lagoon, is wildly popular with locals Tuesday (southern fried chicken or flounder), Wednesday (pasta galore), and Friday (BBQ) nights, where you get huge portions (and seconds) for only $10 or $12. Dining à la carte will net you big slabs of mahi mahi and snapper floating in creole or lemon-butter sauce and a great spicy pasta puttanesca. Saturdays also pack them in for lobster.... *Tel 809/773-5762. Mill Harbour, Concordia. Reservations recommended. D, DC not accepted. $$*

South Shore Cafe. This convivial little bistro overlooking the Great Salt Pond has yet to be discovered by tourists. Chef Chris Merola is a whiz at homemade pastas, with zippy sauces alive with tomatoes, basil, and garlic; seafood includes uniformly excellent specials like swordfish puttanesca, with lusty olives, capers, and tomatoes.... *Tel 809/773-9311. Rtes. 62 & 624. No credit cards. $$–$$$*

Tommy and Susan's Taverna. It's just as nonchalant as it sounds, a local favorite for Mediterranean lunches like shrimp broiled with feta and tortellini in pesto.... *Tel 809/773-8666. Apothecary Hall Courtyard, Company St., Christiansted. Reservations not accepted. No credit cards. $*

Top Hat. Aptly named, this restaurant is as soigné as Astaire and Rogers in their prime. The interior is a vision in red and black, with beamed ceilings, latticework, and black-and-white photos, but the food is a tad stolid, emphasizing Danish specialties like roast duck stuffed with apples and prunes and garnished with red cabbage; fried camembert with lingonberries; and frikadeller (meatballs in snappy cocktail sauce). You can also get lighter fare like Danish open-face sandwiches at the intimate bar.... *Tel 809/773-2346. 52 Company St., Christiansted. Reservations necessary. D, DC not accepted. $$$–$$$$*

Tutto Bene. St. Croix's trendiest-looking restaurant, with a teal ceiling and mustard-colored walls, painted wood tables, piebald cushions, and striking black-and-white photos; the food is nowhere near as hip—unimaginative versions of shrimp scampi and veal piccata and the like.... *Tel 809/773-5229. 2 Company St., Christiansted. Reservations recommended. D, DC not accepted. $$–$$$*

UCA Vegetarian Restaurant. You'll recognize the UCA center by the vivid Rastafarian hues splashed across the ancient stone building. No decor to speak of, but if you like crisp, colorful veggies simmered in piquant sauces, refreshing bush teas, and mounds of rice, make a beeline.... *No telephone. 66 King St., Frederiksted. Reservations not accepted. No credit cards. $*

Vel's. You'd never know from the humble digs (green-and-white checked tablecloths topped with bud vases), but this is a favorite haunt of local politicos. The governor himself swears by the delicious local fare, including stewed chicken, conch salad, arroz con pollo, and tasty tostones (corn fritters).... *Tel 809/772-2160. 16A King St., Frederiksted. No credit cards. $–$$*

Villa Madeleine Greathouse. It's like a private home profiled in *HG*—Chinese Chippendale chairs, Japanese prints, Oriental rugs, brick-and-tile terrace with wrought iron tables, and fanciful driftwood sculpture. But you'll feast on Caribbean lobster and sea scallop Napoleon in red pepper cream; veal chop with morels; or lobster ravioli in sauternes sauce. Watch for rotating celebrity chef weeks in season, which have lured the likes of Randy Daigle (Patout's, New Orleans) and David Lawson (Blantyre Castle, the Berkshires). Top-notch wine list.... *Tel 809/778–7377. Teague Bay (take Rte. 82 out of Christiansted and turn right at the Reef Condominiums). Reservations necessary. D not accepted.* $$$$

Villa Morales. Some plain tables on the terrace and several more inside in a burnished-wood barn, where locals (and the Lions Club) stage impromptu jump-ups some weekends. The hearty, spicy local food includes fried plantains, meat and conch empanadillas, and succulent fried chicken.... *Tel 809/772–0556. 52C Estate Whim. No credit cards.* $–$$

St. John

Asolare. A converted stone-and-wood private home, with throw rugs, vases, teal fabrics, and an exquisite rock pool garden lit by torches, Asolare may be the most sophisticated restaurant on island. Do whatever you can to reserve a table on the terrace in season, to watch fireball sunsets. Chef Robert Smith's food is sensuously textured and subtly flavored: tandoori salmon with lemon dal; rare, roasted chinois duck with tamarind-mustard glaze; and an astonishing spiced shellfish consommé with crispy dumplings, galangal (an Asian herb) and cilantro.... *Tel 809/779–4747. Cruz Bay. Reservations necessary. D, DC not accepted.* $$$$

Cafe Grand. Marble tables and bleached rattan chairs add a touch of elegance to this airy beachfront cafe that serves the most bountiful buffets on St. John—Surf and Turf, Prime Rib, Lobster, and Chicken-and-Ribs nights draw crowds.... *Tel 809/693–8000. Hyatt Regency Beach Hotel. Reservations recommended. DC not accepted.* $$$

Chateau Bordeaux. Perched on a cliff overlooking the B.V.I.s, this romantic restaurant has cozy Caribbean Victorian decor—lace tablecloths, antiques, and a rotating gallery of local artworks. Start with house-smoked chicken spring roll crowning angel-hair pasta blazing with ancho coulis, or delicate saffron ravioli with smoked salmon and a caper, leek, tomato, and white wine sauce; then sail into pan-seared yellowtail brushed with a light wasabi-soy glaze with ginger-shallot confit, or slow-roasted Cornish hen seared with lemon-thyme-lingonberry *jus lie*..... *Tel 809/776–6611. Rte. 10, just east of Centerline Rd. D, DC not accepted. $$$$*

Ciao Mein. This sleek, soaring, severe space is the closest thing in the U.S.V.I. to a high-tech L.A. nightspot, with taupe and olive columns, black lacquer tables, Oriental screens, brass fixtures, and marble floors. The "transcultural" menu offers Chinese on one page, Italian on the other; both are surprisingly good, though portions are most charitably described as nouvelle. Sample the Mein platter for two, a glorified pu pu platter including spring rolls, potstickers, and light crispy fried calamari; seafood orecchiette features wok-seared scallops, clams, and mussels with cilantro over roasted garlic pasta.... *Tel 809/693–8000. Hyatt Regency Beach Hotel. Reservations recommended. DC not accepted. $$$$*

Ellington's. A very attractive space with rattan furnishings and black-and-white accents, and excellent sunset-watching on the veranda. The seafood is often sublime: sweet, succulent coconut shrimp in mango sauce; a fish chowder that would do a Marseillais proud; velvety zucchini-lobster bisque; or perfectly seared sea scallops in pesto. The home-baked desserts are just sinful, especially the white-chocolate brownie... *Tel 809/776–7166. Gallows Point Suite Resort, Cruz Bay. D, DC not accepted. $$$*

Equator. This 19th-century sugar mill was completely renovated when Rosewood Hotels took over; a trendy open kitchen is the focal point of the vast circular space. Renowned executive chef Dean Fearing (of Mansion at Turtle Creek fame) fearlessly contrasts tastes and textures: chili-crusted shrimp and smoked scallop on peanut sauce with black bean relish; sugarcane-glazed salmon on habañero mashed potatoes with fermented guava rum sauce; and Hawaiian chocolate fudge tart in cashew crust are all standouts.... *Tel 809/776–6111. Caneel Bay Resort. Reservations necessary. D not accepted. $$$$*

Etta's. This is a simple affair, with a trickling fountain and virtual jungle taking over the courtyard. Come here to mingle with locals, dance the night away to hot bands, and most of all, to sample calaloo (a soup made from okra and dasheen, a tuber leaf resembling bitter spinach), chicken or lamb curry, and heavenly conch or grouper fritters served with blazing sauces.... *Tel 809/776–6378. 34E Enighed, Cruz Bay. DC not accepted. $–$$*

The Fish Trap. This rickety, split-level wooden structure seems propped up by banana trees and coconut palms; fish nets dangle everywhere, with hand-carved fish and crustaceans struggling to free themselves. Chef Aaron Willis dishes out several kinds of fresh fish nightly, including wahoo, grouper, and yellowtail, and a manly fish chowder (and adequate steak and chicken for unrepentant carnivores).... *Tel 809/693–9994. 5A Cruz Bay. DC not accepted. $$–$$$*

JJ's Texas Coast Cafe. White wrought-iron tables and chairs in this shady courtyard across from the ferry dock see a brisk trade in day-trippers (early) and heavy drinkers (late).... *Tel 809/776–6908. 6D Cruz Bay. Reservations not accepted. No credit cards. $–$$*

Lime Inn. Another appealing courtyard alive with greenery, furnished with wrought-iron tables and green beach chairs, The Lime Inn serves probably the most staid food on St. John—steak and prime rib.... *Tel 809/776–6425. Lemon Tree Mall, Cruz Bay. D, DC not accepted. $$–$$$*

Luscious Licks. Each unadorned wood table sports its own pithy saying; drinks of choice are carrot juice and soy shakes; the strictly vegetarian food runs toward wholewheat oatmeal pancakes, black bean burritos, garden pita pizzas, and veggie burgers and sandwiches. The green highback chairs encourage ramrod posture; fortunately a massage therapist often floats about offering neck rubs.... *Tel 809/693–8400. 18A Enighed, next to Mongoose Junction, Cruz Bay. No credit cards. $*

Miss Lucy's. This easygoing beachside spot is a cut above most local cafes, with pretty maroon and lavender trellises and coral-colored linens. You could happily make a meal of the velvety conch fritters and sassy red bean soup alone, but continue on to the mahi mahi creole, curried goat, or conch in lemon butter. Chef Albert Huey can also whip up surprisingly fine veal medallions in port sauce. Finish up with a banana cake that would make Sara Lee hang up her apron.... *Tel 809/779–4404. Calabash, Friis Bay. D, DC not accepted. $$–$$$*

Morgan's Mango. Dine here under peach, turquoise, and white gazebos, with live classical guitar or a samba combo. The pan-Caribbean menu offers a travelogue of tastes: New Orleans Cajun shrimp, Haitian voodoo snapper (très authentic), Jamaican pickapepper steak, mahi mahi with Cruzan rum mango sauce. Knockout drinks and desserts.... *Tel 809/693–8141. Across from National Park dock, Cruz Bay. Reservations recommended. $$–$$$*

Paradiso. Well-heeled yachties and docksiders alike flock to this handsome space, with parquet floors, stone walls studded with glass shards, cathedral ceilings, and cognac and movie posters. The new owners (who also run Asolare and Chateau Bordeaux) have upgraded the Italian menu: even the fettucine primavera is scented with saffron.... *Tel 809/693–8899. Mongoose Junction, Cruz Bay. Reservations recommended. D not accepted. $$–$$$*

The Purple Door. Break out your dashikis: This 19th-century building (yes, the doors are purple), which has been in owner Kim Lyons' family for generations, is transformed with Nigerian batik wall hangings, Yomba carvings, Adire paintings, Maroon baskets, and assorted gourds and instruments. Standouts include great, chunky fungi; melting conch in butter; and fabulous stir-fries incorporating things like okra, pumpkin, and yam..... *Tel 809/693–8940. 1F Cruz Bay. D, DC not accepted. $$–$$$*

Pusser's. At this faux–Somerset Maugham-ish tropical pub—brass fixtures, hardwood paneling, whirring ceiling fans, old ad posters (Yorkshire Relish, Parkinson's Sugar Pills)—you can get pub grub like fish and chips, juicy burgers, and reasonably edible pastas gussied up with island spices.... *Tel*

809/693–8489. Wharfside Village, Cruz Bay. D, DC not accepted. $$

Saychelles. The green-and-white awnings and blue shutters are reminiscent of St. Tropez, as is the bar crammed with beautiful tanned people; a casual wooden terrace fronts the beach, while the interior gleams with tile floors, ceramic lamps, and Italian fabrics. Chris Coble's food duplicates the robust, sun- and garlic-drenched flavors of Provence.... *Tel 809/693–7030. 4 Cruz Bay, Wharfside Village, Cruz Bay. Reservations recommended. D, DC not accepted. $$$*

Seabreeze Cafe. This laid-back local hangout with masks and seascapes hanging on the walls is the kind of place where you're expected to linger over your coffee. The eats are basic—lemon chicken, garlic shrimp, BBQ beef sandwiches.... *Tel 809/693–5824. 4F Little Plantation. Reservations not accepted. No credit cards. $*

Skinny Legs. Little more than a corrugated tin-and-wood shack seemingly held together with Christmas lights, peeling posters, and curling business cards, but impecunious yachties descend like locusts to scarf down burgers and chili dogs.... *Tel 809/779–4982. Emmaus, Coral Bay. Reservations not accepted. No credit cards. $–$$*

Woody's Seafood Saloon. There's no decor at this glorified bar, unless you count the stringy-haired, tattooed, emaciated youths (they look French but aren't) slouching beneath the umbrellas on the tiny patio. Woody's does have a few advantages: it offers several beers on tap, excellent conch fritters, and six different kinds of shrimp, plus a full late menu—until 1am Mon–Thurs, and 2am Fri–Sun.... *Tel 809/779–4625. Cruz Bay. Reservations not accepted. No credit cards. $–$$*

St. Thomas Dining

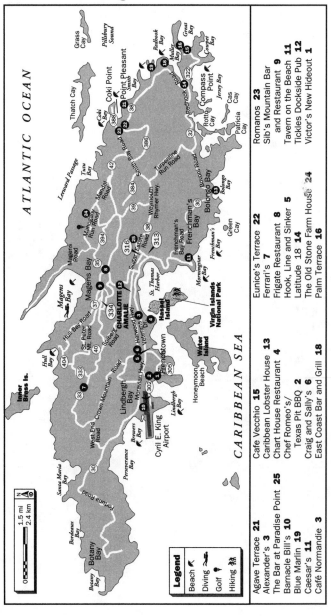

Agave Terrace **21**
Alexander's **3**
The Bar at Paradise Point **25**
Barnacle Bill's **10**
Blue Marlin **19**
Caesar's **11**
Café Normandie **3**

Cafe Vecchio **15**
Caribbean Lobster House **13**
Chart House Restaurant **4**
Chez Romeo's/
Texas Pit BBQ **2**
Craig and Sally's **6**
East Coast Bar and Grill **18**

Eunice's Terrace **22**
Ferrari's **7**
Frigate Restaurant **8**
Hook, Line and Sinker **5**
Latitude 18 **14**
The Old Stone Farm House **24**
Palm Terrace **16**

Romanos **23**
Sib's Mountain Bar
and Restaurant **9**
Tavern on the Beach **11**
Tickles Dockside Pub **12**
Victor's New Hideout **1**

Charlotte Amalie Dining

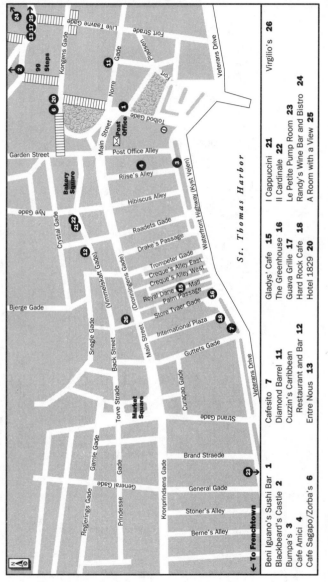

Beni Iguano's Sushi Bar **1**
Blackbeard's Castle **2**
Bumpa's **3**
Cafe Amici **4**
Cafe Sagapo/Zorba's **6**
Cafesito **7**
Diamond Barrel **11**
Cuzzin's Caribbean Restaurant and Bar **12**
Entre Nous **13**
Gladys' Cafe **15**
The Greenhouse **16**
Guava Grille **17**
Hard Rock Cafe **18**
Hotel 1829 **20**
I Cappuccini **21**
Il Cardinale **22**
Le Petite Pump Room **23**
Randy's Wine Bar and Bistro **24**
A Room with a View **25**
Virgilio's **26**

St. Croix Dining

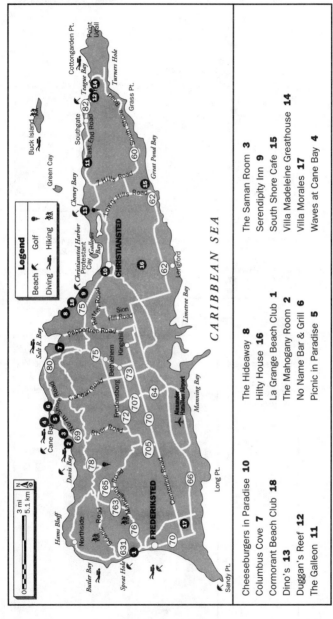

Christiansted Dining

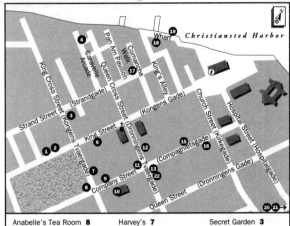

Anabelle's Tea Room **8**	Harvey's **7**	Secret Garden **3**
Antoine's **18**	Indies **15**	Tommy and Susan's
Banana Bay Club **4**	Jackie's Courtyard **2**	Taverna **22**
Bombay Club **6**	Kendrick's **20**	Top Hat **9**
Camille's **11**	Kim's **1**	Tutto Bene **16**
The Chart House **19**	Luncheria **13**	
Club Comanche **17**	Morning Glory **21**	
Eeez's Specialty Cafe **10**	Pangaea **12**	

Frederiksted Dining

Café du Soleil **5**
Le St-Tropez **2**
Market Street Cafe **3**
On the Beach Bar and Grill **6**
UCA Vegetarian Restaurant **1**
Vel's **4**

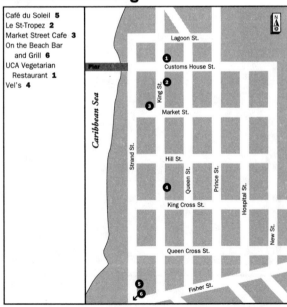

St. John Dining

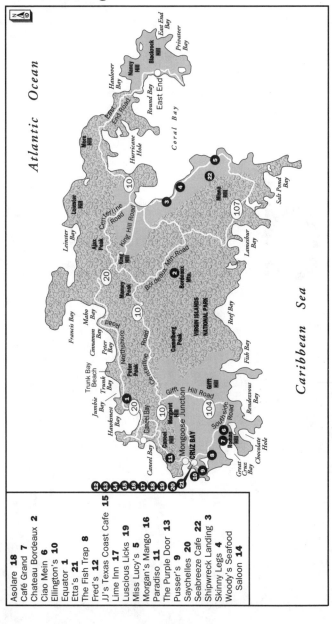

Asolare **18**
Café Grand **7**
Chateau Bordeaux **2**
Ciao Mein **6**
Ellington's **10**
Equator **1**
Etta's **21**
The Fish Trap **8**
Fred's **12**
JJ's Texas Coast Cafe **15**
Lime Inn **17**
Luscious Licks **19**
Miss Lucy's **5**
Morgan's Mango **16**
Paradiso **11**
The Purple Door **13**
Pusser's **9**
Saychelles **20**
Seabreeze Cafe **22**
Shipwreck Landing **3**
Skinny Legs **4**
Woody's Seafood Saloon **14**

3
sions

Most visitors
descend on the
U.S. Virgin
Islands to
scrounge in the
stores and lounge
on the shores, the

next piña colada conveniently within arm's reach. But once you're down here and this regimen starts to get old, what next? Of course you can go sailing, take a nature hike, or snorkel around (see Getting Outside for help with all this). Or you can hunt up a little culture—emphasis on the world "little." No fewer than seven flags have flown over the Virgin Islands in its crazy-quilt history; marauding pirates (Edward "Blackbeard" Teach) and dashing corsairs (Sir Francis Drake) fought over them like dogs over a bone. As a result, the handsome towns of Charlotte Amalie, Christiansted, and Frederiksted each developed distinct colonial personalities. Charlotte Amalie shows the most wear and tear, overrun with commercialism and continually encroaching on the (formerly) green countryside; Christiansted and Frederiksted have maintained more architectural integrity, including graceful arcades of 18th-century Danish design. Ruins poke up like restless spirits amidst the tangle of undergrowth on St. John, while banks of purple and pink bougainvillaea tumble over St. Croix's numerous derelict sugar mills (though none of these relics have ever been fully developed as bona fide tourist attractions). The forts and sugar plantation greathouses down here are among the best-preserved in the Caribbean, but there aren't all that many—you won't need more than a day to take them in. Still, once you've got a good start on your tan, you may want to distract yourself for an afternoon with some of the amusements offered here.

Top five reasons given by locals for driving on the left
1. It's a holdover from the Danes, except they drive on the right.
2. Because we're always drunk.
3. Because we'd kill people driving on the right.
4. Because we're militant and it's our way of subverting the U.S. government.
5. Because it'll mean fewer but better cruise ship passengers (wink wink).

Getting Your Bearings
St. Thomas's main arteries are Route 30, which skirts the south shore; Routes 33, 37, 40, and 42, which careen madly up, down, and around the hills of the interior, often affording fabulous views as they crest; and Route 38, which traverses the ugly Anywhere-U.S.A. wasteland of strip malls and fast-food joints that define central St. Thomas, before

turning into Smith Bay Road, which takes you to the magnificent northeastern beaches. On St. John, Northshore Road (Route 20) weaves in and out of thick stands of mahogany and bay trees, yielding glimpses of incredibly romantic, champagne-colored coves, while Centerline Road (Route 10) bisects the island before hugging the pristine East End coast. On St. Croix, Routes 66 and 70 provide a fairly straight shot between Christiansted, the airport, and Frederiksted. But the north-coast road, Route 80, zigs and zags wildly between the resorts before merging with Route 75, which circles around central St. Croix, in and out of Christiansted. Route 82 is a more serene coastal drive, passing the resorts east of Christiansted before spiraling through the arid, scrubby East End and ending at the easternmost point in the United States, Point Udall.

The Lowdown

Overrated... For some reason, tour groups (especially off the cruise ships) descend like locusts on St. Thomas's **Estate St. Peter Greathouse and Botanical Gardens**, which are not worth the $8 admission on a good day, even less so when overrun. Since the greathouse also happens to be the owner's home, unwelcoming signs ("Please do not sit") bristle throughout the living room/art gallery. A rum punch that tastes like Kool-Aid with a thimbleful of alcohol is included in the admission, which hardly makes it worth it. You can drive up the mountain from Charlotte Amalie for free, or take a $3 cab ride from downtown, so why pay $10 to ride the **Paradise Point Gondolas**? It's tramway robbery. And you'll spend even more money drinking or shopping up top—not that these can't be fun, especially with such amazing views all round. On St. Croix, the **Cruzan Rum Distillery** extracts $3 for a rum tasting (during which you get the hard-sell along with the hard stuff), a brief explanation of the distilling process, and a tour of the plant. Pretty much a rip-off, considering that most of its Caribbean counterparts don't charge anything, and many also offer museums on the history of rum-making. **Salt River Bay National Historical Park and Ecological Preserve** isn't a rip-off, since entry is technically free (there are no facilities), but if you believe the pompous assertion by Jesse Thomson, president of the Columbus Jubilee Committee, that Salt River is "a microcosm of the continuum of human history in the West Indies," you'll be sadly disappointed. At present, it's mostly just nature preserve, and two-thirds of that is underwater; a few archaeological sites exist, but laypeople can't really appreciate them in their current state. The plan is to create interpretive nature trails along the biodiverse wetlands and perhaps even the surrounding coral reefs, while building a replica of a traditional Carib village that would serve as a heritage museum. Great idea—we'll come back when it's finished.

Tourist traps you won't mind getting caught in...

Tillett Gardens on St. Thomas was developed by artist Jim Tillett, known for his silk-screened maps superimposed over island scenes; it's a collection of brightly colored, typical West Indian cottages with red tin roofs and gingerbread trim, which now host various shops and artists' studios. Small, fanciful murals (a frog munching on hibiscus, a mongoose sipping a martini, an iguana in a wine glass) march across some of the exteriors, and rock gardens, fountains, and gazebos in the courtyard make it a cool oasis under the fierce sun. Well-hyped evening musicales, from classical to jazz (see Nightlife and Entertainment) are held here throughout the year. Another all-too-well-known St. Thomas attraction, **Coral World**, is crowded and noisy, filled with screeching children and tour groups, but there's no better or cheaper way to explore the wonders of the deep without donning scuba gear or spitting into a snorkel.

Fortifying yourself...

St. Thomas and St. Croix offer three of the most perfectly preserved citadels in the Caribbean, decked out in brilliant hues like some Technicolor fantasy. Constructed between 1672 and 1687, the brick-red **Fort Christian** stands sentinel over Charlotte Amalie harbor on St. Thomas. An antique still and animal-driven sugarcane mill sit in the spacious interior courtyard; several musty rooms are devoted to history, including documentation and photographs of the Danish-American transfer, and a re-creation of a typical 18th-century burgher's home. There's also an exhibit on bird life in the Virgin Islands, and noted folklorist Arona

Peterson's collection of medicinal plants (including charming drawings by schoolchildren of various native herbs). Rotating exhibitions of local artworks are also featured, with a "meet the artists" program the first Tuesday of each month. The active museum board also schedules special events like dinner dances and Beaux Arts masquerade balls, to which the public is sometimes invited (check local papers or call the fort for information). On St. Croix, mustard-colored **Fort Christiansvaern** overlooks the sparkling Christiansted harbor. Gazing at the perfect geometry of ocher stone, white trim, jade-green grass, and azure sky, it's hard to imagine that the dank dungeons and detention cells (replete with serious shackles) were ever used for more than drying out the occasional drunk. (As the Danish Governor General tartly evaluated his garrison in 1747, "[We have] only 20 living soldiers, one of whom is over 60 and the rest are drunkards.") Just down Company Street, the burgundy-and-white **Steeple Building** (included on the same admission ticket) was St. Croix's first Lutheran church, completed in 1753 and deconsecrated in 1831. Its exhibits, including archeological artifacts of the native Arawak tribes and displays on black culture (music, food, dance, folklore) are of greater interest than the dry-as-

> **Sightseeing for shopaholics**
>
> Some of the larger shopping malls in the U.S.V.I. are sightseeing attractions in themselves, if only for gawking at frenzied crowds of cruise shippers exclaiming over the merchandise. On St. Thomas, the leviathans dock right at **Havensight Mall** (Rte. 30, Long Bay), which offers the best people-watching; you'll find their opposite nautical number—yachties who need a taste of terra firma—at the **American Yacht Harbor Mall** in Red Hook. At **Mountain Top Mall** and **Paradise Point**, also on St. Thomas, the shops are secondary to the views and hopping, happening bars. **Tillett Gardens** offers unique items like batik clothing and handmade gold jewelry in the most refined setting on St. Thomas, a scene of tinkling fountains and gingerbread-style buildings. In St. John's Cruz Bay, **Wharfside Village** occupies a killer setting right on the harbor, while **Mongoose Junction**, a contemporary take on classic stone–and–wood 18th-century architecture, is as upscale as the Virgin Islands—indeed the Caribbean—gets.

dust military memorabilia in the fort. Constructed in 1760, the small, symmetrical **Fort Frederik** (in Frederiksted) is exceptionally pretty in maroon with white trim, with its original cobblestone interior courtyard. Its primary claim to fame is that its cannons fired the first unofficial salute to a U.S. ship on October 25, 1776. The dungeons and artillery rooms have been converted into exhibit halls, with a decidedly minor collection—mostly xeroxes of historic documents, yellowing newspapers, and a few related artifacts (although an entire room devoted to the transfer of the islands from Denmark to the United States is kind of interesting to browse through). But there are often fine rotating local art shows, as well as neat science exhibits like "In the Eye of the Storm," which traces the history of hurricanes throughout the Carribbean.

When sugar was king... **Estate Whim Plantation Museum** on St. Croix is tiny—only three rooms—but it's superbly restored, a mid-18th-century plantation greathouse with a simple oval design that was unusual for its time. Inside, the furnishings include period Duncan Phyfe mahogany and cool little touches like whist and cribbage boards. Other buildings include a re-creation of an apothecary, the stables, and a traditional colonial kitchen, where an impassive woman in period garb and sneakers fries up delicious johnnycakes. All the estate's buildings were constructed of coral and native limestone—look closely at the mortar, which was made of molasses and crushed seashells. Built in the 1780s, **Annaberg Plantation** on St. John was once one of the most significant sugar mills in the Virgin Islands. The ruins, silhouetted against Leinster Bay and several British Virgin Islands in the distance, provide perhaps the best Kodak moment on St. John. Regrettably, the government has discontinued the morning crafts demonstrations they used to have here, but rumor has it they may be reinstated in 1996. A good thing, since it was the best place on the island to get a cheap, filling breakfast (still more tasty johnnycakes). The history on display at another of St. John's restored greathouses, the **Elaine Ione Sprauve Library and Museum**, is confined to shards of Arawak pottery, chipped colonial china, and yellowing newspaper cuttings.

Gimme that old-time religion... While the whitewashed or cotton-candy façades of the islands' many historic churches make for pretty photo ops, the interiors are humble indeed. If you visit one, make it **Frederick Lutheran Church** in Charlotte Amalie, the second-oldest Lutheran place of worship in the Western Hemisphere. Although the congregation was established in 1666, the current building was completed in 1793 and remodeled after numerous fires and hurricanes ravaged the interior in the 1870s. Notice the striking altar, chancel, pulpit, and ceiling, all fashioned from local mahogany. The St. Thomas **Synagogue** (its full name is **Beracha Vershalom Vegmiluth Hasidim**, which translates as "Congregation of Blessing, Peace, and Loving Deeds") has held a weekly Sabbath service since 1833, making it the second-oldest temple in the Western Hemisphere. The architecture is exquisitely textured: stark white Greco-Roman pillars, dark mahogany altar and pews, rough gray limestone walls, and sand floors (not merely a primitive touch—it's supposed to represent the exodus from Egypt). Incidentally, no matter what your creed, Sunday services throughout the islands give you a wonderful window on life down here, especially at the Baptist churches, whose congregations sing joyfully and lustily.

Only in the Cruzan rain forest... Most of the western half of St. Croix is blanketed with a thick tangle of rain forest. A single paved road jigs determinedly under a canopy of mahogany and turpentine trees, until suddenly you come into a clearing dominated by a bamboo-and-thatch hut that leans drunkenly in all directions, seemingly glued together by business cards and Christmas lights. Welcome to the **Mt. Pellier Hut Domino Club**. If you stop for a drink in the heat of the day you'll hear the impatient grunts of a sow named Miss Piggy. As one of the barkeeps trundles over to her sty with a brew, she fixes him with a bleary eye; the hiss of the can opening elicits a torrent of orgasmic squeals as she charges, snout thrust pugnaciously forward, awaiting her fix. Don't share your Bud with her though—since she's the owner's meal ticket, Miss Piggy has been weaned off the hard stuff and onto non-alcoholic beer (Kaliber seems to be her favorite). Further down Mahogany Road is the **St. Croix LEAP**

(Life and Environmental Arts Project), dedicated to helping jobless Cruzans find a vocation working with native woods like saman, tibet, and mahogany, and thereby keep local craft traditions alive.

Museums without walls... There are no art museums in the Virgin Islands, and few galleries, at least of the Soho sort where the art lovers are as well worth watching as the artworks themselves. St. Thomas, however, offers something possibly better: colorful murals splashed all over walls in unlikely places. If your time is limited, the first two are the most conveniently located. **Mural One** adorns the back wall of the Government House in Charlotte Amalie. Commissioned by the WPA (Works Project Administration) in the 1930s, the three panels are an artist's rendering of major events in U.S.V.I. history. The first is a typical Caribbean scene—two black sugar workers (perhaps slaves) in a canefield, faces impassive, shoulders sloping, indicating the dignity of labor (the most overt social commentary in the work). The second panel shows the transfer of the islands from Denmark to the U.S. as battleships steam into the harbor. The third panel shows Columbus landing on St. Croix in 1493, a ludicrous scene of a bound Indian kneeling in supplication to the Spaniards as a monk looks on, ready to convert the heathen. Politically correct it ain't. **Mural Two**'s panels confront one another across the Charlotte Amalie post office. They're the work of another 1930s WPA artist, Stephen Dohanos (who illustrated numerous *Saturday Evening Post* covers, though these murals are definitely not Norman Rockwellian). The first trumpets the importance of shipping to the local economy, with curves of green bananas, the folds of burlap sacks and billowing sails, and the skewed perspective of a curved horizon all creating an impression of tremendous forward movement. The second panel is hardly subtle in its socialist message, all about the triumph of industry over agriculture and the oppression of the local population: there are solid earth tones in the foreground, with bright colors relegated to the background; an anchor on one side, looking suspiciously like the Soviet hammer and sickle, is balanced by oil derricks on the other; an enormous cannon seems to be trained directly on a cruise ship in the distance.

(You may sympathize, at least on a day when you find hundreds of cruise passengers crowding you off the streets of Charlotte Amalie.) An even more overtly political statement, **Mural Three** defiantly unrolls down Route 38 East (Weymouth Rhymer Highway) near the **Fort Mylner Shopping Center** outside of Charlotte Amalie. The work is an ongoing community project, entitled *Black Utopia Lane*; artists sometimes ask for donations of money or supplies at the roadside. Occasionally, they'll paint over their own work when the mood or inspiration strikes. Panel one, titled *Portraits of Africa*, celebrates African Americans' links to Africa, with the proud images of Queen Nefertiti and a lion. In panel two, a black Moses brandishes the Ten Commandments, set against a stylized Nile scene, reminding us that all civilization emerged from Africa. The third panel recites a litany of grievances against white society, with various mottoes incribed around a single image, giant clasped hands labeled "rich" and "poor." The fourth panel symbolically depicts the dispersal of African tribes (look for the spreading banyan tree with one trunk contorted into a figure straight out of Munch's *The Scream*). The next panel admonishes blacks to "Stand firm by any means" (Malcolm X); the sixth mourns deaths from AIDS and recommends the use of condoms; the final panel simply warns us that "Those who do a kindness because they expect to be repaid are always DISAPPOINTED." The whole mural is totally didactic, without a whiff of compromise or apology—and refreshingly uncommercial. Also just outside Charlotte Amalie, **Mural Four**—oddly set in the bustling Tutu Park Shopping Center—was begun in 1993 when students from Charlotte Amalie High School painted the first panel, a historical diorama with crude, blockish figures of surprising power; the colors are wonderfully vibrant, reminiscent of the best Haitian art. A professional artist, Eric Winter, was then commissioned to paint the other murals, and an interesting choice it was, too—Mr. Winter is white, in his 60s, and hails from New England, so he's not just another local artist working in the primitive tradition. His four murals depict timeless island scenes. The first two are idealized views of waterfront life—happy tourists snapping photos of one another, juxtaposed with locals going about their daily business—but check out the locals' ramrod posture and averted eyes, conveying (intentionally or not) that these are people just barely surviving. Two more Winter murals are in the food court: the first again portrays the Charlotte Amalie waterfront, as it might have been in the 1930s (not a cruise ship in sight); the second contrasts a beach scene with market day. Here too the figures' eyes are averted and most are depicted from the rear, save for one woman in the foreground, her eyes hauntingly shaded by her hat. It's quietly compelling, in dignified contrast to the fast-food hustle it hangs above.

Do-it-yourself museums... Historic museums are a dime a dozen in the Caribbean, but the **Seven Arches Museum** in downtown Charlotte Amalie is something special. Yes, it offers the usual haphazard assortment of rusting cannonballs, chipped china, and tchotchkes like a chicken carousel, all displayed with fine contempt for the curator's art; it *is* the only historic private home open to the public on St. Thomas, but that and its touchingly paltry collection are not the real reasons to visit. This museum is, well, homey—genial proprietors Barbara Demaras and Philibert Fluck, artists and amateur archaeologists, actually live in this 18th-century burgher's home, and it has taken on their quirks. Entrance to Seven Arches is through a courtyard brimming with bougainvillea, fragrant with clove and cinnamon, and crowned with a majestic night-blooming cirrus cactus that resembles a thousand writhing snakes. It's also home to a thriving iguana colony (they're partial to hibiscus, and will nibble the flowers from your hand). Barbara conducts most of the tours personally, even taking visitors into the couple's bedroom. Four cats have the run of the house (watch where you walk—they're usually sunning on the steps). You can even sip a complimentary fruit punch in the garden, chatting with Barbara and Philibert. In the same vein, though not as much fun, is the **Estate Mt. Washington Plantation** on St. Croix, which dates from the 1750s. Owners Nancy and Tony Ayer have gradually restored the estate; ruins of a rum cistern and factory now rise dramatically amid the surrounding mango and guava trees. The "tour" is self-guided and the estate house is not open to visitors, so don't go knocking on their door except on Sundays, when Nancy opens her antique store (see Shopping).

Save it for a rainy day... You'll be singing "How Dry I Am" at the **Cruzan Rum Distillery** on St. Croix as you wait out a typically brief but torrential tropical thunderstorm, sipping piña coladas or tasting the white, gold, spiced, and overproof (151) products, after touring the grounds. **Seven Arches Museum** (St. Thomas) is another spot best left for a rainy day, since you may end up lingering over punch with the owners. St. Thomas also crawls with malls (see Shopping); why waste a sunny day inside?

Local color... An old-time Caribbean marketplace is a jambalaya of sights, sounds, and smells: local ladies, garbed in bright bandannas and shifts, fan the flies off the luscious produce of the islands, from papayas to plantains; dreadlocked herb doctors hawk potions and cures; shining-eyed schoolgirls in starched uniforms pool their resources and skip off with sticky coconut tarts. It's the best free show in town; you can view it at pulsating **Market Square** in Charlotte Amalie on St. Thomas daily, and on St. Croix at Christiansted's **Christian "Shan" Hendricks Market** on Wednesdays and Saturdays. On St. Thomas, **Vendors Plaza**, at the corner of Emancipation Gardens (so named for the regrettably undistinguished statue that commemorates the freeing of the slaves in 1848), is where, in 1992, the government gathered all those pesky pushcart peddlers who used to roam Charlotte Amalie. It now has the air, if not the aroma, of a Moroccan souk. Fishermen casually toss their 100-pound catches from boldly colored boats to waiting trucks at the harbor in St. Thomas's Frenchtown. Also on St. Thomas, **Clinton Phipps Racetrack** attracts a pan-Caribbean field to its haphazardly scheduled races. Everyone on-island shows up, soaking up the ambience, munching on heavenly island fried chicken—and happily losing money. Betting is secondary here—it's probably the world's only race course where you can place $20 to win and get only $10 back. On Sundays, the strong of heart and stomach can follow the blood-curdling cheers just around the corner from the track, where a plain, unlabeled shack hosts grisly (illegal) pit-bull and cock fights; many of the handlers look like they've seen their share of brawls themselves. St. Croix's **Mt. Pellier Hut Domino Club** is famed not only for Miss Piggy—a sow whose penchant for beer would shame frat boys—but also for a Sunday brunch that draws locals and tourists alike for savory barbecue and a one-man steel band. With that combination, the brunches range from merely festive to downright rowdy. They're never dangerous, but unaccompanied women will have to endure more than their usual share of leers from louts. Local vendors selling the usual T-shirts and tchotchkes cluster at the **Ferry Dock** at Cruz Bay on St. John, and the taxi (actually safari van) lineups rival those at the Ritz.

Bird's-eye views... On St. Croix, the hotel known as **Blackbeard's Castle** occupies the site of the 1679 Fort Skytsford, though all that remains is a small lookout tower (which the hotel, with an utter lack of imagination, uses for storage). It casts a bullying shadow over the pool, which itself boasts sweeping views of Charlotte Amalie. A rival hotel, **Bluebeard's Castle**, has its own authentic lookout tower staring Blackbeard's down across the town and harbor; these hotel grounds reveal a different but equally stunning perspective. The bench at **Drake's Seat**, St. Thomas's most famous lookout spot, probably dates from the 1950s, but local lore insists that Sir Francis Drake made this summit his personal lookout post. West from Drake's Seat, the somewhat less romantic **Mountain Top Mall** has its own claim to fame: the Mountain Top bar here bills itself as the place that invented the banana daiquiri. (It sells so many daily—estimates run as high as 3,000 in season—that they switched from glass to plastic go-cups.) But the observation deck does have glorious views of Magens Bay, and the green isles of Hans Lollik, Jost Van Dyke, and Tortola undulate like sea serpents in the distance. Though ridiculously overpriced, the **Paradise Point Gondolas** (catch them on Route 30, next to Buccaneer Mall) offer incredible views of the harbor on the five-minute ride up and down, and even more sensational 360-degree panoramas up top. **Seabourne Seaplanes** offers "flightseeing," an hour's tour of St. Thomas, St. John, and several British Virgin Islands from the air, while the **St. Thomas/St. John Ferry** also offers a bird's-eye view—at least, the perspective of a gull cruising for its lunch—plus a vista of the ragged St. Thomas coastline, scissored with coves like a child's paper cutouts. On St. John, **Chateau Bordeaux/Cheeseburger Cheeseburger** is like the Jekyll and Hyde of restaurants. The latter is a rickety wooden shack that serves as a terrace for the former, come evening. You'll get nothing fancier here than a daiquiri and cheeseburger, served by punked-out, body-pierced Brad Pitt wannabes with flashy smiles—but what sublime views of the British Virgin Islands, their color shifting with the sun's progress from emerald and taupe to indigo and jet.

Fish-eye views... **Atlantis Submarines** (St. Thomas) is like something out of Jules Verne. The 50-minute ride plunges 90 feet below the surface, where divers shoo all the denizens of the deep—from darting iridescent parrotfish to gliding stingrays to lumbering groupers—past your private porthole. The rival **Coral World**, also on St. Thomas, counters with a state-of-the-art observatory tank sunk over a particularly dazzling reef. Come feeding time, it's a toss-up whether there's a bigger frenzy inside the shark tank or outside, with hordes of families jockeying for position. **St. Croix Aquarium** is small-fry by comparison, with just one room. Where else, though, will the resident marine biologist take visitors on a personalized tour of each tank, culminating in a touch-pond that never fails to make kids giggle with delight?

Great walks... Stroll along **Kongen's Gade** (King Street) up Government Hill in downtown Charlotte Amalie to sample a fascinating hodgepodge of architectural styles handed down from various European rulers across the years. Elegant mansions, including the 1867 Government House and Hotel 1829, incorporate Spanish terracotta patios, Dutch carved wood doors, Danish red tile roofs, French iron grillwork, and English gingerbread trim; the ubiquitous yellow brickwork is made from bricks originally used for ballast on the trading ships. Between the mansions run narrow alleys called freeways, once used exclusively by slaves (who weren't allowed to walk the main streets) to shield their comings and goings from their masters. Halfway up the hill, between Hotel 1829 and Government House, you'll see a vaulting staircase, cracked and crawling with undergrowth, named the 99 Steps (there are actually 103 steps, though—go figure). It's hilarious to watch the tourists trudging up and down this stairway, dutifully counting the steps, in the steamy, sultry air. Also in Charlotte Amalie, **Dronningen's Gade**, or Main Street (it actually means Queen Street), is one of the Caribbean's great shopping thoroughfares—the ornamental flourishes of its lovely architecture are plastered over with signs advertising "Sale!" or "Best Prices in Town!" Linking Main Street to the waterfront drive are a series of narrow, sun-streaked passages (mini-malls unto themselves, aflutter with pennants and sale signs), their coral and canary-yellow façades shaded by palm trees that vault like the arches of Chartres Cathedral. Among the historic sights along Main Street are the 1818 von Bretton house, now the Enid M. Baa Public Library, and the Camille Pissarro Building, where the artist was born Jacob Pizarro in 1830. Downtown Christiansted, on St. Croix, is a bit like a Hans Christian Andersen fairy tale transplanted to the Caribbean. Start at the harbor at **King Street**, perhaps the most historic street. You'll find yourself in a square dominated by the lemon-hued 1856 Old Scalehouse, where taxable goods (including immense barrels of rum and molasses weighing up to a ton) were weighed by 19th-century customs agents. Nowadays it's occupied by the **Visitor's Bureau**, agent for St. Croix's most lucrative 20th-century industry. Across the square is the Old Customs House, today the National Park Service headquarters, with its gracefully sweeping staircase. The 1830s Government House, at the corner of King and Queen Cross streets, has elaborate formal gardens, now sadly running to seed. At the other end of St. Croix, the stately, somewhat dour buildings lining Frederiksted's **Strand Street** date mostly from the late 19th century, in contrast to the rest of town, where flocks of Victorian gingerbread drowse in the sun as if this were New Orleans. But Strand Street is worth visiting for a splendid waterfront walk, where—unlike Charlotte Amalie—the views aren't spoiled by circling tour buses and taxis, honking horns, and squealing shoppers.

A walk on the wild side... Once you stroll above Queen Cross Street in the town of Christiansted on St. Croix, **King, Company, and Queen streets** take on an unmistakable Hispanic flavor, thanks to the resident—mostly illegal—Dominican immigrants. Local cops confide that, as they make their island rounds in the dead of night, they often come upon troops of shivering, soaking wet, scantily clad women fresh off the boats, who have made the trip to work as prostitutes in Christiansted's red-light district. At night, buxom ladies poured into tight spandex dresses frame themselves in the doorways of the nondescript, no-name bars that line Company and King streets. (King Street—not Queen Street, as locals crudely joke—is where male prostitutes tend to hang out, at times literally.) Even during the day, when you can admire the decaying but still lovely arcaded buildings, single men are likely to be propositioned. The Dominican influence is just as pronounced at the other end of St. Croix on Frederiksted's **Queen and Prince streets**, though these have more of a family, neighborhood feel than their Christiansted counterpart. Throughout the day, pulsing salsa and merengue blare from the bodegas, while the smell of strong coffee and last night's *asado* (barbecue) wafts on the breeze. On St. Thomas, the **Savan**—the working-class district of Charlotte Amalie—draws all kinds of Caribbean immigrants, especially Jamaicans; you can usually inhale the sweet scents of ganja and garlic in its streets. General Gade, in particular, has a great selection of Rasta shops and holes-in-the-wall serving Ital fare, the Rastafarian version of vegan cuisine.

Kid stuff... Surprisingly, there are few activities geared especially toward children in the U.S.V.I. And their idea of a playground is a crayon-colored flag outside the local McDonalds. But several hotels (see Accommodations) offer day-care centers whose activities might include treasure hunts, local crafts workshops, even Caribbean cooking classes. On St. Thomas, **Coral World** provides plenty of hands-on experience for the tots (they love getting their hands slimy in the touch pools, feeling up starfish and cucumbers). Kids invariably find submerging in the **Atlantis Submarines** way cool, and parents will appreciate the fact that the entire Caribbean suddenly becomes a personal aquarium. While the **St. Croix**

Aquarium is the proverbial small fish in a big pond when it comes to tourist attractions, its curator delights in taking kids around personally and introducing them to the marine environment.

Where to escape the crowds... Just outside downtown Charlotte Amalie on St. Thomas, **Frenchtown** is the place to escape the shopping Huns. Savor its quiet, workaday rhythm, watch the fishermen (many of them descended from the original fair-haired Norman settlers), or wander past the ramshackle wooden houses daubed in cotton-candy colors and obscured by a jungle of laundry hung out to dry. There's little to see at St. Croix's **Salt River Bay National Historical Park and Ecological Preserve**, aside from a plaque marking the site of Columbus' landing and a few partially unearthed pre-Columbian archaeological sites—and that's its saving grace. It's a delightfully deserted, almost desolate site, where you can be left alone to commune with the resident flocks of seabirds. St. John's **East End** is another peaceful area, where goats huddle for warmth during a thunderstorm in a bus stop splashed with colorful Rasta graffiti, or even wander right into impeccable balconied houses sporting lacy gingerbread trim.

Green spaces... Located in the more lush part of St. Thomas, where rainfall is heavier, **Estate St. Peter Greathouse and Botanical Gardens** is an uncommonly peaceful place—when the tour groups aren't in. The name is deceiving; while an estate did sit here once upon a very distant time, the greathouse is actually owner Howard Wolf's residence, built in the 1980s. Hurricane Hugo entirely wiped out the original greathouse, so Wolf started again from scratch (a series of vivid photos documents the destruction), and finally opened to the public in 1993, raking in $8 a head to view the place. Wolf's living room rather uneasily doubles as an art gallery, showcasing work by members of the local arts council, from batik prints to underwater photographs. The real reason to come here is to explore the nature trails, which cling precariously to the hillside and snake through the jungle-like grounds, or to dally on the observation decks, which offer terrific views of Magen's Bay and Tortola. St. Croix spirals from rain forest to semi-arid desert, and the **St. George Village Botanical Gardens** has examples of each, including a cactus grove and a miniature rain forest. Some of the plantings are imaginatively incorporated into the ruins of a 19th-century sugar plantation. Also on St. Croix, the **Salt River Bay National Historical Park and Ecological Preserve**—dedicated November 14, 1993, to commemorate the quincentennial of Columbus' landing—gives you a chance to explore a watery ecosystem, with approximately two-thirds of its 912 acres submerged under water. This coastal estuary contains the largest remaining mangrove forest in the U.S.V.I., as well as a submarine canyon and a habitat for endangered species such as roseate terns, peregrine falcons, brown pelicans, and hawksbill turtles. And as if that's not enough, archaeologists have unearthed all sorts of fascinating stuff here—the only remains in the Caribbean of a prehistoric ceremonial ball court, evidence of various Taino and Carib settlements and burials, and a 16th-century fort. The promontory Cabo de las Flechas (Cape of the Arrows) is the site of the first recorded skirmish between Europeans and indigenous American people, in 1493.

The Index

St. Thomas

Atlantis Submarines. The price includes a free rum or fruit punch and round-trip catamaran cruise in the Charlotte Amalie harbor on the way to the sub, which is docked off Buck Island National Wildlife Refuge. The 46-passenger submarines are air-conditioned, with large portholes; the captain's running narration is informative if a bit hokey (along the lines of, "Look, on the starboard side, there's Big John, our resident friendly grouper.").... *Tel 809/776–5650, 800/253–0493. Building VI, Havensight Mall, Rte. 30, Long Bay. $72 adults, $36 children 13–18, $25 4–12. Times vary; call ahead for reservations. Service was slated to begin from Red Hook and St. John to the waters surrounding Grass Cay in late winter 1996.*

Blackbeard's Castle. The views from this hotel/restaurant are a textbook definition of the word "panoramic." And yes, Edward "Blackbeard" Teach himself posted lookouts from the 17th-century (1679) "castle," which is on the National Register of Historic Places.... *Tel 809/776–1234. Blackbeard's Hill, Charlotte Amalie. Open daily. Admission free.*

Bluebeard's Castle. Still more amazing views of Charlotte Amalie and the harbor, and another piratical lookout post, this one dating from the 18th century.... *Tel 809/774–1600. Bluebeard's Hill, Charlotte Amalie. Open daily. Admission free.*

Clinton Phipps Racetrack. Churchill Downs it's not (though the drinking is just as heavy), but the raucous crowds suggest that the sport of kings has truly been given back to the people.... *Tel 809/775–4555. Nadir, off Rte. 30. Race days vary, but are usually on weekends. Admission $5.*

Coral World. If you don't want to get your feet wet snorkeling or scuba diving, this is the next best thing. The real attraction is the sunken glass-enclosed observatory, 20 feet beneath sea level. There are also predator- and reef-encounter feedings (starring the sharks and rays), hands-on displays, a flamingo exhibit, a semi-sub, and bird shows (parrots, macaws, and cockatoos ride bikes, roller-skate, and play ring toss). (The big predator tank was destroyed by Marilyn, but it should re-open by spring '96.)... *Tel 809/775–1555. Coki Point. Open daily, 9–6. Admission $16 adults, $10 children. Sea Explorer Semi-sub: half-hour tours several times daily, adults $19, children under 18, $12.*

Drake's Seat. Sir Francis Drake reputedly kept watch over his ships (and looked for the Spanish galleons that made his fortune) from this mountain viewpoint. Even on a cloudy day, you can see Magens and Hull bays, Inner and Outer Brass, Jost Van Dyke, and Tortola. A stop on every cruise-ship tour itinerary—to avoid crowds (and persistent T-shirt vendors), come after 4pm.... *Rte. 40, near intersection with Rte. 35.*

Estate St. Peter Greathouse and Botanical Gardens. This contemporary variation on a Caribbean greathouse is home to a rotating local art exhibition. The nature trails are not extensive, though plans are afoot to expand them; nearly 200 species of flora are identified along the walking routes.... *Tel 809/774–4999. Rte. 40, St. Peter Mountain Rd. Open daily 9–5 Nov–Apr. Closed Sun May–Oct. Admission $8 adults, $4 children under 12.*

Fort Christian. The fort holds intriguing displays on local herbs and birdlife, as well as the usual garden-variety historic exhibits and rotating art shows, with fine harbor views from the ramparts as a bonus.... *Tel 809/776–4566. Across from Norre Gade off the waterfront. Open Mon–Fri 8:30–4:30, Sat 9:30–4, Sun noon–4. Admission free.*

Frederick Lutheran Church. The present church was completed in 1793; the interior, rebuilt several times following fires and hurricanes, is notable for its lovely local woodwork.... *Tel 809/776–1315. 7 Norre Gade, open Mon–Sat 9–4. Admission free.*

Market Square. The big St. Thomas marketplace, where fruits and vegetables of all descriptions are sold by vendors of all descriptions. Get there early to see the wares at their finest and freshest.... *Off Strand Gade between Dronningens Gade (Main St.) and Vimmelskaft Gade (Back St.). Open daily 9–5.*

Mountain Top Mall. Sensational views of surrounding islands, a few indifferent shops hawking mostly local products, and the reputed birthplace of the banana daiquiri make this a compulsory stop for herds of tourists.... *Rte. 33. Open daily 9–9.*

Mural One. This series of vividly colored 1930s WPA murals pays tribute to important moments in U.S.V.I. history. They're located in the rear of the ground floor of the governor's traditional residence, so you'll have to pass through a metal detector—and submit to a frisking if the guard has nothing better to do.... *Tel 809/774–0001. Government House, Government Hill, Charlotte Amalie. Open Mon–Fri 9–5. Admission free.*

Mural Two. More WPA murals, but by a different artist, these moodier pieces glare down on usually oblivious postal customers.... *Charlotte Amalie Post Office, intersection of Norre Gade and Tolbod Gade. Open Mon–Fri 9–5, Sat 10–4. Admission free.*

Mural Three. This lengthy mural along one of the busiest highways on St. Thomas is a militant paean to black pride. Malcolm X would have approved.... *East Side of Rte. 38 (Weymouth Rhymer Hwy.) near Fort Mylner Shopping Center. Park at the mall or by the adjacent outdoor fruit stand, cross the highway, and stroll up the sidewalk.*

Mural Four. Several different works, one by a group of schoolchildren, in the delightfully incongruous setting of an otherwise unremarkable shopping center.... *Tutu Shopping Mall, Rte. 38. Mall open daily 9–9.*

Paradise Point Gondolas. The five-minute ride up Flag Hill is outrageously priced, but the harbor views going up and down are almost worth it.... *Tel 809/774–9809. Rte. 30, next to Buccaneer Mall. Runs continuously 9–7 daily. $10 adults, $5 children 6–12, 5 and under free.*

Seabourne Seaplanes. Aside from taking off and landing on the water, the pilots' skills include giving an entertaining spiel about the area. They weave history, tidbits of local folklore, and island gossip together while you fly over St. Thomas, St. John, and such B.V.I.s as Necker, Salt, Peter, Norman, and Fallen Jerusalem islands.... *Tel 809/777–4491. 5305 Long Bay Rd., Yacht Haven Marina, Charlotte Amalie. $78/person for 1-hour tour. Day trips range from $99 to $179 per person.*

Seven Arches Museum. The interior is full of mahogany moldings, 19th-century Bajan and Haitian furnishings, and an authentic Danish kitchen with cistern and brick oven. Look for the original gun slots on the exterior of the bedroom walls.... *Tel 809/776–9295. Government Hill, Charlotte Amalie. Open Tue–Sat 10–3, or by appointment. Admission $5.*

St. Thomas/St. John Ferry. The ferry from Red Hook is much faster, but the one leaving from the Charlotte Amalie waterfront has one big plus: dazzling views of the coast.... *Tel 809/776–6111. Charlotte Amalie waterfront. Daily, every two hours 9–4, and noon, 5:30pm, and 7pm. $7 each way.*

Synagogue. The synagogue is most notable for the sheer fact that such a place exists at all in the Caribbean, but the cool interior with its mahogany moldings, brickwork, and sand floors is worth a quick look as you wander Charlotte Amalie.... *Tel 809/774–4312. 15 Crystal Gade, Charlotte Amalie. Open weekdays 9–4. Service days and times vary according to season. Admission free.*

Tillett Gardens. This imaginative shopping mall (created by artist Jim Tillett) occupies what was an 18th-century Danish farm. Shops and artists' ateliers are housed in little pastel buildings with whimsical gingerbread trim, surrounding the original garden courtyard with fountain.... *Tel 809/775–1929. Rte. 38. Open daily 9–9.*

Vendors Plaza. This outdoor bazaar is usually packed with shoppers looking for last-minute gifts.... *Emancipation Gardens, Charlotte Amalie. Open daily.*

St. Croix

Christian "Shan" Hendricks Market. This small market bustles on Wednesdays and Saturdays, when you'll find everyone shopping here—old women balancing on their heads buckets crawling with scaly sea things, or chefs in toques nearly as tall as they are.... *Company Street, Christiansted. Open 7–5.*

Cruzan Rum Distillery. Founded the day after prohibition ended in 1932, this is one of only four rum distilleries left in the U.S. A 20-minute tour of the premises and an explanation of how rum is made are followed by the inevitable tasting (fruit juices are served to children).... *Tel 809/772–*

0280. Airport Rd. Open Mon–Fri 9–11:30 and 1–4, admission $3 adults, $1 children under 18.

Estate Mt. Washington Plantation. No reason to stop here unless you're in the neighborhood, browsing in owner Nancy Ayer's antique store, or researching a term paper on 1750s rum factories.... *Tel 809/772–1026. Rte. 63. Open daily sunrise–sunset, self-guided. Admission free.*

Estate Whim Plantation Museum. This impeccably restored plantation greathouse is especially impressive during evening candlelight classical concerts (see Entertainment and Nightlife). Unfortunately, the unenthusiastic volunteer staff seems more interested in yakking among themselves than in explaining the history on view.... *Tel 809/772–0598. Centerline Rd. near Frederiksted and Airport. Open Mon–Sat 10–4. Admission $5 adults, $1 children.*

Fort Christiansvaern. The most impressive part of the Christiansted National Historic Site, this fort has a glorious location surveying the harbor and King's Wharf, which has made it a favorite hangout of locals and tourists. Down the street, the **Steeple Building** houses exhibits on local history and culture.... *Tel 809/773–1460 (both). Waterfront, Christiansted; Steeple Building, Company St. Fort open weekdays 8–5, weekends and holidays 9–5; Steeple Building open Wed and weekends 9–4. Admission adults $2 for both, seniors over 62 and children under 16 free.*

Fort Frederik. This relatively small fort has been turned into a local-history museum, more notable for its rotating art and science exhibits than its permanent collection.... *Tel 809/772–2021. End of King St., Frederiksted. Open Mon–Fri 9–4, Sat 1–4. Admission free.*

Mt. Pellier Hut Domino Club. One of the wackiest bars in the Virgin Islands, thanks to a beer-swilling sow named Miss Piggy and her equally bibulous offspring.... *Tel 809/772–9914. Route 76, Montpellier. Open daily 9am–1am.*

Salt River Bay National Historical Park and Ecological Preserve. Dedicated in 1993, this wild tangle of mangrove, surf, and rock is the site not only of Columbus' landing in 1493 on his second voyage, but also of several pre-Columbian artifacts and richly diverse bird, plant, and marine life.... *Call St. Croix Environmental Association, tel 809/773–1989, for information on walking tours. Salt River Landing.*

St. Croix Aquarium. Enthusiastic director Lonnie Kaczmarsky personally conducts tours of his one-room marine world, giving special weight to the responsibilities of snorkelers and scuba divers in protecting the fragile underwater environment. He also leads snorkeling expeditions (see Getting Outside). Over 100 indigenous Cruzan species are on display, from dancing sea horses to sensuously waving sea fans.... *Tel 809/772–1345. Strand St., Frederiksted. Open Wed–Sun 11–4. Admission $3 adults, $1.50 children under 18.*

St. Croix LEAP. This workshop in the middle of the rain forest is fragrant with the scent of fresh-cut wood; you can talk with the craftsmen as they chip, saw, and whittle away.... *Tel 809/772–0421. Rte. 76. Open daily 9–6. Admission free.*

St. George Village Botanical Gardens. This 17-acre park, standing on the site of a pre-Columbian settlement, showcases every major ecosystem on St. Croix.... *Tel 809/772–3874. Centerline Rd., Kingshill. Open daily 9–5 except national holidays. Admission $5 adults, $1 children under 18.*

St. John

Annaberg Plantation. The best-preserved of many sugar plantation ruins on St. John, though hauntingly swallowed up by weeds.... *No telephone. Leinster Bay. Open daily 9–6. Admission free.*

Chateau Bordeaux/Cheeseburger Cheeseburger. These eateries (the cheeseburger half occupies the terrace during the day and serves mediocre food by comparison) offer a jaw-dropping vista of several British Virgin Islands.... *Tel 809/776–6611. Rte. 108 (Bordeaux Mountain Rd.). Cheeseburger Cheeseburger open daily 9–5.*

Elaine Ione Sprauve Library and Museum. This restored plantation functions as a combination history museum and art gallery; it's one of the better places to escape the crowds or heat.... *Tel 809/776–6359. Enighed, Cruz Bay. Open weekdays 9–1 and 2–5. Donations accepted and encouraged.*

Ferry Dock. Great free people-watching as the dinghies cruise in and out of town. There are also a few vendors, and a bunch of cabbies looking half-heartedly for a fare.... *Tel 809/776–6111. Wharf, Cruz Bay. Ferry departs daily every hour 9:15–2:15, and 7:15am, 3:45pm, and 5:15pm. $7 each way.*

St. Thomas Diversions

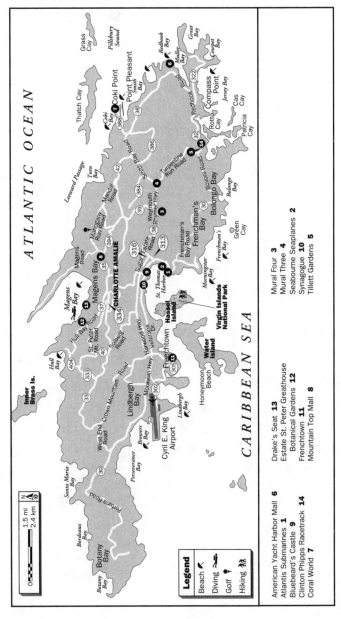

Charlotte Amalie Diversions

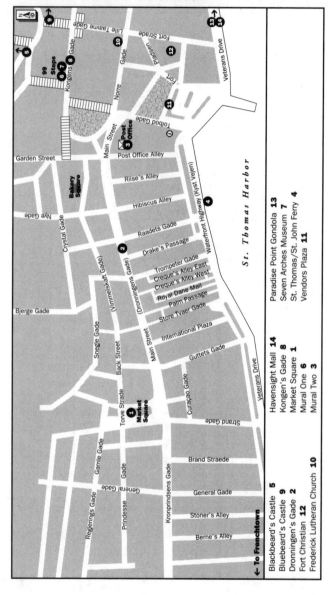

Blackbeard's Castle **5**
Bluebeard's Castle **9**
Dronningen's Gade **2**
Fort Christian **12**
Frederick Lutheran Church **10**

Havensight Mall **14**
Kongen's Gade **8**
Market Square **1**
Mural One **6**
Mural Two **3**

Paradise Point Gondola **13**
Seven Arches Museum **7**
St. Thomas/St. John Ferry **4**
Vendors Plaza **11**

St. Croix Diversions

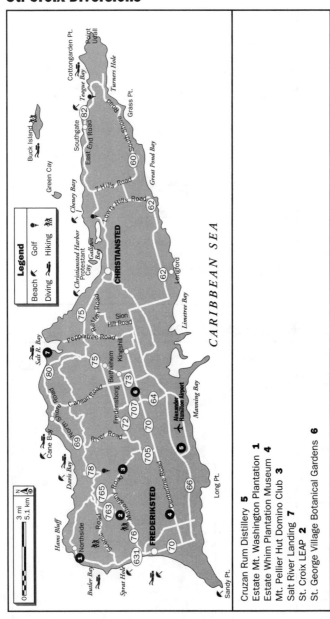

Cruzan Rum Distillery **5**
Estate Mt. Washington Plantation **1**
Estate Whim Plantation Museum **4**
Mt. Pellier Hut Domino Club **3**
Salt River Landing **7**
St. Croix LEAP **2**
St. George Village Botanical Gardens **6**

Christiansted Diversions

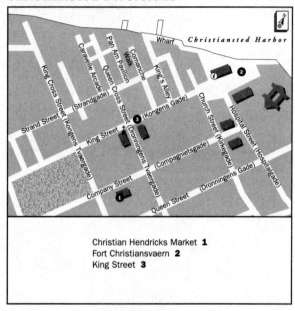

Christian Hendricks Market **1**
Fort Christiansvaern **2**
King Street **3**

Frederiksted Diversions

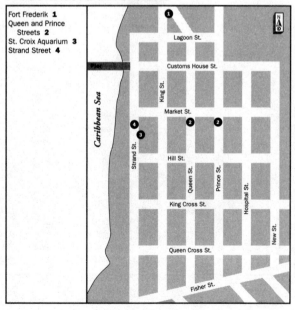

Fort Frederik **1**
Queen and Prince Streets **2**
St. Croix Aquarium **3**
Strand Street **4**

St. John Diversions

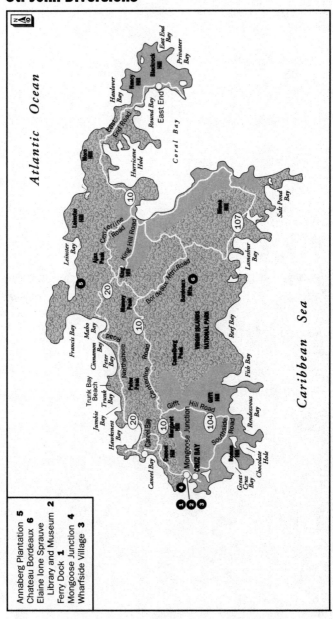

getting

4 outside

You'd be nuts to come down here and not hit the beach. Or plunge into the water—Bonaire, Dominica, and

Saba may be hotter dive sites these days, but the Virgin Islands take a back seat to none of them. Failing that, rent, borrow, or hijack anything you can to get out *on* the water: sailboats, booze cruises, yachts, windsurfers, kayaks, jet skis, whatever. Wherever there's a pier, you can bet there'll be some salty type seadogging you with a boat for hire. As Nike puts it, "just do it."

The ecotourism thing is a big draw, particularly on lush St. John; quite possibly the greenest island in the Caribbean, it's mostly national park. St. Croix also has some gorgeous rain forest, with guides as gung-ho as scout-troop leaders to tromp you through the bush, pointing out exotic flora and fauna as you go. Ecowatch organizations run fascinating expeditions to study endangered birds and turtles, too. As far as golf goes—well, it ain't Bermuda, but the three championship courses down here offer plenty of challenge and variety, as well as ocean views so distracting, they're the ultimate water hazard.

Until the double whammy of hurricanes Luis and Marilyn in September 1995, the Virgin Islands were considered by many the recreational capital of the Caribbean. It's all still here, but not necessarily in the same shape, unfortunately—nearly half the boats sustained damage, some beaches have at least partially disappeared, and the golf courses are not nearly as well manicured as the golfers are. Ah well. Just another day's work in the American Paradise. While you're playing outdoors, the residents are laboring mightily to restore things to normal.

The Lowdown

Many recreational facilities are attached to resorts; for phone numbers and addresses, see Accommodations.

Hitting the beach... All U.S.V.I. beaches are open to the public without charge. Many are best accessible via a resort; usually the beach boys don't demand IDs, but at some of the tonier resorts, it *will* look odd if you spread out your hotel towel amid a sea of chaise longues (at these times a well-placed tip may come in handy unless you want to swim back to *your* hotel). Theft on the beaches, while not approaching the legendary proportions of, say, Rio, is common. Take the usual precautions: lock any valuables in your car (or hotel safe) and don't leave purses or Walkmans unattended when you go for a dip.

On St. Thomas, cruise-ship passengers swarm all over **Coki Beach**, thanks to its convenient position right next to Coral World (a favorite stop on cruise-tour itineraries) and the excellent snorkeling right offshore. There are several water-sports concessions, offering everything from parasailing to waterskiing. Often cited in lists of the world's top 10 beaches, **Magens Bay** actually lives up to its picture-perfect postcard billing. Of course, almost every tourist stops by to see what all the fuss is about, so try to get here on slower cruise-ship days (check the local newspaper listings) or after 3pm. Because it's situated between two peninsulas, the waters are remarkably calm and ideal for swimming; the fast-food stand offers terrific pizza and even better local gossip. Unfortunately, there have been many reports of harassment here recently: local men showing off their wares to anyone who'll look, regardless of sex. They're a nuisance, but harmless. (One named Bill is affectionately dubbed "Peg Leg" by locals; they even have a song about him, for which, alas, we

> **Working up a sweat**
> For people who can't do without an indoor workout during their stay in this tropical paradise, most major resorts offer some sort of fitness room with at least free weights and nautilus, if not cardiovascular equipment. In many cases, non-guests can just sneak right in. The following are exceptions—in great part because they offer the most extensive facilities—but day passes are available. **Bayside Fitness Center and Spa** is everything its name implies. The fitness section has ten work stations, including lifecycles, treadmills, stairclimbers, weight training, and a huge pool with hydrotoning classes. The spa offers saunas, massages, facials, wraps, and a full-service beauty salon. The all-inclusive **Bolongo Elysian** and **Club Everything** between them offer free weights, nautilus and Universal equipment, aerobic classes, saunas, massages, and facials. On St. John, the **Hyatt Regency** offers two rooms, one devoted to weight training, the other to cardiovascular workouts. **Buccaneer Hotel** on St. Croix is most notable for its combined health club and spa, with facials, massages, and body wraps on tap.

can't provide sheet music.) If you *really* like that sort of thing, or want to do it yourself, **Little Magens Bay**, a short hike away along a marked trail, is the peninsula to the right as you face the water, emphatically jabbing itself into the sea. This is where locals and those in the know let it all hang out.

St. Thomas's **Secret Harbour** condominium complex opens onto a serene cove that offers great snorkeling near the rocks toward the left. The sensuous strand of **Morningstar Beach**, shared by Marriott's Morningstar and Frenchman's Reef resorts, is a favorite of the pretty young things (of both sexes and all sexual orientations) who work the cruise ships. You can usually catch a fairly competitive game of volleyball here, too. **Sapphire Beach** is the other classic resort beach, with smashing vistas of St. John and some of the best shore snorkeling and diving to the east, off Pettyklip Point. It also has the most water-sports concessions for those who wish to zoom in a waverunner or glide under a parasail.

Hull Bay, on the north shore, has a rugged beach that faces Inner and Outer Brass cays and attracts fishermen, sea kayakers, surfer dudes, and beachcombers. It's the place to be on Sunday afternoons, when locals head here in droves for an informal barbecue and live bands. **West Carot** is the big kahuna of surfing beaches, with swell swells; isolated **East Carot** has a reputation as the place for necking.

St. Croix's big deal isn't even on St. Croix itself: **Buck Island**'s reef is a protected national monument, accessible only by a half-hour boat ride (and there are plenty of boats and captains bobbing in the Christiansted harbor waiting to pounce). Buoys mark the "sightseeing" trail; snorkelers are discouraged from wandering off. If you're a veteran of coral-reef pyrotechnics, you might be disappointed, but anyone else will make the requisite oohs and ahhs at the hawksbill turtles, lumbering groupers, and gliding rays. The magnificent beach is ideal for picnics and barbecues, but you'll probably spend the bulk of your time underwater. **Cane Bay** is a wild, wind-whipped north-shore beach, but it's often deserted; less than 200 yards out to sea, the extraordinary Cane Bay Wall drop-off (reaching depths of 12,000 feet, almost Jules Verne level) is a favorite with divers.

Among the resort beaches, check out **Tamarind Reef Beach**, the **Buccaneer Hotel**'s three strands (the main one, Cutlass Cove, has great protected swimming; the Grotto has the finest snorkeling; and Whistle is the perfect place for a romantic sunset stroll), and **Chenay Bay Beach**. All afford glorious views of Buck Island, Thatch Cay, and Green Cay; and all offer water sports and eating facilities and have excellent snorkeling right offshore.

There are several secluded, rockier beaches on St. Croix's East End, most accessible only after a 5- to 15-minute hike. "Naturists" obey the laws of gravity at the lengthiest, calmest strand, **Jack's Beach**. A bit farther along the same path is **Isaac Bay**, with its pristine barrier reef featuring a voluptuous tumble of marine life, one ecosystem encased within another like a series of Chinese boxes.

The entire west coast of St. Croix seems like one long, tawny, palm-fringed stretch, basking like a cat in the sun. The most popular sections, closer to Frederiksted, offer beach bars and restaurants: the **West End Beach Club** north of town; the **La Grange Beach Club**; and the gay-owned (and gay-friendly) **On the Beach Hotel and Restaurant**, just to the south. Finally, there's **Sandy Point Beach**, a protected reserve that's only open to the public weekends 9–5. (It's a favored nesting spot of endangered sea turtles, especially from March to June, but you're unlikely to see any during the day.) Unfortunately, the sand is marred by fences that look like they were laid out by some drunken landowner, zigging and zagging everywhere you look.

The beaches on St. John are incredible: idyllic, sweeping, palm-lined crescents of champagne-colored sand. **Caneel Bay Resort** enjoys the most exquisite situation in the Caribbean, bordering seven gorgeous beaches that glitter like crushed diamonds. And now that Rosewood Hotels has instituted a policy allowing day guests, all are readily accessible (prior to that, six were reachable only by boat). **Hawksnest Beach**—a thin ribbon of vanilla-colored sand anchored by sea-grape trees—has restrooms and cooking grills, the latter increasingly popular with locals on weekends, when it's *the* social beach. **Trunk Bay** is Magens Bay revisited, a glorious stretch crawling with cruise-ship passengers who come for the justly celebrated 225-yard-long snorkeling trail. It has the most facilities of any beach on island, including changing rooms, a snack bar, picnic tables, and snorkeling equipment for rent. **Cinnamon Bay** is just as lovely, a graceful arc of sand with smashing views of several tiny cays; its campground facilities are open to the public. Snorkeling is wondrous here, too—inquisitive angelfish, neon parrotfish, and mauve triggerfish swim right into your hand. **Maho Bay** is actually a trio of interlocking crescents; it includes the isolated **Francis Bay**, though the bay is reached by an easy 10-minute hike. Several beaches along St. John's south and east coasts are accessible only by hiking, four-wheel-drive vehicle, or boat. **Salt Pond Bay** and the even rockier, more desolate **Drunk Bay** are get-away-from-it-all, unmaintained spots. Swimming is not advised, owing to heavy surf, but snorkeling is quite good if you hug the coast. **Lameshur Bay**, **Reef Bay**, **Hurricane Hole**, and **Haulover Bay** are magnificent, secluded half-moon coves, and even more difficult to reach, only accessible by boat or four-wheel-drive and then a hike.

Windsurfing and other macho stuff... On St. Croix, **Chenay Bay Beach Resort** (tel 809/773–2918, Chenay Bay) offers the services of women's world windsurfing champion Lisa Neuberger; the surrounding waters are fairly calm, making this a superb place for beginners. **St. Croix Water Sports Center** (tel 809/773–7060, Hotel on the Cay, Christiansted harbor) offers windsurfing, too, in addition to parasailing, and they rent jet skis, wave runners, and sea kayaks, and book trips to Buck Island. **Caribbean Watersports** (tel 809/776–8500, ext. 625 or 676, several resort locations) is their equivalent on St. Thomas. **Caribbean Boardsailing** is the only BIC- and Mistral-certified windsurfing center on St. Thomas (tel 809/776–3486, Ramada Yacht Haven Motel and Marina; tel 809/776–1730, Point Pleasant Resort). They can also arrange sea-kayaking expeditions along St. Thomas's more rugged north coast; as can **Aqua Action Watersports** (tel 809/

775–6285, Red Hook). On St. John, **Low Key Watersports** (tel 809/776-7048, Box 431, Wharfside Village, Cruz Bay 00831) and **Arawak Expeditions** (tel 809/693-8312, Box 853, Cruz Bay, 00831) also run sea-kayaking adventures.

With a tube in your face... Even though the hurricanes of 1995 shifted and/or destroyed many coral reefs and left the normally translucent waters cloudy for weeks—even months—the U.S.V.I. and their British cousins remain one of the great unsung snorkel/dive destinations in the Caribbean. In fact, the hurricanes may have done divers a favor by unearthing cannons, anchors, and other relics of wreckage that will create new homes for sealife and provide new diving destinations. Certain B.V.I. sites are so spectacular that many U.S.V.I. dive outfits go through the nuisance of clearing customs (it just involves bureaucratic paperwork, but you may need to produce photo ID). These include the wreck of the **H.M.S.** *Rhone* (immortalized in Peter Benchley's book *The Deep*) and the numerous caves and grottoes dotting the littoral of **Norman Island**.

In the U.S.V.I. off St. Thomas, **Thatch Cay** and **Hans Lollik** are a marine Disneyland of arches and pinnacles. St. Croix is beloved for the **Cane Bay Wall**, plummeting hundreds of feet and blooming with coral gardens. Salt River Bay also boasts a dramatic submarine canyon and abundant marine life. St. John's waters are mostly protected national park, closed to divers, but a snorkeler's paradise; outside Coral Bay there are several spots worth visiting for divers, including the **Cathedral**, an underwater cavern 300 feet in circumference and 15 feet high.

Snorkelers will enjoy trips to the two **Buck Islands**: the one off St. Thomas, little more than a rock jutting up from the sea, perpetually shadowed by swooping gulls; and the larger National Wildlife Refuge off St. Croix, which you can only visit under the auspices of **Dive St. Croix** (see below). (At the former, the wreck of the World War I cargo ship *Cartenser Sr.* is a particular lure here for divers, who also can marvel at huge gardens of fire coral populated by black sea urchins, barracudas, and stingrays.) The **St. Croix Aquarium** (tel 809/772-1345, Strand St., Frederiksted—see Diversions) specializes in environmentally aware snorkeling expeditions, led by the resident marine biologist. The **National Park Service** (tel 809/776–6201, Cruz Bay wharf) on St. John runs several special ranger-guided trips during the week at Trunk Bay, also with an emphasis on preserving the environment. And if you love snorkeling but can't quite go all the way down, try Trunk Bay's **Snuba** (tel 809/776–6922, Box 37, St. John, 00831), a combination of diving and snorkeling without all that restrictive gear.

So how do you get out to these sites? No problem, mon. All three islands swarm with dive outfits (many of which also run snorkeling trips), and most major resorts offer dive packages. The following operators are all PADI and/or NAUI certified, and offer both resort and certification courses as well as night dives. Costs start at $40 for a single-tank dive. Snorkeling equipment usually rents for $10; half-day trips run $35 and up. On St. Thomas, try **Aqua Action Watersports** (tel 809/775–6285, Box 15, Red Hook 00802); **Joe Vogel Diving** (tel 809/775–7610, Box 7322, Charlotte Amalie, 00801), the oldest certified diving operation in the U.S.V.I.; **Seahorse Dive Boats** (tel 809/774–2001, Crown Bay Marina, Suite 505, Charlotte Amalie, 00802); and **Underwater Safaris** (tel 809/774–1530, Box 8469, Long Bay, 00801; Yacht Haven Marina).

Reputable St. Croix outfits include **Anchor Dive** (tel 809/778–1522 or 800/532–DIVE, Box 5588, Salt River Marina, Sunny Isle 00823); **Cane Bay Dive Shop** (tel 809/773–9913, Cane Bay); **Dive Experience** (tel 809/773–3307 or 800/235–9047, Box 4254, Strand St., Christiansted 00822-4254); **Dive St. Croix** (tel 809/773–3434 or 800/523–3483, 59 King's Wharf, Box 3045, Christiansted 00820), the only operation permitted to dive around Buck Island; and **V.I. Divers, Ltd.** (tel 809/773–6045 or 800/544–5911, Pan Am Pavilion, Christiansted 00820).

On St. John, reliable operations include **Cruz Bay Watersports** (tel 809/776–6234 or 800/835–7730, Box 252, Cruz Bay 00830); **Coral Bay Watersports** (tel 809/776–6850, Coral Bay); **Low Key Water Sports** (tel 809/776–7048, Box 431, Wharfside Village, Cruz Bay 00831); and **St. John Watersports** (tel 809/776–6256, Box 70, Mongoose Junction, Cruz Bay 00830).

Par for the course... Luis and Marilyn really did a number on the three classic championship courses on the U.S.V.I. St. Thomas's **Mahogany Run** (tel 809/775-5000) had just completed a $4 million re-landscaping when the hurricanes hit—much of which had to be redone. This par-70, 6,022-yard, 18-hole course has really breathtaking views of the B.V.I., especially from the trio of holes—13, 14, and 15—known as the Devil's Triangle (announced by a huge sign sporting a skull and crossbones; you actually win a prize if you make it through without a penalty shot). The 13th hole's green is a ledge set on a cliff; 14 has jaw-dropping views of Tortola, Hans Lollik, and the crashing surf; and 15 has an impossibly narrow fairway leading straight to a pond filled with contented ducks (try not to hit them). And, oh yes, iguanas sunning themselves on the rocks make for the ultimate hazard. Bruce Devlin and Chi Chi Rodriguez are among the many pros who've raved about this course. Greens fee $50; clubs $18; cart $15.

St. Croix's hotels offer two fine resort courses, the par-71, 6,117-yard **Buccaneer** (tel 809/773-2100) and par-72, 6,843-yard **Carambola** (tel 809/778-5638). The Buccaneer has some knockout views, especially from its trademark third hole, with a vista that sweeps from Christiansted to Buck Island. Greens fees are $20 for non-guests; clubs $16; carts $13. Carambola, a Robert Trent Jones–designed beauty, is far more challenging, with 96 bunkers (including one the size of the Sahara on the eighth hole), four straight holes that play right into the wind, and a very tricky winding layout up and down the valley. This is more a mountain course than a resort course; there are no ocean views, although the 18th hole has lovely valley vistas. Greens fees for non-guests are $55; clubs $15; carts $25.

The tennis racket... Public courts are available on all three islands. The only thing to recommend them is that they're free, and available on a first-come, first-served basis. But don't even bother, unless you're seeking the ultimate challenge of some extremely weird bounces, owing to cracks in the concrete and flowering weeds of every description. (And that was *before* the hurricanes hit.) Likewise, hotel courts, except at the largest resorts, are often in states of disrepair. Even those that are open to non-guests are usually booked at the most desirable hours (just after dawn and before sunset); whoever wants to play tennis in the heat of day may wish to consult other listings in the local phone book (such as psychotherapists) or just dial 1-900-masochist.

That said, there are a few excellent tennis programs. On St. Thomas, **Marriott's Morningstar and Frenchman's Reef**, **Sapphire Beach Resort**, and the **Stouffer Renaissance** offer tennis packages as well as lessons for non-guests. The **Buccaneer**, where Teddy Kennedy plays when he's on St. Croix, is a member of the highly regarded Peter Burwash International Special Tennis Programs. Both the **Hyatt Regency** and **Caneel Bay** on St. John have accredited tennis pros and extensive facilities.

With the wind at your back... Many charter companies have developed a reputation for "booze cruises," where unlimited rum punches are included in the price. You can either step aboard on a particular day trip or custom-design your own itinerary (for more moolah, of course). Favorite day trips are to various British Virgin Islands. **Tortola**, the largest and most populated, is a series of undulating emerald humps that slope precipitously down to honey-hued beaches renowned among surfers; it's one of the Caribbean's most engagingly laid-back islands, with fine restaurants and even finer bars. **Virgin Gorda** seems almost primeval, its moody coast dotted with hulking boulders that resemble abstract sculptures. The most popular spot here is the Baths, a series of sun-dappled grottoes at the island's southern tip. **Jost van Dyke** is an unexpected delight, one of the Caribbean's great party islands, especially during the famed Foxy's Wooden Regatta held every September and on New Year's Eve, a required pilgrimage for every yachtie worth his or her sea salt. And, there are dozens more—some virtually private islands, home only to luxury resorts; others deserted specks noted for their dive sites.

If you want to explore on your own, consider renting a daysailer (18- to 20-foot Hobie Cat or Sunfish) at your resort. Or if you'd rather venture farther afield (or stream), try a powerboat; they vary in length from 20 to 28 feet and can comfortably accommodate two people. On St. Thomas, **Club Nautico** (tel 809/779-2555, American Yacht Harbor, Red Hook) and **Nauti Nymph** (tel 809/779-5066, American Yacht Harbor, Red Hook) are both highly recommended. Several of St. Thomas's charter companies specialize in captained day trips, from parasailing to jet skiing, snorkeling to light tackle fishing. Contact the **Red Hook Charter** office (tel 809/775-9333, Box 57, Red Hook, 00802) or **Coconut Charters** (tel 809/775-5959, Box 59, Suite 202, Red Hook Plaza, 00802). Their vessels range from Hobie Cats to 100-foot catamarans and trimarans. (the best for boozing, since they guarantee a smoother ride). The **Kon Tiki** (tel 809/775-5055, Box 8803, Charlotte Amalie, 00801; West Indian Company Dock, Havensight Mall, Charlotte Amalie) is perhaps the craziest booze cruise in the islands, with unlimited frozen concoctions and rum punches that pack a real wallop.

The thing to do on St. Croix is snorkel around Buck Island. Call **Mile-Mark Charters** (tel 809/773-2628 or 800/524-2012, 59 King's Wharf, Christiansted) for a variety of boats of all speeds and sizes. **Big Beard's Adventure Tours** (tel 809/773-4482, Pan Am Pavilion, Christiansted) offers two catamarans departing from Kings Wharf, one with a glass bottom, while **Buck Island Charters** counters with Captain Heinz's trimaran, the *Teroro II* (tel 809/773-3161, Green Cay Marina).

On St. John, try **St. John Proper Yachts** (tel 809/776-6256, Mongoose Junction) or **Cruz Bay Watersports** (tel 809/776-6234, Hyatt Regency and Cruz Bay) whose 45-foot vessel, *Blast*, provides revelers with just that.

Ahoy there, matey... Another option is yachting, the original all-inclusive vacation, only without the madding crowd and no fixed itinerary. Even a crewed charter complete with gourmet chef costs little more than a week at a deluxe landlocked resort. You save still more money if you're qualified to sail, since you can then charter a bareboat and provision it yourself. Remember that even on the most deluxe yachts (hovering around 100 feet) you'll be in close quarters; many friendships (and even marriages) have been wrecked like a galleon on treacherous reefs. Make sure you're comfortable with your fellow sailors; this is not the time to find out if the Joneses down the block are as much fun on the bridge as at the bridge table. Otherwise you'll be shivering more than your timbers.

Prior to Luis and Marilyn, the U.S.V.I. boasted the largest charter-boat fleet base in the Western Hemisphere; it's rebuilding as fast as possible. You can either book a boat through a broker or contact a charter-boat company directly. In either case, you'll be deluged with brochures on each available yacht (including captains' and chefs' bios and sample menus on crewed boats), and may be required to fill out a lengthy, even nosy questionnaire to help determine which boat (and crew) makes the ideal match for you (from party-hearty types to more sedate foodie/wine snobs). The top fleets are centered in St. Thomas at **American Yacht Harbor** in Red Hook or **Yacht Haven Marina** in Charlotte Amalie. (Several more companies of international repute are based in Tortola, in the B.V.I.)

Blue Water Cruises (tel 800/524-2020, Box 292, Islboro, MA 04848) and **Regency Yacht Vacations** (tel 800/524-7676, fax 809/776-7631, Long Bay Rd., St. Thomas 00802) have enviable reputations as brokers for the Virgin Islands. Charter-boat companies on St. Thomas include **Avery's Marine, Inc.** (tel 809/776-0113, Box 5248, Charlotte Amalie 00803); **Virgin Island Yacht Charters** (tel 800/524-2061, fax 809/776-4468, Yacht Haven Marina, Charlotte Amalie); **Caribbean Yacht Charters** (tel 800/225-2520, fax 617/639-0216, Box 583, Marblehead, MA 01945); and **Island Yachts** (tel 809/775-6666 or 800/524-2019, 6100 Red Hook, Suite 4, Red Hook 00802). On St. John, **Hinckley Charters Caribbean** (tel 809/776-6256, Box 70, Cruz Bay 00830), based out of Caneel Bay, is your best—and practically only—bet.

Island-hopping, the easy way... For those who have the urge to see the islands by water, but don't want to drink themselves sick on a booze cruise or go Top-sider by Top-sider with the yachties, there are still the ferries. The **Virgin Island Hydrofoil** (tel 809/776-7416) goes between Charlotte Amalie and Christiansted three times daily. The trip takes 75 minutes, costs $32 one way or $60 round trip and is a fun, quick skim over the ocean. There are also ferries between Cruz Bay on St. John and Red Hook and Charlotte Amalie on St. Thomas, as well as ones to Tortola, Jost van Dyke and Virgin Gorda from Charlotte Amalie. Call 809/776-6111 for more information. Though the ferries are probably not the way your average over-tanned, chest-thumping thrill-seeker would spend the day, they might be the right thing for those who just want to go on a ride.

Something's fishy... While the sportfishing around the U.S.V.I. doesn't rank as high as that in the Bahamas, Trinidad, or the Dominican Republic, over 20 world records, many for blue marlin, have been set here. The lion's share of leviathan deep-sea monsters hang out at St. Thomas's world-renowned North Drop. **St. Thomas Sportfishing Center** (tel 809/775–7990, American Yacht Harbor, Red Hook), **Frenchman's Reef Adventure Center** (tel 809/774–2990, Marriott's Frenchman's Reef, Morningstar Beach), or **American Yacht Harbor Charters** (tel 809/775–0685, American Yacht Harbor, Red Hook) are reliable bookers for U.S. Coast Guard–licensed deep-sea fishing boats. On St. Croix, contact **Mile-Mark Charters** (tel 809/773–2628, 59 King's Wharf, Christiansted), or **Ruffian Enterprises** (tel 809/773–6011 or 809/773–7165 day, 809/773–0917 night, St. Croix Marina, Gallows Bay). And on St. John, give **World Class Anglers** (tel 809/779–4281, Box 8327, Cruz Bay, 00831) a call. Don't choke on the prices: they start at $600 for a full day, $350 for a half day. The boats usually are between 35 and 50 feet long and most are limited to six passengers.

Stretching your legs... St. Croix Environmental Association (tel 809/773–1989, Apothecary Hall Courtyard, Christiansted) is a remarkable group, intensely dedicated to preserving St. Croix's natural beauty. They run several "walks on the wild side": through the rain forest under a canopy of 200-foot-tall kapok trees; across the semi-arid desert around Point Udall (easternmost point in the U.S.); and in the Salt River Bay National Historical Park and Ecological Preserve, pointing out Taino burial grounds, the site of Columbus' landing, nesting sites, and mangrove swamps. The enthusiastic guides spout plenty of natural history and native lore along the way. There are two hikes daily, Monday–Friday, for $20 per person. Hey, it's for a good cause, and it's good exercise, if nothing else. You can also ask them about the status of Earthwatch, a private research group that used to take small groups out at night to study nesting sea turtles.

Also on St. Croix, **Olassie Davis** (call Tourist Office at 809/773–0495 for information) leads tours through the rain forest, pointing out medicinal herbs and other sources of local lore, ending up at the remote, rugged Ham's Bay beach. He's quite a sight himself, with long, graying dreadlocks swaying in the breeze. **Take-a-Hike** (tel 809/778–6997, Box 7937, Sunny Isle, Christiansted, 00823) offers walking tours of Christiansted and Frederiksted, as well as nature hikes all over the island. If you'd rather not hoof it, try mountain biking through the rain forest or along the northwest coast with the guides at **St. Croix Bike and Tours** (tel 809/772–2343, 70 King St., Frederiksted), which will also rent bikes by the day.

The **National Park Service** (tel 809/776–6201, Cruz Bay wharf) on St. John conducts several walks during the week. The most memorable is the Reef Bay hike, a fairly arduous two-hour guided tour; participants descend dizzying slopes, passing the ghostly remains of sugar plantations swallowed up in rain forest and a colorwheel of flowering trees and shrubs (each lovingly described by the park rangers) on the way to the beautiful Reef Bay beach, where there are several Taino petroglyphs. This is a marvelous history and botany lesson rolled into one. Be sure to book passage on the boat ($10) that picks up hikers at the bottom—it's a long way back up. Birders should check out the two-hour walks led by naturalists at Francis Bay and the Seashore Walk among the mangrove lagoons and coral flats below the Annaberg Plantation. There is a nominal fee for each hike. St. John's best self-guided hikes are along Leinster Bay beach, passing a crumbling plantation (bring your snorkeling gear along on this one, and swim out to Watermelon Cay) and down to Salt Pond and Drunk Bays (see above).

Back in the saddle... Paul and Jill's Equestrian **Stables** (tel 809/772–2880 or 809/772–2627) is located at St. Croix's Sprat Hall Plantation Great House (see Accommodations), a moody, dour place that looks like something out of a novel by one of the Bronte sisters (as do the three, uh, intriguing sisters who run various parts of the family estate). Jill Hurd and her husband Paul operate the stables, which are perfectly situated for both rain-forest and beach rides. Both are fonts of local history and gossip (much of it unprintable), and they natter on happily about the local flora and fauna you encounter along the way.

shop

ping 5

Shopper's paradise? Hardly. For all the cruise-ship hype about Charlotte Amalie, the fact is that savvy shoppers can probably do better at year-end sales back home in New York or La-La-Land. But there's no denying the temptation offered by an unbroken street of stores vying to outdo (and undo) one another. Window-shopping alone provides an eye-popping display of wares for conspicuous consumption; you can find Cartier and Chanel, Versace and Vuitton—anything from appliances to appliqué.

The U.S.V.I.'s rep as a haven for discount shopping stems from the fact that there's no sales tax here, and loads of duty-free shops. American citizens are allowed $1,200 in duty-free goods per family member, and an additional 10 percent discount on the duty on the next $1,000 worth of goods. (Be sure to save your receipts just in case the customs officer is in a bad mood that day.) The most substantial discounts are in perfume, cosmetics, electronics, jewelry, china, crystal, lace and linens, and liquor. Savings can be as much as 50 percent, but for the most part the stores here are the equivalent of factory outlets back home: in other words, they sell odds, ends, and any other merchandise that doesn't move. It may be a Calvin—but is chartreuse really your color?

Target Zones

The big complex catering to cruise-ship daytrippers is St. Thomas's **Havensight Mall**, located right next to the cruise-ship dock. You'll find many branches of top downtown retailers in its six rather ugly buildings. **Vendors Plaza**, a collection of pushcarts, is ideally situated for last-minute shopping on the waterfront at Emancipation Gardens; here you'll find everything from tacky T-shirts to finely detailed local jewelry and wood carvings.

The many side streets of Charlotte Amalie, between the waterfront and Main Street, function as mini-malls unto themselves, each with its own distinct personality. They are remarkably pretty, with colorful pennants fluttering like sea birds and palm trees piercing the sky like cathedral spires. Because of horrific traffic snarls during post-Marilyn reconstruction, Main Street has been turned into a pedestrian mall on heavy cruise-ship days, an ingenious idea that will probably be kept. By far the ritziest shops are in **Riise Alley** (complete with bronze sculptures of Mercury and Venus), followed by the hipper **Palm Passage**, which regrettably just lost three distinctive stores, but rumor has it that Versace and Armani may open outlets here. **Royal Dane Mall**, in yet another alley, essentially caters to a younger, poorer crowd looking for bargains in perfume and jewelry.

Then there's the chic enclave **A Taste of Italy**. Like many Charlotte Amalie buildings, it has a fascinating history, from Moravian mission to dance school to newspaper office to crack house. Today, it houses a collection of shops as well as a capuccino bar and a rather gloomy pasta joint, Il Cardinale (see Dining). **Tillett Gardens** (see Diversions) houses some of the island's more appealing galleries in a set of charming colonial buildings, remnants of an 18th-century farmhouse.

On the East End, near the top resort hotels, the **American Yacht Harbor Mall** in Red Hook offers everything from pottery to potpourri in its mostly high-profile stores. Elsewhere on St. Thomas, the vast, sterile **Tutu Park Mall** appeals mainly to locals, though its colorful murals (see Diversions) are worth a look. **Frenchman's Reef**, the huge Marriott resort (see Accommodations), has enough stores to qualify as a mall, including branches of many top downtown stores. **Mountaintop** no longer offers the variety of stores it once did (though the new owner promises to corral more local retailers with offbeat merchandise), but the views (see Diversions) are tough to beat.

St. Croix doesn't have any malls to speak of, aside from the **Sunny Island Shopping Center**, which caters to locals with hardware stores, pharmacies, and the like. Christiansted's most stylish shopping areas are the **Pan Am Pavilion** off Strand Street and **Caravelle Arcade** along King and Company streets. On St. John, the most upscale shopping can be found in **Mongoose Junction**, a faux Danish colonial structure of stone arches, brick walls, corrugated tin roofs, wooden beams and galleries, teak doors, and graceful shaded courtyards brimming with bougainvillea. (The overall effect is quite delightful; just don't look too closely, or you'll notice the shoddy plastering and uneven construction.) By comparison, the **Wharfside Village** shops seem far more downhome, but the faded, peeling pastel clapboard buildings feature several fine restaurants with stunning harbor vistas—ideal for a quick break.

Bargain Hunting

Technically, everything in the U.S.V.I qualifies as a bargain. But just as with lodging, you'll find the biggest savings off-season, from May to November, when "Everything must go!" signs dangle in practically every shop window. Of course, that sometimes means the prices were inflated first, then discounted....

Trading with the Natives
Other than haggling with salespeople in Vendors Plaza on St. Thomas, bargaining is frowned upon in the U.S.V.I. Of course, there's always the time-honored trick of asking the price and pretending to leave in disgust. Casually mentioning that the shop three buildings down offers the same item for 20 bucks less works occasionally; but store owners here are no dummies. They usually know their competitors' ledger books and inventory intimately.

Hours of Business
Most shops are open Monday–Saturday from 9am to 5pm, although the shops in Havensight Mall, oh-so-conveniently located right by the cruise-ship docks, often stay open until 9pm and on Sundays when several boats are in.

The Lowdown

If you want to attract attention on the beach...
On St. Thomas, **G'Day** is for those who want the beachwear equivalent of those piebald Coogi sweaters from the Land Down Under; there's even a line for youngsters, in bold, brassy colors. **Local Color** specializes in Scoop Jones' dazzling hand-painted fashions—think Jackson Pollock on acid. **Lovers Lane** sells by far the skimpiest bathing attire on island (along with sexy lingerie and bedtime board games). **Painting in the Garden** sells floppy sunbonnets painted with shocking-pink lizards, electric-blue fish, and abstract swirls. The swimwear at St. Croix's **Gold Coast** doesn't look like an explosion of fireworks (except for beach bags in tropical-drink colors), but Brazilians have been known to shop here for dental-floss bikinis when they tire of the shops on Copacabana and Ipanema.

Fashion forward... The Indonesian batiks at the three **Java Wraps** stores on St. Thomas and St. Croix may not boast an impressive label, but they're among the most stylish threads anywhere. The staffers at **Liz Claiborne** now rank as St. Thomas's prettiest, but you may not feel the same way about the selection; at least Liz's clothes always drape well. The salespeople at **Louis Vuitton** act like vultures circling their prey; no wonder, considering that the LV insignia has been outré for years. **Gucci** offers its trademark link design in leather, luggage, jewelry, and the like, along with the most attitude on island. **Janine's Boutique** offers DKNY, YSL, and everything in between, from Balmain to Balenciaga, and caters to the island's richest, most powerful women.

Wayne James Boutique and **Yemaya** are beginning to develop a reputation outside tiny St. Croix, the former for sassy, brightly colored designs, the latter for sensuous, flowing, hand-painted silks. **The Little Mermaid** offers the Junior League's fave designers (DKNY, Claiborne, etc.) at major-league prices. **Urban Threadz** casually leaves the latest copies of *W*, *Spin*, and *Details* around, in case you didn't get the point about its aggressively trendy sportswear collections, including the latest in "rave" and "urban" designs. On St. John, you might luck into a label at **Bougainvillea**, much of whose clothes are otherwise appliquéd or beaded to the hilt to look designer chic.

Natty threads for him... On St. Thomas, **Nicole Miller** carries that designer's costly, way-out ties plastered with images ranging from sailboats to champagne labels. **Big Planet Adventure Outfitters**, with stores on both St. Thomas and St. John, appeals to the macho man (and woman), with outdoorsy clothes from big names such as Timberland. The occasional Ralph Lauren threads to be found at St. Croix's **Caribbean Clothing Company** will remind you that Lauren's really just a guy from the Bronx, and that golf clothes will never qualify as haute couture.

Tackiest tchotchkes... The tackiest shop, bar none, on St. Thomas, and perhaps the entire Virgin Island archipelago, is the **Old Danish Warehouse**. The setting, in a classic colonial building with high brick arches, is tasteful as can be. Otherwise, if an item can be emblazoned with the words "St. Thomas," you'll find it here, from miniature bathyspheres to glow-in-the-dark plastic bracelets. **Caribbean Safari** is a worthy runner-up, if only for the Aunt Jemima panama hats (to be fair, though, there is a shelf sporting some rather unusual Christmas ornaments). The **Gem Palace/T-Shirt Factory** sells jewelry that looks costume but isn't, and T-shirts of the "Top Ten Reasons a Cucumber Is Better Than a Man" ilk. On St. Croix, **Le Shoppe** and **Nano's** take great pride in their selections of cheap made-in-Taiwan wares, including porcelain bells, "silver" spoons, and truly ugly fake African carvings.

Tchotchkes with cachet... Only in **Paradise** (St. Croix) sells some expensive glass baubles and porcelain bric-a-brac in questionable taste, from hand-painted carnival dolls to larimar (a light blue semiprecious stone) jewelry to mother-of-pearl inlaid boxes to shell windchimes to cheesy fake chinoiserie. **Karavan**, also on St. Croix, displays unusual abstract glassware, nutcrackers, and jewelry fashioned from buttons and magical beads (Louise Tice, the owner, points out that the word "bead" is derived from the Saxon *bodden*, meaning prayers). **Island Glass Treasures** sells miniature hand-blown fish that would make nice paperweights or end-table dust-catchers, as well as some beautiful hand-carved chess sets. On St. John, **Island Hoppers** has those calabash bowls and metal Creole houses you were looking for. And if you can't go snorkeling, swim into **Tropical Fantasies**, where starfish, turtles, and fishies are fashioned from glass, wood, and metal.

Where money talks... Other than Merrill Lynch and the U.S.V.I. legislature, **Gucci** and **Cartier** (St. Thomas) are perhaps the only Virgin Island locations where money doesn't merely talk, it screams. The obsequious salespeople descend on you like locusts if you reek bucks; otherwise their noses jut so high, you can look right up their nostrils.

Wacky and one-of-a-kind... On St. Thomas, **Rhiannon's Mystical Gifts** delivers on that promise, with amulets to ward off evil spirits, healing incenses (musk for courage, vanilla for reinvigoration), drum sets from Burkina Faso, and even clay pipes (the mystical part depends on what you smoke in them).

On St. Croix, **Karavan** sells all manner of toys for adults (and get your mind out of the gutter): Enesco's intricate miniature calliopes, ferris wheels, popcorn wagons, and telephone boxes. **Grateful Bones** bills itself as an "Art and Relaxation Studio," where owner Barbara (Babs)

Keller will provide an inexpensive, invigorating neck or foot massage if you're stressed out from having to choose from her glitzy array of hand-painted beaded vests, jackets, boxes, and Christmas ornaments. **Rare Designs** is a very local shop with a very African-American theme, specializing in oils, incenses, herbal products, astrological candles, and African fabrics by the yard for those wanting to create their own chic dashikis.

On St. John, **Donald Schnell Studio** produces fanciful, almost Gaudiesque ceramic fountains. It's hard to imagine where to place them once you're home, though. Several less intriguing pottery and glass items are also on display. You can play the shell game at **Mermaid's Garden**, where gifts include bottles painted with underwater scenes, terra-cotta vases (daubed in Caribbean colors, of course) with shells dangling from them, and stationery embossed with shell patterns. **Silverlining** will cloud your mind with an array of unusual knick knacks, from Carnival masks to hand-carved chess sets.

Precious old stuff... **Carson Company Antiques** (St. Thomas) will keep antiquers happily busy for hours with a dizzying, dazzling collection of artifacts and trinkets from around the world, ranging from painted Mayan pottery to Ashanti gold weights to Ming bowls. **Estate Mt. Washington Antiques** (on St. Croix) specializes in magnificent 18th- and 19th-century furnishings and artwork crafted in the Caribbean, collected and refurbished painstakingly by owners Nancy and Tony Ayer, who are also restoring the ruins of a 1750s sugar plantation on their property, including a cistern and rum factory. **Quin House Galleries** is cluttered with potential gems for your collection, from antique jewelry reinvented in various traditions to authentic old nautical prints and maps.

Fake old stuff... At its St. Thomas and St. John branches, **MAPes MONDe** features lovely Italian-made faux historical prints, maps, postcards, and posters depicting various aspects of West Indian life. Charlotte Amalie's **Shipwreckers** (formerly Nautical Collectibles) is a treasure trove of sailing prints, model ships in bottles, steering wheels, mariners' compasses, and the like; some are reproductions but most are genuine, straight from *The Ghost and Mrs. Muir*. On St. Croix, **Estate Whim Plantation**

Museum rents a studio to David Dennis, who custom-designs mahogany furniture in grand colonial style.

Unusual book nooks... On St. Thomas, **Dockside Book Shop** is unusual only for its wide selection of books on the both the U.S. and British Virgin Islands, from birding manuals to folklore collections; it's also a great source for last week's stateside magazines. The shelves at St. Croix's **Jeltrups' Books** look topsy-turvy, but there's a method to the madness. The staff seems intimately knowledgeable about every tome ever printed. It should come as no surprise that the **National Park Visitors Center** on St. John has an incredible selection of books on the flora, fauna, cuisine, history, and ecosystems of the U.S.V.I., from Audubon to Peterson.

The island beat... The beat goes on at St. Thomas's **Parrot Fish Records and Tapes**, where ska, soca, steel band, calypso, and reggae reign supreme; they're also an excellent source for live "pirate" tapes (without labels) of up-and-coming Caribbean bands. On St. Croix, **Island Rhythms** features a smaller, but still choice, selection of island artists.

Incredible edibles... **Caribbean Cookie Company** on St. Thomas uses fresh tropical fruits and spices to provide a twist to the old-fashioned chocolate chip cookie. **Down Island Traders** serves up ginger or passion fruit teas; mango chutney; scotch bonnet hot sauce; jerk seasoning; spicy fish pâté; coconut candy; guava, papaya, and cinnamon jellies; Jamaican coffee: practically the entire bounty of the Caribbean, if it can be preserved, canned, freeze-dried, or bottled. St. Croix's **Royal Poinciana** will bathe you in bath gels, herbal teas, and sassy seasonings, all regionally made. On St. John, **Cruz Bay Emporium** has a wide selection of condiments, jams, perfumes, sauces (try the tangy tamarind), and herb teas, all made from local plants.

Putting your two scents in... On St. Thomas, the two **A.H. Riise** stores seem to have a virtual monopoly on elegant goods of all descriptions; their perfume and cosmetics counters are no exception, with all the latest from Adolfo to Carolina Herrera. **Tropicana Perfumes** probably boasts the largest selection of perfumes, including many fragrances unavailable stateside; **St. Croix Perfume Shoppes** sprays it all, from Lagerfeld to La Liz' "creations"; **St. Croix Shoppes** offers ye olde classics like Chanel and ye latest faves like Adolfo. **Violette Boutique** has a superb collection of cosmetics, from Clarins to Clinique. St. John's **Cruz Bay Emporium** specializes in bath salts, soaps, body splashes, and fragrances coaxed from local plants like jasmine, gardenia, coconut, and pineapple.

Diamonds are a girl's best friend... Colombian Emeralds, with branches on all three islands, is the jewelry equivalent of a fast-food chain (bracelet, that is), but the gems—including the trademark emeralds—are first-rate. **H. Stern**, with several stores on St. Thomas, could be dubbed the cut-rate Tiffany's of the Caribbean. Also on St. Thomas, **Irmela's Jewel Studio** has been turning out remarkably fine jewelry in Caribbean colors and images for nearly a quarter century. The several branches of **Cardow's** feature a "chain bar" of neckwear in precious metals, in addition to cheapie rings, bracelets, brooches, and the like. And then there's **Cartier**—need we say more?

Brian Bishop, the proprietor of St. Croix's **Crucian Gold**, has developed an admiring following for his savvy designs, including knot rings and lovely sugar-mill pins and pendants. **Sonya**, a tiny store just off the Christiansted harbor, catapulted to fame for its "hurricane bracelet" design—two interlocking links—that has become the unofficial symbol of St. Croix. **Karavan** creates groovy bead jewelry (from semiprecious stones) that owner/designer Louise Tice swears has magical properties.

On St. John, **Caravan** offers both gorgeous antique stones and settings and fashionable, hand-crafted ethnic jewelry. **R&I Patton Goldsmiths** features the elegant designs of Rudy and Irene Patton; they base their work on local themes, creating such lovely trinkets as silver hibiscus pendants and gold petroglyph pins. **Freebird Creations** carries funky, clunky, ethnic jewelry of the sort popular with the Love Generation.

For those born with silver spoons in their mouths... Little Switzerland, with two branches on St. Thomas and one on St. Croix, nearly requires the Swiss Guard to protect its vast array of china, crystal, watches, and more. Customers are never neutral about the excellent price/quality ratio. **The English Shop** always seems to have a "white" sale going on, with such top-notch marks as Royal Doulton and Wedgwood represented. **A.H. Riise** has it all, from Ainsley to Daum to Orrefors to Rosenthal (including little glass and porcelain somethings designed by artists like Dali, Lichtenstein, and Hundertwasser). On St. Croix, **The Royal English Shop** is the place for tea things and dinnerware; on St. John, **Island Galleria** devotes two floors to everything from Wedgwood to Waterford.

Clothes to make you look grown up... On St. Thomas, **Bliss** has Blass and de la Renta. **Base**'s New-Agey combination of unstructured lines, monochromes (black, white, taupe), and art-naif patterns (heart, fish, sun) is the latest rage to sweep the Caribbean. In Christiansted, **From the Gecko** sells ultrasoigné hand-painted cotton shirts, silk scarves, sarongs, and hammocks. **Java Wraps** has become a Caribbean institution for its soft, flowy Indonesian batik items. **Wayne James Boutique** showcases the vividly colored haute couture of this native Cruzan, who has designed both vestments for the pope and evening wear for the queen of Denmark. **Yemaya** is known for her elegant painted-silk clothes that always seem to drape just right, the ultimate in casual chic.

Clothes to make you look young... **G'Day** (St. Thomas) has skimpy bikinis and Speedos (as well as more substantial cover-ups) in wild splashes of color designed to outdo the Caribbean sunsets. Its equivalent for silkscreened T-shirts and hand-painted caps and dresses is the delightful **Local Color**. On St. Croix, **Caribbean Clothing Company** and **Urban Threadz** both sell the kind of antidesigner designer duds that fit loosely and comfortably; the former is more sports-oriented, with California looks and labels like Guess?, Putumayo, and Betsey Johnson, while the latter tries to be hipper, with a selection ranging from streetwear to swimwear. **Big Planet**'s St. John and St. Thomas stores will do until they open an Abercrombie and Fitch; come here if you want to look like you're going on safari. Outfit your favorite captain for his or her yacht with the marine duds at **Pusser's of the West Indies**, also on St. John and

St. Thomas: white ducks, Docksiders, sailor suits for the young'uns, T-shirts bearing the unmistakable Pusser's logo…you get the drill. **Best of Both Worlds**, in Cruz Bay's Mongoose Junction, is a gallery that features some enchanting wearable art on its second floor.

Objets for the home… Infrati's (St. Thomas) ceramicware comes straight from La Bella Italia in a variety of sun-drenched colors. **Emerald Lady** imports beautiful, vividly hued glass from Murano, that famed island staring down the Venetian Lido. **Shanghai Linen** and its sister shop, **Shanghai Silk and Handicrafts**, sit side by side on the St. Thomas waterfront; their tablecloths and napery are almost too good to use. **The Linen House** purveys the finest in Irish linens and Belgian lace, at prices that belie their imported status. **Bernard K. Passman Gallery** sells drop-dead black coral dishware, while **Satori Pottery** creates everything from ashtrays to vases in Caribbean hues from turquoise to sapphire. **Kilnworks Pottery** is for those who like their ceramics unglazed and rough textured. **Mango Tango** gallery has opened an extension that sells superlative reproductions of colonial mahogany furnishings. **Afrocentric Essentials** is a bit of a misnomer; they carry anything with an ethnic theme, from Indonesian batiks to brass napkin rings from Mali. **Scandinavian Center** lives up to its name, with everything you could ever covet from Kosta Boda, Georg Jensen, Royal Copenhagen, and the like.

St. Croix LEAP (see Diversions) is a workshop dedicated to preserving native craft traditions and providing jobs for homeless Cruzans. Avoid anything with "St. Croix" burned into the woodwork (the clocks just won't do), and opt instead for the masks and statues (carved from local woods like mahogany and teak) that celebrate African tribal traditions. **Estate Whim Plantation Museum** collaborates with Baker Furniture in North Carolina to reproduce 18th-century furnishings. Carpenter extraordinaire David Dennis also has a studio on the property, where he carves credenzas, four-poster beds, armoires, and planter's chairs according to time-honored colonial traditions. **Quin House Galleries** sells estimable hand-painted porcelain and napery in addition to colonial-era antiques. **America West India Trading Company** sells miniature painted metal Creole houses, papier mâché tap-taps (those brightly painted minivans), and ceramic animal masks (lions and pigs and bulls, oh my), which make marvelous wall hangings; there's also a second floor devoted to local paintings. At the outstanding **Folk Art Traders**, check out the beautiful hand-painted ceramic tiles, the terrifying *cojuelos* (devil) masks from the Dominican Republic, and *molas* (shawls) woven by the Cuna Indians of Panama. **Java Wraps Home Store** chimes in with ceramic platters and tiles, eerie Modiglianiesque dolls, intricately carved teak boxes and mahogany beds, and other items culled from owner Twila Wilson's travels abroad. **Jan R. Mitchell Studio and Gallery** produces glorious glass pieces and intriguing bas-relief bronzes. **Green Papaya** is a clutter of items—some magnificent, some kitschy—that resembles an indoor garage sale. **Gone Tropic** had merchandise for mad dogs and Englishmen alike: elaborately carved stools, hand-painted pillows and throw rugs, fanciful candlesticks, Balinese masks, and brass hangings from sunbursts to men in the moon.

St. John's **Bamboula** carries an assortment of crafts from around the Third World, from Lombok rice baskets to hand-painted and -carved Balinese bed ornaments to Chinese bamboo screens. **Isola** runs the gamut from playful seashell lampshades to "dream" pillows stuffed with herbs, seeds, and flowers (to guarantee pleasant dreams), to hand-carved and -painted Madura chests. **Fabric Mill** carries the inspired Sloop Jones rugs, sarongs, and linens, all splashed with vivid color.

The art bug... St. Thomas's **Camille Pissarro Gallery** is most notable as the birthplace of the influential Impressionist painter; today the canvases range from schlocky to sublime, at prices slightly higher than the competition's. Aside from having the coolest name, **Mango Tango** boasts the sunniest, most spacious exhibit space on St. Thomas, showcasing top artists from around the Caribbean. **A.H. Riise Caribbean Print Gallery** is the source for pretty, inexpensive prints in a riot of desert colors. **Jim Tillett Gallery** sells Jim's inventive silk-screened maps; some of his more abstract patterns make great wall hangings. **Painting in the Garden** creates fetching pastel birdhouses and hand-painted silk scarves that can either be worn or mounted and displayed.

The indefatigable Linda Colón has done an impressive job with her **Frederiksted Gallery**. The four rooms showcase rotating exhibits of the work of leading local artists and craftspeople, as well as selected visiting artists from around the Caribbean. **Gilliam-King Gallery**, set in a neat West Indian cottage, displays the work of Trudi Gilliam, a sculptor who works in metal, and Joanna King, a landscape painter. The **Jan R. Mitchell Studio and Gallery** features exquisite hand-blown and -painted glass sculpture. If that doesn't leave you glassy-eyed, check out the fluid dolphins and rays created by Larry Coxe at **Island Glass Treasures**.

On St. John, **Coconut Coast Studio** traffics in those soft pastel watercolors and prints that never fail to elicit oohs and ahhs from Junior League grandmothers. **Bajo el Sol** sells the work of "local" artists who hail from Michigan and Long Island, but who claim Mexican and Haitian influences.

Ethnic goodies... In addition to Caribbean foodstuffs, St. Thomas's **Down Island Traders** trades in papier mâché masks, hand-crafted wooden horses, model tap-taps (the wildly colored, ubiquitous Caribbean buses), abstract Haitian metal sculpture, hand-painted Christmas ornaments, and *mocko jumbies* (spirits) mounted on mahogany. **The Caribbean Marketplace** celebrates, well, the Caribbean marketplace, hawking crafts ranging from established brands like St. Lucia's Caribelle Batik and Tortola's Sunny Caribbee products (spices, jams, oils, soaps, etc.) to straw mats from Dominica and gourds from Trinidad. **Touba Homeland** carries Rasta hats, piecework quilt bags, and cotton outerwear in all the colors of the rainbow. **Afreekan** produces sculptures from various native woods: polished mahogany and redwood with flowing, sensuous lines, or rougher-textured guavaberry and ironwood. Who knows what it's doing in St. Thomas, but **Cowboys and Indians** is the only place on the island where you can locate genuine Zuni fetishes and pewter bolos.

Oddly enough, some of the most distinctive international crafts can be found on St. Croix at **Folk Art Traders**; owners Patty and Charles Eitzen comb the planet for exotic finds. You might happen upon hammered-gold jewelry fashioned from Spanish pieces of eight, brass and ceramic candlesticks, striking (even disturbing) black-and-white photos, or stunning mahogany sculpture. **American West India Trading Company** carries various typically Caribbean items, from hot sauce to hand-painted hammocks. **Java Wraps** and its sister **Java Wraps Home Store** offer Indonesian silks, batiks, textiles, Ikats, bedclothes, baskets, ottomans, and teak or mahogany furnishings. Many of the items at **St. Croix LEAP** are inspired by ancient African tribal designs, though regrettably the artisans' talents are usually steered in tackier directions: fish mobiles, clocks, and bud vases, all aimed at souvenir-hunters. **Third World Traders** carries everything from Haitian paintings to African masks.

St. John's **Bamboula** appeals to all the senses as you shop: the aroma of incense and essential oils wafts about, the insistent rhythm of African tribal music makes it hard to stand still, and the multicultural merchandise—from silk kimonos to whimsically carved teak furnishings, from ornate Persian rugs to frilly lace dresses—will keep you touching and feeling for ages. **Caravan** entices with Senegalese brass figurines, Ecuadorian pottery, Italian stained glass, and Ashanti carvings. **Tu Tu Tango** carries locally produced stained glass, pottery, hand-painted T-shirts and shoulder bags, jewelry, and dainty dolls in traditional island dress.

Leather trade... **Zora's** is a St. Thomas hole-in-the-wall that has been plying its trade (beautifully crafted sandals) for years. **Gucci** and **Louis Vuitton** live up to their reputations for supple and pricey leather goods. The **Leather Shop** is the most upscale joint of the lot, especially since they've got an exclusive on Fendi; there's a new outlet on Back Street where you can pick up some amazing buys. **Traveler's Haven** is just that for the American tourist(er) who's done too much shopping and needs another suitcase or has worn out his or her wallet. **Seoul Trade** traffics solely in eelskin wallets, belts, and purses, some in outlandish colors that would shock any eel that slithered by. On St. Croix, you won't get your kicks casing the leather goods at **Kicks**, but it's the finest the island has to offer, from belts to bags. At **Leather or Not**, Lisa Hutchinson is trying to duplicate Zora's success with her painstakingly handcrafted sandals.

Kid stuff... On St. Thomas, the **Land of Oz** may make you wish you could click your ruby slippers and be back home at F.A.O. Schwarz, or at least Toys R Us, but its rather silly collection of bright trinkets, many of them motorized and correspondingly pricey, will do as a quick bribe. St. Croix's **Small Wonder** features some fun island-style clothes for children. Kids will be entranced by the colors alone on bountiful display in the **Fabric Mill**, but sooner or later they'll start fondling the fanciful soft sculptures of sea creatures (like lobsters and octopi) or the patchwork-quilt Creole houses.

How much can I bring back duty-free?... A.H. Riise Liquors dwarfs everyone else when it comes to sheer variety and volume; the list of high-end potables like Armagnac and single-malt scotch is mind-boggling. **Woolworth's**, believe it or not, offers some of the lowest prices in the islands. (It's probably not worth a special trip if you're only buying a couple of bottles, but if you're a large family traveling together...) **Randy's**, also a fine bistro (see Dining), boasts the most sophisticated selection of wines from around the globe, atdown-to-earth prices.

St. Thomas

Afreekan. The artisans here work in redwood, ironwood, and mahogany, fashioning haunting sculptures patterned after tribal traditions.... *Tel 809/777–3301. Tillett Gardens.*

Afrocentric Essentials. Owner Al White combs the Third World (not just Africa) for his unique home furnishings....

Tel 809/774–5326. 1A–C Willemstad (Back St.), Charlotte Amalie.

A.H. Riise Caribbean Print Gallery. If pastel islandscapes are to your taste, you'll discover a wide assortment here.... *Tel 809/776–2303. Riise Alley off Main St., Charlotte Amalie.*

A.H. Riise Gift Shops. Consumerism runs rampant at this elegant luxury bazaar, its tables and shelves brimming with every great brand name in china, crystal, jewelry, watches, perfumes, silver, and more.... *Tel 809/776–2010, Riise's Alley; tel 809/776–2303, Havensight Mall; Charlotte Amalie.*

A.H. Riise Liquors. The stock of liqueurs, brandies, eaux de vie, ports, sherries, single malts, and cigars (none Cuban, alas) would keep the royals in dinner parties for generations.... *Tel 809/774–6900, Havensight Mall; also in Riise Alley, Charlotte Amalie.*

Base. English designer Steven Giles opened Base a few years ago in Antigua; his, uh, *basic* solid and striped cotton-and-Lycra T-shirts and sundresses in earthy colors are beyond hip.... *Tel 809/777–8050. Grand Hotel Court, 151 Tolbod Gade, Charlotte Amalie.*

Bernard K. Passman Gallery. A treasure trove of Passman's breathtaking creations in black coral and diamonds, from willowy candelabras to silverware designed for Charles and Di. The shop is ostentatiously guarded by two British grenadiers in full regalia (well, all right, the rifles are wood).... *Tel 809/777–4500. 37 Main St. at Riise Alley, Charlotte Amalie.*

Big Planet Adventure Outfitters. Think Banana Republic, only a bit more environmentally aware, with such labels as Patagonia and Birkenstock. As the owners put it, "products for people who embrace, perform, and celebrate life with color, freedom, difference, and love."... *Tel 809/774–2700. Palm Passage, Charlotte Amalie.*

Bliss. Most of the threads at this shop, which caters almost exclusively to locals, are rather ordinary, but occasionally you might luck into an off-the-rack number from Herrera or

St. Laurent.... *Tel 809/774–2547. 11 Wimmelskafts Gade, Charlotte Amalie.*

Camille Pissarro Gallery. Ignore the front room, where the cheesier canvases usually hang, and check out the back room, where you might find an exhibit of superb work by Haitian expats (like Sacha Tebo) experimenting in new, exciting media such as encaustic (applying dry pigments on beeswax).... *Tel 809/777–5511. 14 Dronningens Gade, Charlotte Amalie.*

Cardow's. By far the largest selection of jewelry, mostly of the gold chain variety, in the U.S.V.I., at guaranteed 30–50% off mainland retail prices, or your money back within 30 days of purchase.... *Two shops on Main Street, tel 809/776–1140 and 809/774–7983; three in Havensight Mall, tel 809/774–5905, 809/774–0530, and 809/774–0053; all in Charlotte Amalie.*

Caribbean Cookie Company. Delectable, crispy variations on old favorites, adding such classic Caribbean ingredients as rum, coconut, passion fruit, ginger, or mango into the mix.... *Tel 809/775–3559, or fax orders to 809/777–7155. Al Cohen's Plaza, Raphune Hill; or mail orders to P.O. Box 306497.*

The Caribbean Marketplace. In the market for Jamaican Blue Mountain coffee, Dominican masks, Tortolan hot sauce, Grenadian spice baskets, St. Lucian hand-painted T-shirts? Then you can do worse than this one-stop shopping center for Caribbean crafts.... *Tel 809/776–5400. Havensight Mall Bldg. III, Charlotte Amalie.*

Caribbean Safari. Fake Balinese masks and garishly painted papier mâché fish are the order of the day, in addition to a vast selection of T-shirts, most of them forgettable.... *Tel 809/777–8795. 6 Wimmelskafts Gade, Charlotte Amalie.*

Carson Company Antiques. Marvelous shop crammed with goodies, as if every attic around the globe had emptied its contents—from wonderful 1920s Bakelite costume jewelry to Spanish gold medallions to Etruscan vases.... *Tel 809/774–6175. Royal Dane Mall, Charlotte Amalie.*

Cartier. Well, at least the pins and pens are reasonably priced here.... *Tel 809/774–1590. 30 Trompeter Gade, Charlotte Amalie.*

Colombian Emeralds. The name is misleading—emeralds are only one type of exquisitely cut gem on sale at this Caribbean staple.... *Two shops on Main St., tel 809/774–9400 and 809/774–2280; tel 809/774–1033, on the waterfront; tel 809/774–2442, Havensight Mall; all in Charlotte Amalie.*

Cowboys and Indians. From plastic pistols to genuine Pendleton blankets, you'll find them all here. The store is located on the second floor of the gorgeous Grand Hotel, which hasn't received guests in decades.... *Tel 809/777–5900. 43–46 Norre Gade, Grand Hotel Court, Charlotte Amalie.*

Dockside Book Shop. From sailing to shelling and pirates to parrots, Dockside offers books on every subject of interest pertaining to the Virgin Islands.... *Tel 809/774–4937. Havensight Mall Bldg. IV, Charlotte Amalie.*

Down Island Traders. Gourds, pottery, jams, paintings: a Caribbean cornucopia on tap.... *Tel 809/776–4641, Veteran's Dr., Charlotte Amalie; tel 809/774–3419, Frenchman's Reef.*

Emerald Lady. Some lovely jewelry is on display, but the Venetian glass is the real lure here.... *Tel 809/777–5665. A Taste of Italy Mall, Back St., Charlotte Amalie.*

The English Shop. Not just English china and crystal, but also Japanese (Mikasa), Spanish (Lladro), French (Limoges), and German (Dresden): a veritable United Nations of dinnerware.... *Tel 809/776–5399, waterfront; tel 809/776–3776, Havensight Mall; Charlotte Amalie.*

G'Day. This emporium sports Aussie artist Ken Done's splashy beachwear designs, which are perfect for splashing around in.... *Tel 809/774–8855. Waterfront at Royal Dane Mall, Charlotte Amalie.*

Gem Palace/T-Shirt Factory. The diamond jewelry here looks like it would move well on the Home Shopping Network.

And what can you say about a large selection of T-shirts along the lines of, "Men are like pantyhose: When you're counting on them, they run."... *No telephone. Havensight Mall, Bldg. III, Charlotte Amalie.*

Gucci. You can get trademark leather bags and belts or silk items at the Caribbean flagship store; some of the bags are dyed exotic tropical colors, which makes them a bit more fun.... *Tel 809/774–7841, Riise's Alley off Main St.; tel 809/774–4090, Havensight Mall; Charlotte Amalie.*

H. Stern. This is by far the classiest jewelry franchise in the Caribbean.... *Tel 809/776–1939, 12 Main St.; tel 809/776–1146, 32AB Main; tel 809/776–3550, Raadets Gade and Main St.; tel 809/776–1223, Havensight Mall; tel 809/774–3158, Bluebeard's Castle; all in Charlotte Amalie. Tel 809/774–7658, Frenchman's Reef.*

Infrati. Italian ceramics colored like toucans and Mexican primitive art are just two of the reasons to stop by.... *Tel 809/777–5665. A Taste of Italy Mall, Back St., Charlotte Amalie.*

Irmela's Jewel Studio. Irmela Neumann has been creating wondrous designs in gold, lapis, lavender jade, and coral for nearly 25 years.... *Tel 809/774–5875. Tolbod Gade, Grand Hotel Court, Charlotte Amalie.*

Janine's Boutique. This upscale shop is popular with trophy wives who come here to nab designer duds from Chanel, Cardin, et al., all at off-the-rack prices.... *Tel 809/774–8243. Palm Passage, Charlotte Amalie.*

Java Wraps. The beachwear and coverups at this store, which originated on St. Croix, are mostly batiks, Ikats, and silks imported from Indonesia.... *Tel 809/777–3450. Royal Dane Mall, Charlotte Amalie.*

Jim Tillett Gallery. For Jim Tillett's silkscreened maps superimposed over delicate underwater fantasies. Jim's assistants will explain the silkscreening process if you visit the adjacent workshop.... *Tel 809/775–1929. Tillett Gardens, Rte. 38.*

Kilnworks Pottery. Peggy Seiwert and her apprentices putter about their potters' wheels, turning out ceramics in colors that duplicate those of seashells and rich earth.... *Tel 809/775–3979. Rte. 38, 6029 Estate Smith Bay.*

Land of Oz. Porcelain dolls, coconut-husk piggy banks, and Bavarian nutcrackers—the toy stock here is stock indeed, but it will do in a pinch.... *Tel 809/776–7888. Royal Dane Mall, Charlotte Amalie.*

Leather Shop. The ABCs of leather are sold here: attachés, belts, coats. Fendi, Bottega Veneta, Moschino, Prima Classe, Gucci, you get the picture.... *Tel 809/779–0290. Main St. and Havensight Mall, Bldg. 1. Outlet on Back St. off Taste of Italy Mall (no telephone). Charlotte Amalie.*

The Linen House. You'll bolt out of here with terrific bargains on the kind of stuff your great-great-grandmother used to labor over for her daughters' hope chests, including Battenburg lace and hand-crocheted doilies.... *Tel 809/774–8117. 7A Royal Dane Mall off Main St., Charlotte Amalie.*

Little Switzerland. The best buys are in china, crystal, and watches: Lalique, Lladro, Kosta Boda, Waterford, Wedgwood, Spode, Rolex, and Swatch are among the names to watch for.... *Tel 809/776–2010, Havensight Mall, Charlotte Amalie; tel 809/777–3100, American Yacht Harbor, Red Hook.*

Liz Claiborne. Another factory outlet with last year's clothes (for both men and women) at last year's prices.... *Tel 809/774–8050. 15 Main St., Charlotte Amalie.*

Local Color. Whimsical wearable art by several local designers, including Scoop Jones, are on vivid display here in colors that rival the daiquiri selection at the bars.... *Tel 809/774–3727. Kommandant Gade, Charlotte Amalie.*

Louis Vuitton. Does anyone still buy authentic Vuitton bags? If so, you'll run into them here.... *Tel 809/774–3644. 24 Main St. at Palm Passage, Charlotte Amalie.*

Lovers Lane. You'll find teeny bikinis along with intimate apparel (mostly in silk and lace, with a whiff of leather) for both women and men. Sensuous bath oils and board games to play in bed... *Tel 809/777–9616. Waterfront, Charlotte Amalie.*

Mango Tango. Superlative exhibitions of regional artists in the most light-filled space in the U.S.V.I.... *Tel 809/777–3995. Al Cohen's Plaza, 4002 Raphune Hill.*

MAPes MONDe. These island prints and maps will fill out any bathroom, nook, or cranny.... *Tel 809/776–2886. Riise Alley, Charlotte Amalie.*

Nicole Miller. Wacked-out tie designs for men.... *Tel 809/774–8286. Main St. off Riise Alley, Charlotte Amalie.*

Old Danish Warehouse. Cheap bead earrings, dogs fashioned from shells, mugs, bells, and serving spoons, all proudly proclaiming "St. Thomas." Get the picture?... *Tel 809/774–8432. Grand Hotel Court, Charlotte Amalie.*

Painting in the Garden. Rugs, straw hats, bird feeders, silk scarves, and pottery, all daubed and glazed in pastels or bolder colors.... *Tel 809/775–4800. Tillett Gardens, Rte. 38.*

Parrot Fish Records and Tapes. The joyous sounds of reggae, calypso, and soca pulse from this tiny shop that carries both stateside and local recording artists. The selection on display is just a sampler; you can send for their complete catalogue at Parrot Fish, Box 9206, St. Thomas 00801.... *Tel 809/776–4514. 2 Store Tvaer Gade, Charlotte Amalie.*

Randy's. This marvelous wine store and bistro (see Dining) racks up the most varied selection of international fine wines on St. Thomas.... *Tel 809/775–5001. Al Cohen's Plaza, 4002 Raphune Hill.*

Rhiannon's Mystical Gifts. Crystals, amulets, incense; the only thing missing is voodoo dolls.... *No telephone. American Yacht Harbor, Red Hook.*

Satori Pottery. Eclectic selection of ceramics, from cookware to sculpture.... *Tel 809/775–1700. American Yacht Harbor, Red Hook.*

Scandinavian Center. Georg Jensen watches and silver, Dansk cutlery, Royal Copenhagen porcelain, Orrefors crystal, and that marvelous Kosta Boda glass almost too pretty to use.... *Tel 809/776–5030. Havensight Mall, Bldg. III, Charlotte Amalie.*

Seoul Trade. Eelskin wallets, purses, belts, and luggage are the draw here; eel is surprisingly durable and wears to a sensual softness with use.... *Tel 809/777–8900. 33 Raadets Gade, Charlotte Amalie.*

Shanghai Linen. Fine shop sells linens from around the world, including Belgian and Irish lace tablecloths, napkins, and doilies.... *Tel 809/776–2828. 30 Main St., Charlotte Amalie.*

Shanghai Silk and Handicrafts. Sister shop to Shanghai Linen (above). Just don't come here for dresses (all right, you can buy a kimono).... *Tel 809/776–8118. Royal Dane Mall, Charlotte Amalie.*

Shipwrecks. Head here if you like your shopping ship-shape and want your living room to resemble a British pub. Most of the items on display were salvaged from wrecks; some of them still look it.... *Tel 809/774–2074. Royal Dane Mall, Charlotte Amalie.*

Touba Homeland. If it's reggae and Rasta, you'll find it here, including those wildly colored hats. Sorry, no ganja.... *No telephone. International Plaza, Charlotte Amalie.*

Traveler's Haven. From cheap fanny packs to Fendi, this store sells leather travel accessories in all shapes, sizes, and prices.... *Tel 809/775–1798. Havensight Mall, Charlotte Amalie.*

Tropicana Perfume Shoppes. The stench of perfume here is almost unbearable. Arguably the widest selection of fragrances in the U.S.V.I., if not the Caribbean, and the staff squirts free samples at everyone within spitting distance.... *Tel 809/774–0010, 2 Main St.; tel 809/774–1834, 14 Main St.; Charlotte Amalie.*

Woolworth's. The place to buy liquor, especially in bulk.... *Tel 809/774–3330. Lockhart Gardens (one block up from Havensight Mall), Charlotte Amallie.*

Zora's. If you forgot your moccasins or thongs, stop by this St. Thomas institution where sandals are made to order.... *Tel 809/774–2559. Norre Gade across from Roosevelt Park, Charlotte Amalie.*

St. Croix

American West India Trading Company. You can find locally made jewelry, pottery, prints, masks, hand-carved salad bowls, and (in the "Tonsil Torture Zone") hot sauces from around the Caribbean.... *Tel 809/773–7325. 1 Strand St., Christiansted.*

Caribbean Clothing Company. Loose-fitting, comfortable (mostly American) designer casual clothes at designer prices.... *Tel 809/773–5012. 55 Company St., Christiansted.*

Colombian Emeralds. All that glitters is not just emeralds at this monstrous Caribbean jeweler.... *Tel 809/773–1928 or 809/773–9189. 43 Queen Cross St., Christiansted.*

Crucian Gold. Brian Bishop creates refined, elegant designs in gold at his small shop, including Cruzan sugar-mill pins, steel-drum pins, and cannon pendants (complete with onyx cannonballs).... *Tel 809/773–5241. 57A Company St., Christiansted.*

Estate Mt. Washington Antiques. Remarkable store specializes in authentic colonial Caribbean furnishings and bric-a-brac. Open only on Sundays—call ahead, since owners Nancy and Tony Ayer are often out of town. After browsing, you can stroll through the grounds, where the Ayers are gradually restoring the ruins of an 18th-century sugar plantation.... *Tel 809/772–1026. 2 Estate Mt. Washington.*

Estate Whim Plantation Museum. The museum's gift shop carries little souvenirs and is an excellent source for books on local culture. Carries superlative Baker reproductions of Duncan Phyfes and similar furniture of the past, and David Dennis' remarkable (and expensive) re-creations of classic colonial mahogany furnishings.... *Tel 809/772–0598.*

Centerline Rd. near Frederiksted and Airport. David Dennis: tel 809/772–1697.

Folk Art Traders. Perhaps the most distinctive store in the U.S.V.I., with both original tribal artworks and dazzling reinterpretations of ancient traditions by contemporary artisans... *Tel 809/773–1900. 1B Queen Cross St. at Strand St., Christiansted.*

Frederiksted Gallery. Linda Colon is a patron of Cruzan arts, and her expansive sunny new space displays their works to great advantage. Linda can also arrange tours of the artists' ateliers.... *Tel 809/772–1611. 12 King St., Frederiksted.*

From the Gecko. "From the Chameleon" might be more appropriate, given the jungle of extravagantly hued hand-painted silk scarves, sarongs, hammocks, and straw hats hanging on the walls and racks.... *Tel 809/778–9433. 1233 Queen Cross St., Christiansted.*

Gilliam-King Gallery. King's watercolors are pretty but ordinary; Trudi Gilliam's copper, brass, and steel sculptures, imaginatively incorporating local woods like mahogany and saman, are stunning.... *Tel 809/773–9377. 2111 Company St., Christiansted.*

Gold Coast. Fun, practical beachwear, from bikinis and Speedos to cover-ups (the kind of nifty T-shirts that will end up as your favorite grungewear).... *Tel 809/773–2006. 2220 Queen Cross St., Christiansted.*

Gone Tropic. The goods here all hail from equatorial countries, hence the name. It's very New Age, with overpowering incense, but you'll find some superb buys here, especially if you're looking for fabulously ornate or theatrical touches for your home.... *Tel 809/773–4696. 55 Company St., Christiansted.*

Grateful Bones. Both an atelier and a massage parlor—Barbara (Babs) Keller offers Shiatsu foot massage and striking hand-painted vests, jackets, boxes, and Christmas ornaments. Odd hours, so call ahead.... *Tel 809/772–1480. Limetree Court off King St., Frederiksted.*

Green Papaya. A jumble of stuff that should appeal to "specialty" collectors, from hand-painted bamboo boxes to whimsically elaborate teapots to gigantic stone toads.... *Tel 809/773–8848. Caravelk Circade, 15 Strand St., Christiansted.*

Island Glass Treasures. Treasure might be overstating it, but Larry Coxe creates some attractive, free-flowing sea creatures. David Burnette also sells his intricate mahogany and saman carvings.... *Tel 809/778–2485. Palms Arcade, Christiansted.*

Island Rhythms. Parrot Fish's St. Croix branch has a smaller selection, but you can find leading artists in every Caribbean tradition, from soca to calypso to reggae to zouk to the beguine.... *Tel 809/773–3006. 48 King Cross St., Christiansted.*

Jan R. Mitchell Studio and Gallery. Delicate glass creations, ranging from abstract sculpture to Christmas ornaments, and unusual bas-relief bronze hangings.... *Tel 809/773–2676. 1102 Strand St., Pan Am Pavilion, Christiansted.*

Java Wraps. Owner Twila Wilson is one of the Caribbean's most stylish entrepreneurs, and her original store is a triumph of good taste. She's become so successful, she employs an entire Javanese town to create her wares.... *Tel 809/773–3770. Pan Am Pavilion, 42–43 Strand St., Christiansted.*

Java Wraps Home Store. Indonesian fabrics and textiles, especially Ikat, make amazing clothes, hangings, slipcovers, upholstery, bed linens, even drapes; owner Twila Wilson is a former interior designer, so she knows her stuff.... *Tel 809/773–7529. 51 ABC Company St., Christiansted.*

Jeltrups' Books. Janis James' wonderful jumble of new and used books is a delight to browse. Come here for the occasional poetry and book reading, as well as for long out-of-print titles on the Caribbean.... *Tel 809/773–1018. 2132 Company St., Christiansted.*

Karavan. Louise Tice's fun, funky store is a shrine to the kid in us all, with kicky clothes, porcelain dolls, Christmas villages and crèches, and Enesco's "Small World of Music" sculpture collection, where adorable mice might run rampant over an old-fashioned English telephone box or ride on a ferris wheel.... *Tel 809/773–9999. Gallows Bay.*

Kicks. You'd swear you're sauntering into a saddlery when that tanned scent smacks you in the face, but the belts, bags, wallets, and vests here are definitely upscale.... *Tel 809/773–7801. 10 Company St., Christiansted.*

Le Shoppe. Deliriously tacky. Fake African art labeled "We be jammin", mini airline bottles of Cruzan rum topped with plastic nipples ("the St. Croix hangover cure"), and the usual assortment of T-shirts and mugs.... *No telephone. 2106 Company St., Christiansted.*

Leather or Not. Lisa Hutchinson handcrafts a wonderful selection of sandals, from simple to extravagant.... *Tel 809/773–3898. 102 Strand St., Christiansted.*

The Little Mermaid. Here's where Republican ladies of leisure head when they've forgotten their favorite sundress, bonnet, or "casual chic" evening wear; others will find some surprisingly sexy beachwear.... *Tel 809/773–2100. Buccaneer Hotel, Shoys.*

Little Switzerland. Break the piggy bank here to buy anything from Lladro to Lalique.... *Tel 809/773–1976. Hamilton House, 56 King St., Christiansted.*

Nano's. The "souvenirs" at this el cheapo store truly define bad taste, but they're perfect for that joke gift: salt and pepper shakers and shot glasses emblazoned "St. Croix," even black Barbies with straw hats.... *Tel 809/773–8487. 1 King Cross St., Christiansted.*

Only In Paradise. Several well-lit rooms filled with trinkets that should appeal to some taste or other; few items are locally made, however.... *Tel 809/773–0331. 5 Company St., Christiansted.*

Quin House Galleries. Don't be deceived by the dusty, dimly lit clutter: this is a first-rate antique store, with especially tasteful antique glass, jewelry, and odds and ends like an elaborate Danish Colonial metal and wood rocking horse.... *Tel 809/773–0404. 51 ABC Company St., Christiansted.*

Rare Designs. They may not be rare, but the "voodoo" herbs and oils sold here set this shop apart from its brethren.... *No telephone. 19AB Strand St., Frederiksted.*

The Royal English Shop. While no match for the great St. Thomas china emporia, you could still register here and come away with booty (or at least Bernadaud).... *Tel 809/772–2040. 5 Strand St., Frederiksted.*

Royal Poinciana. A very pretty store, fragrant with all manner of West Indian scents, from frangipani perfume or soap to passion-fruit tea.... *Tel 809/773–9892. Caravelle Arcade, Christiansted.*

St. Croix LEAP. This workshop is worth a visit just to talk with the craftspeople keeping island traditions in woodwork alive.... *Tel 809/772–0421. Mahogany Rd. (Rte. 76).*

St. Croix Perfume Shoppes. A vast selection of classics, from Joy to Windsong (and for the guys, Obsession to Paco Rabanne), perfume the air in this chi-chi store; as a bonus, the air-conditioning seems to be the most powerful on island.... *Tel 809/773–7604. 53 King St., Christiansted.*

St. Croix Shoppes. One half of the shoppe is given over completely to Estée Lauder and Clinique products; the other offers just about any other cosmetic or perfume you'd want.... *Tel 809/773–2727. 53AB Company St., Christiansted.*

Small Wonder. Toys and clothes, nothing special (well, the island designs with fishies swimming everywhere are cute).... *Tel 809/773–5551. 4 Company St., Christiansted.*

Sonya. Owner Sonya Hough created St. Croix's trademark hook bracelet, which still sells briskly.... *Tel 809/778–8605. 1 Company St., Christiansted.*

Third World Traders. Two rooms, filled with incense and the sound of wind chimes, crammed with merchandise culled from the owners' world travels, from Dominican straw work to Kenyan soapstone sculpture.... *No telephone. Merwyn's Courtyard off Strand St., Frederiksted.*

Urban Threadz. This store sells both savvy street clothes (Urban Youth and No Fear) popular with the club set, and more upscale resortwear (Mossimo and Calvin Klein), as well as embroidered T-shirts in vivid Rasta colors and Guess? jeans.... *Tel 809/773–2883. 52C Company St., Christiansted.*

Violette Boutique. Lâncome to Lauder, you'll find everything that smells, feels, or looks good (including Fendi bags and Gucci watches).... *Tel 809/773–2148. 38 Strand St., Christiansted.*

Wayne James Boutique. Wayne James is bidding to become St. Croix's most famous son; his vivid clothes are as bold as Mizrahi, yet as classic as Chanel and Dior. He also makes delicious, equally sassy seasonings (try Carnivale) that pay loving tribute to his Cruzan roots.... *Tel 809/773–8585. 42 Queen Cross St., Christiansted. (Please note: he was moving at press time, so check first.)*

Woolworth's. On duty-free booze, Woolworth's offers even better buys than the airport shops. And you can buy thongs and sunscreen, too.... *Tel 809/778–5466. Sunny Isle Shopping Center, Centerline Rd.*

Yemaya. Exquisite, feathery hand-painted silk dresses and scarves that duplicate the soft colors of the Caribbean at dawn.... *Tel 809/773–1169. Waterfront behind St. Croix Library, Frederiksted.*

St. John

Bajo El Sol. Three artists-in-residence—Kat Sowa, Aimee Trayser, and Gail Vandy Bogurt—all hail from the States but have lived on St. John for several years; their creations range from ordinary islandscapes to extraordinary hand-painted boxes.... *Tel 809/693–7070. Mongoose Junction, Cruz Bay.*

Bamboula. Owner Jo Sterling culls eclectic, electric objects from her Third World travels, from fabulous mahogany or teak chess sets to splashy Indonesian sarongs.... *Tel 809/693–8699. Mongoose Junction, Cruz Bay.*

Best of Both Worlds. The first floor of this gallery showcases local artists and artisans whose work includes photos, ceramics, and fabric paintings. The most interesting items are upstairs: gorgeous hand-painted silk, linen, or cotton dress ensembles, ties, tablecloths, umbrellas, and throw pillows.... *Tel 809/693–7005. Mongoose Junction, Cruz Bay.*

Big Planet Adventure Outfitters. Hemingway himself might have enjoyed browsing in this store; so will environmentalists, as some of the casualwear is made from recycled materials. There are also some way-cool, way-garish ties.... *Tel 809/776–6638. Mongoose Junction, Cruz Bay.*

Bougainvillea. Bright, sunny, rustic home furnishings and tableware, as well as glitzy, ritzy fashions.... *Tel 809/776–6993. Mongoose Junction, Cruz Bay.*

Caravan. This tiny store is jammed with fascinating items from around the globe, some antique, others contemporary takes, still others quite fine reproductions. Looking for that perfect bamboo-and-fruitwood box or Hellenist-inspired bead necklace? You've come to the right bazaar.... *Tel 809/693–8550. Mongoose Junction, Cruz Bay.*

Coconut Coast Studio. Elaine Estern and Lucinda Shutt's studio is set in a picturesque West Indian cottage—just the sort of scene they paint. They are, respectively, the "appointed" artists-in-residence for the Hyatt Regency and Caneel Bay. Their works are pretty, but pretty pricy, too, though their note cards make a nice gift.... *Tel 809/776–6944. Frank Bay.*

Colombian Emeralds. Though smaller than its sister stores on the other islands, this branch still offers a surprising number of fine gems at prices under $100.... *Tel 809/776–6007. Mongoose Junction, Cruz Bay.*

Cruz Bay Emporium. A general store for souvenirs, from cheap pottery to sensuous bath salts, all made locally.... *Tel 809/693–8686. Wharfside Village, Cruz Bay.*

Donald Schnell Studio. This ceramicist is celebrated for his elaborate fountains, but you'll also find rough-textured coral dinnerware, wind chimes, and lovely hand-blown glass vases.... *Tel 809/776–6420. Mongoose Junction, Cruz Bay.*

Fabric Mill. An explosion of colors, from the Sloop Jones–designed rugs, sarongs, and napery to the bolts of fabric for creating your own. Kids adore the whimsical soft sculptures.... *Tel 809/776–6194. Mongoose Junction, Cruz Bay.*

Freebird Creations. Make your own bead necklaces with larimar and amber, or ask the owner to create a special charmed amulet. You can also buy droopy silver earrings, ornate heavy necklaces from India, and genuine tribal masks from Benin or the Ivory Coast.... *Tel 809/693–9625. Wharfside Village, Cruz Bay.*

Island Galleria. The salespeople here are far less pushy and obsequious than at other establishments of this type. They won't even hover protectively if you dare to handle the Orrefors and Lladro, and they answer all your questions patiently at the perfume/cosmetics counter.... *Tel 809/779–4644. Mongoose Junction, Cruz Bay.*

Island Hoppers. The place to go for island-themed items when you don't want to spend more than $20—bush teas and hot sauce to mocko jumbies made from coconut husks and intricately pleated basketry.... *Tel 809/693–7200. Wharfside Village, Cruz Bay.*

Isola. This neat little store carries a wide assortment of intriguing, original designs, from hand-painted sarongs and throw pillows to Javanese wedding cabinets.... *Tel 809/779–4212. Wharfside Village, Cruz Bay.*

MAPes MONDe. For replicas of old-fashioned maps and island genre scenes.... *Tel 809/693–8123. Mongoose Junction, Cruz Bay.*

Mermaid's Garden. Everything here relates to the sea in some way, from conch shells and pieces of coral to vases and jewelry cleverly fashioned from them.... *Tel 809/693–7150. Wharfside Village, Cruz Bay.*

National Park Visitors Center. Vast array of books pertaining to all aspects of U.S.V.I. life, especially the environment.... *Tel 809/776–6201. Waterfront, Cruz Bay.*

Pusser's of the West Indies. You may feel like singing "Yo ho ho and a bottle of rum" at this establishment for nautical nuts. The décor runs toward steering wheels, buoys, oars, and sailing prints; the merchandise is mostly tropicalwear for that swabbie look.... *Tel 809/693–8489. Wharfside Village, Cruz Bay.*

R&I Patton Goldsmiths. Rudy and Irene's graceful jewelry creations in hammered gold and filigreed silver include sea fan and starfish motifs.... *Tel 809/776–6548. Mongoose Junction, Cruz Bay.*

Silverlining. Nearly everything here is in remarkable taste—incredible carved Balinese chess sets, whimsically painted Christmas ornaments, and metal wall hangings from mermaids to moons.... *Tel 809/693–7766. Frangipani Square, Cruz Bay.*

Tropical Fantasies. Your first impression is of a floral fantasia, from real bouquets to hand-painted silk flowers. Then you see the iridescent sea creatures, from dolphins to tortoises, swimming everywhere, and crafted in a variety of media.... *Tel 809/693–7090. Wharfside Village, Cruz Bay.*

Tu Tu Tango. The only shopping experience of any value on St. John's eastern half, with charming native crafts.... *Tel 809/693–5900. 1 Estate Emmaus.*

night
enterta

life & entertainment

Most nightlife in the U.S.V.I. is of the rum-soaked variety, usually conducted to the lethargic strains of a steel band tapping out "Sunny" or "La Bamba." If you're looking for sin, sex, and squalor as the antidote to civilization, you'd best go elsewhere. Of course, every hangout has its share of middle-aged men on the prowl; watching these barflies may well be the most entertaining show in town. Still, you'll find more variety than on most islands. Every major resort holds theme-buffet evenings throughout the week with flamboyant live entertainment; look in particular for West Indian nights. The hotels all employ the same rotating troupes of fire-eaters, jugglers, broken-bottle and limbo dancers, and mocko jumbies (extravagantly costumed spirits teetering on stilts). It's surprisingly fun—the first time. Consult local papers for listings or ask at your hotel's front desk. Many restaurants also have live music of some sort—from acoustic to zydeco—especially on weekends, usually without a cover charge. The music of the islands—reggae, calypso, and soca—is, predictably, the most popular, but jazz combos, string quartets, and even square-dance bands all take turns on the Virgin Islands' stages. Live theater, cabaret revues, and standup comedy, however, are pretty scarce, unless you count the turistas baking on the beaches.

Sources
The best source for information on the latest events is *The Quittin' Time Guide*, put out every weekend by the *Virgin Islands Business Journal* and available free at many hotels, restaurants, and shops. There's no need to purchase tickets in advance, except for touring acts at the Reichhold Center for the Arts on St. Thomas or St. Croix's Island Center for the Performing Arts; even these don't need to be bought more than a week ahead.

Liquor Laws and Drinking Hours
Drinking rules and regulations conform to U.S. standards: Twenty-one is the legal age and the laws against drunk driving have become progressively more stringent (though you'll almost never see a cop on the road late at night). Bars close at 2am. Officially, that is.

The Lowdown

Best happy-hour munchies... Happy hours are usually from 4 to 8, just as they are stateside, but you never know where you'll find a 2-for-1 margarita promotion. On St. Thomas, **Cafesito** discounts many of its already inexpensive, tasty tapas to half-price during its happy hour. On St. Croix, **Luncheria** attracts a scruffy bunch who sip their $1 draft beers and heap plates with the free eats ("free" being the good part—Taco Bell couldn't give this stuff away). On St. John, **Woody's Seafood Saloon** sells more $1 draft beer than you can shake a keg at to help wash down their sometimes-good deep-fried denizens of the deep.

Liveliest happy hours...

On St. Thomas, **Iggie's** is where the all-inclusive crowd hangs out; since drinks are free, these folks can go from live wire to dead drunk in no time flat. The **Bar at Paradise Point** practically has a monopoly on great sunsets and equally explosive drinks. **Frenchman's Reef Pool Bar** is a sensational place to watch the cruise ships glide out to sea. They come so close to the hotel that a Fellini-meets-Woody-Allen scene ensues: cruise passengers take photos of hotel guests snapping photos of them. **Shark Room** does the 2-for-1 drinks thing between 11pm and 1am; they know which side their hot rum is buttered on. **Luncheria** (St. Croix) and **Woody's Seafood Saloon** (St. John) pack the backpack crowd in for the cheap bar food and draft beer. **Don Carlos** (St.

Street talk pickup

The fine art of flirtation is just that in the U.S.V.I. Hardened urbanites might find it sexist (or something straight from a Ru Paul drag queen parody); down here, it's just pure sassy give-and-take, more sport than anything else. Here's a sample of what you might hear on any street corner (with translation).... Two guys are hanging out; a comely maiden sashays by.

Guy 1 (to friend): Hey mon, she be hepsie! (Trans: "look at that chest!")

Guy 2: Yeah, mon, and look at dat maction! (Trans: And look at her swing those hips.)

Guy 1 (to girl): You work that, girl! (Trans: You are one fine looking woman.)

Girl: Yaya, I come work for you anytime! (Trans: Get lost, schmuck!)

Guy 1: Oh you be workin' overtime, mama! (Trans: I can go all night.)

Girl: Oh yeah? And you be payin' me double for my trouble? (Trans: Like you would even buy me dinner!)

Guy 1: Baby, we be workin' it off somehow. (Trans: I got everything you need and more.)

(continued on p. 183)

John) occasionally offers nibbles (taquitos, empanadillas, etc.) at prices lower than those on their regular menu, and strolling mariachis or steel bands to make happy hours as festive as the decor.

Most outrageous bars... Believe it or not, St. Croix's **The Emergency Room** was founded before "ER" became a runaway hit. The bartenders wear surgical masks, gurneys serve as rolling trays, and certain libations are served from IV bags. Cruz Bay's **Bad Art Bar** is a delirious paean to retro-kitsch: It looks as though a child in need of therapy had run amok with psychedelic Playskool fingerpaints. Add black-velvet Elvis paintings, Bugs Bunny pillows, and Rastas sleeping on the banquettes, and you get the idea....

Coziest bars... Not surprisingly, St. Thomas's three wine bars are all perfect for that quiet, intimate tête-à-tête: **Epernay**, all spot lighting and black lacquer; **A Room with a View** (see Dining), with its glorious floor-to-ceiling windows affording sweeping harbor views; and dimly lit, cozy **Randy's Wine Bar and Bistro**. **Hotel 1829** has a delightful little bar, perfect for after-dinner cognac and cigars. The owner, a former backgammon champion, has set up several exquisite old tables. **Ocean Club** re-creates an art-deco ocean liner, all the way down to the portholes and murals of cavorting swells circa the 1920s. **Calico Jack's Courtyard Inne** is set in a welcoming courtyard, its brick walls and wood beams draped with pennants, local murals, and business cards from its international clientele posted on a map. St. Croix's **Bombay Club** bar, with its brick and weathered stone walls, is a preferred spot for power players; the delightful little bar at **Top Hat** is a fine place to nibble on Danish open-face sandwiches, sip a single malt, and schmooze with the tanked-but-not-tank-topped crowd. The handsome bar at **Asolare** occupies the stone and teak kitchen area of a former private home; choose your poison here from the best selection of single malts and brandies on St. John.

Where the locals go... It doesn't get more local on St. Thomas than **Tasha's Place**, tucked away in the Savan and frequented by Rastafarians. White faces will be greeted either humorously or belligerently, sometimes both. **Wet Willy's** is where the local expatriates of all ages hang out (and hang from the rafters) and fall off the high-back rattan chairs lining the Stygian bar. **Wreck Bar** (St. Croix) is that rare tourist trap that appeals to locals, too, with a goofy assortment of live rock and roll, crab races, and the occasional wet T-shirt contest. Despite its hokey nautically themed decor, **Aqualounge** sees mostly local traffic. **Lost Dog Pub** defines neighborhood hangout, with darts, pool, and a great jukebox. **Cap's Place** is an open-air stand opposite the Cruz Bay ferry dock where locals (the ones that resemble refugees from a grunge band who took up residence last year) chow down on superior conch fritters and drink themselves into oblivion.

Where the labels go...

The bars at **Saychelles**, engulfed in a fog of Gauloises, and **Paradiso**, decked out in framed champagne posters from the '20s and '30s, are the two St. John spots where you'll find women thin enough to wear—and carry off—the latest fashions by Mizrahi or de la Renta. When they want to go slumming, the violently beautiful and merely wealthy head for **Copacabana** on St. Thomas, where leather-skinned divorcees fresh off the yachts mingle with up-and-coming, recently crowned drag princesses in a smaller, bargain-basement version of New York's Limelight or Palladium.

Street talk pickup (continued)

Girl: *I got de strumoo on you, boy. You be windward goby.* (Trans: I hear what the girls say about you, you've got swollen cojones.)

Guy 1: *You be barkin' up de right tree den, baby.* (A pun: to bark is an old expression that means applying herbal poultices to the affected area.)

Girl: *Yeah, you be bad sick!* (Trans: You've got the clap.)

Guy 1: *Dat's right. I be bad sick of love.* (No translation necessary.)

Girl: *You need pam pam, mon.* (Trans: I oughta spank you!)

Guy 2 (to guy 1): *She be alabaster baby, mon.* (Snooty bitch!)

Guy 1 (to Guy 2): *Yeah, she well lollis.* (Trans: Talks the talk but can she walk the walk?)

Girl: *You talk lala, bot' of youse.* (Trans: Cut the crap!)

Guy 1 (to girl): *Yah, it been fun. Well t'anks anyway, love, you make my day.* (Okay, I get the picture, I'll stop flirting, but it WAS fun talking to you, thanks.)

Girl: *Okay.* (You're welcome.)

For yachties... St. Thomas's **Latitude 18**, in typical yachtie digs with flags and Christmas lights, is so laid-back, it's nicknamed Lassitude 18; great live bands keep it hopping on weekends, with filling food and plentiful drink doing the trick the rest of the week. On St. John, **Skinny Legs** is renowned among the nautical set for its cheap burgers and brews and haute shanty decor.

For the brunch crowd... **Larry's Hideaway** on Hull Bay (St. Thomas) and **La Grange Beach Club** (St. Croix) throw beach bashes with sensational live bands every Sunday afternoon, which draw an eclectic mix of locals and tourists in loud colors. **Mt. Pellier Hut Domino Club**, also on St. Croix, offers super barbecue Sundays, when the DJ's lineup runs from line-dancing to limbo.

Dance fever... Most of the dancing spots in the U.S.V.I. can be found on St. Thomas. When it was known as Club Z, **Copacabana** was one of the most sophisticated discos in the Caribbean. The sound and lighting equipment still razzle-dazzle—if you never checked in at Studio 54 during its heyday. **The Old Mill** is the fashionable choice for Tuesday nights when the DJ spins house, ska, techno, and otherwise alternative music for a younger, hipper crowd. Think of **Paradise** in the Bolongo Bay Beach Club as the U.S.V.I. equivalent of those New York discos that attract the big-hair set from New Jersey. **Caribbean Disco Club** plays a mix of Latino pop, salsa, and merengue for a mostly Dominican and Puerto Rican crowd, as does **Chocolate Singles**. **The Bounce** attracts an odd mix; some nights an enthusiastic, gayer crowd, others a straight-and-narrow bunch. **Attitudes** (St. Croix) lives up to its name, given the voguing that goes on from people who only wish they were as rich and beautiful as they'd like to think they are. **2 Plus 2** is the glitziest disco on St. Croix, with the best acoustics and laser effects. **Midland Night Club** almost never sees tourists, but locals know it brings in some of the hottest bands from the Dominican Republic and Jamaica.

If you haven't gotten sick of karaoke... **Barnacle Bill's** (St. Thomas), a huge barn decked out with Christmas lights, is renowned for Live Mike Madness Mondays, when B-list celebrities have been known to let their hair down. **Iggie's**, a partly enclosed beach bar, is where everyone who ever wanted to do an Elvis imitation in front of a crowd of total strangers gets a chance—and, regrettably, takes it.

The big game... St. Thomas's big-screen crowd throngs to **Wet Willy's**, the **Greenhouse** (which blasts out both ESPN and ESPN 2), and the Marriott's **Wahoo Saloon** (which has the most screens per square inch in the U.S.V.I.). On St. Croix, you'll find people off the cruise ships and down-at-the-heels ex-pats drinking from 10am on at **Pleasure Spot** while ESPN blares in the background. The huge satellite dish atop the corrugated tin roof of St. John's **The Backyard** is like a beacon for "let's go to the videotape" types.

For drinks that come with those little umbrellas... **Mountain Top** (St. Thomas), an open-air terrace with fab views, claims to have invented the banana daiquiri; no one disputes the contention, least of all the hundreds who come here daily to toast the fabulous sunset. All the other sunset watchers are downing Painkillers (rum, rum, rum, Kahlua, maybe some ice), the drink of choice at the **Bar at Paradise Point**, another St. Thomas terrace overlooking various islands. **Fat Tuesday** has a double-digit list of margarita flavors, all in psychedelic colors whirring around in slush machines. **Coconuts** serves up shots, bushwhackers, and other modern libations in a lovely 18th-century town house. On St. John, **Morgan's Mango** has a drink list a page long. It's a toss-up as to which is prettiest and most colorful: the bartender's concoctions, the pastel gazebos, or the clientele. And for those who can't get by without a piña colada fix, **Pusser's** whips up some potent ones.

Best for one-night stands... If you're looking for a quickie pick up rather than a quick pick-me-up, try **The Greenhouse**, **Wet Willy's**, either location of **Tickles Dockside Pub**, and that old die-hard standby, the **Hard Rock Cafe**, all on St. Thomas.

Best for one-night bands... St. Thomas's **Barnacle Bill's** and the **Shark Room** bring in sometimes phenomenal international acts, mostly jazz, blues, and acoustic rock. The food is strictly burger city at both, but the crowds are an intriguing mix of yachties, tourists, locals, and celebs. A calypso singer wanders **Eunice's Terrace**, strumming his guitar and extemporizing rhymes (sometimes amusing, sometimes annoying) about customers. St. Croix's **Pier 69**, **Footprints Lounge**, **Eeez's Specialty Cafe**, and **Stars in the Night**, and St. John's **Fred's** and **Etta's** always cook with top, up-and-coming local musicians, usually reggae, soca, and calypso types. **Mongoose Restaurant** (St. John) offers jazz, blues, and reggae on weekends. If you're looking for even more sedate music—the type sold on late-night TV—try **Mango Grove** and **Moonraker Lounge** on St. Croix.

Safe after-hours walks... Since most hotels are practically private compounds, especially on St. Thomas, moonlit strolls on the hotel beach are generally the safest. During the week, walking in downtown Charlotte Amalie after dark is not advised; the streets pulse with partiers on weekend nights, though, so proceed with caution as in any big city.

Best beach bars—nocturnal variety... St. Croix's **Sandbar** and **La Grange Beach Club** (both on beaches of the same name) are the best places to boogie barefoot in the sand and surf with crowds of locals and tourists of all ages.

Painting the town pink... For the most part, the Caribbean is woefully conservative. Even if gays and lesbians aren't in the closet, they usually don't stray far from their apartments, conducting their affairs behind closed and double-locked doors. Fortunately, the scene in the U.S.V.I. is relatively open and thriving. Charlotte Amalie is second only to San Juan in terms of nightlife, while the western end of St. Croix has quietly become a mecca for gay and lesbian couples. On St. Thomas, **Blackbeard's Castle** is where all the pretty young things (male) hang out, especially if they have money or pretensions. **Walter's Living Room** attracts an older, more heavily local crowd with its sedate atmosphere. **Copacabana** is where the younger gays vogue on weekends; many claim it's the best place to pick up drunk straight guys for a quickie. On St. Croix, Frederiksted's **On the**

Beach is the only official gay bar. It's actually a gay-owned and -operated resort and small patio restaurant. It's definitely *not* a pickup scene, as the clientele tends to run toward "married" couples, which is precisely what makes it so congenial. A group of local gay men has organized **Planet Q,** a discreet monthly get-together held at various restaurants, clubs, and private homes that attracts eligible locals.

The college scene... Fort Lauderdale and Palm Springs may get the MTV coverage, but St. Thomas also does a brisk trade in Jell-O shots during spring break. We probably shouldn't be telling you this, but many bars are lax when it comes to checking IDs (one bouncer shrugged it off by saying, "We water the drinks down anyway"). **Sib's Mountain Bar and Restaurant** seems to get a younger bunch every year; it's where buzzed buzz-cut dudes wonder aloud why there are no video games. **Hondo's Backyard** on St. Croix usually sees the underage crowd, too, especially upstairs, where there are occasional no-alcohol nights.

For twentysomethings... The **Hard Rock Cafe** in Charlotte Amalie is just like its brethren in New York, London, Toronto, L.A., etc., only with more frozen specialty drinks to go with the rock memorabilia, generic food, and aggressive merchandising. **Wet Willy's** gathers in a weird mix of young hotel workers from the States and older, indigent locals. On St. Croix, **Lizards**—"sleaze-free/drug-free" and decked out with balloons and a few rangy potted plants—is the place where local high schoolers mix with superannuated frat boys and the ponytailed bartenders all wear their baseball caps backward. **Cheeseburgers in Paradise** is a bright yellow strong-margarita-mixing, live-rock-blasting beacon in the middle of nowhere for everyone under 30, especially on weekends. On St. John, the **Bad Art Bar** is *the* hangout. Nothing needs to be nipped or tucked here, and yeah, a few people seem to be practicing pharmacology without a license once they leave the premises.

For thirtysomethings... **Iggie's** karaoke sessions are always fun, if you like broad New Yawk accents singing "Beat It" or "Hound Dog," replete with swiveling hips.

People who never outgrew frat parties are the specialty at **The Greenhouse**, which also does a brisk trade in families as well as fatigued shoppers and tired pick-up lines. **Barnacle Bill's** appeals to the entire family, from kids to grandma and grandpa, but singing (if not swinging) singles also hang out here, especially on Mondays for Live Mike Madness. **Mackenzie's Harbour Pub and Tap Room** attracts a mix of yachties and tourists who have actually been known to sing "Fifteen men on a dead man's chest/Yo ho ho and a bottle of rum" here; otherwise a soft-rock guitarist holds sway. (All on St. Thomas.)

For fortysomethings... Jazz combos make **The Atrium at Windward Passage** an antidote to the shopping hordes in downtown Charlotte Amalie. **Duggan's Reef** (St. Croix) attracts a casual but coiffed crowd to its bar overlooking the beach. There's a congenial mix of twenty-, thirty-, and fortysomethings along with a few willing candidates for eye tucks and liposuction.

For fiftysomethings... Christiansted's tropical **Club Comanche** and Charlotte Amalie's sleekly chic **Blackbeard's Castle** attract the second-honeymoon crowd with romantic dining, sea breezes, and Cole Porter on the piano.

For a little bit o' sleaze... The area of Christiansted above Queen Cross Street (see Diversions) has become a red-light district, where illegal Dominican immigrants of both sexes are for hire. The men are classic rough trade; don't say we didn't warn you. As for the ladies, who hang about in the doorways of depressing, fluorescent-lit bars whose names change every few months, their décolletage is so low it leaves little to the imagination. Whether you think prostitution should be legalized or not, this is one of the saddest scenes in the Caribbean, reminiscent of Times Square pre-Disney, without the live sex shows and XXX movies. An all-too-typical dialogue might unfold as follows (as it did to this writer): "Pssst." "Yes?" "Hey mister, whatchou doin'?" "Just walking around." (Pouting): "You don' wanna make love?" "Oh, no thank you." (Pointing into a shadowy doorway): "My mother? My sister?" We kid you not.

Footprints Lounge (St. Croix) hosts occasional Chippendale's Ladies Night Out evenings, where the men strip farther down than any women do on island. Charlotte Amalie's **Positive Action** is just about the only place to get some (female) striptease action. It is, predictably, a big sailors' hangout, but plenty of local guys too wave their money in the girls'… faces.

On the kinky side… The folks behind St. Croix's **Planet Q** ocasionally throw impromptu drag evenings, and William "Champagne" Chandler, a perennial "King of Carnival" winner, organizes an island-wide drag beauty contest usually held in mid-September at the **Reichhold Center for the Arts** on St. Thomas. But generally, if you're into sexual acts that can be described by initials (i.e., S/M, B&D, WS), you'll be sorely disappointed.

All that jazz… On St. Thomas, the water views and cool ambient music almost make diners forget the hokey seafood-themed decor of **Agavé Terrace**. In high season, **Barnacle Bill's** and the **Shark Room** corral many respectable international acts. **The Atrium at Windward Passage** presents the best in local talent, usually in combos with sax, drums, piano, and bass. The smoky strains of jazz liven up St. Croix's hip bistro **Blue Moon** on weekends, and the staffers at the beachfront **Serendipity Inn** stage some fine cabaret acts on Saturday evenings. The old stone courtyard at **Indies** jives with jazz on Wednesdays and Fridays.

Tickling the ivories… Piano bars are a dime a dozen in the Virgin Islands, where they usually pass as refined background for overpriced, overrated dining. There are four major exceptions to the rule on St. Thomas, where the ambience is truly elegant and the food pricy but worth it. The pianists at **Blackbeard's Castle** and **Old Stone Farm House** know all the Broadway standards, as do their habitués, who are mostly aging, would-be chorus boys. **Palm Terrace** and **Tavern on the Beach** offer a similar musical repertoire, but with a staider, straighter clientele more likely to forget the lyrics to "Memory." On St. Croix, the seedily genteel **Club Comanche** seems ready to welcome the gang from *Casablanca*. Terra-cotta floors, paneled wood roof, sailing prints, and a view of the marina make **The Galleon** a popular piano bar, where locals launch into show tunes once they've put away a few.

Classical sounds... **Tillett Gardens** sponsors a Classics in the Garden series that attracts all the movers and shakers on St. Thomas—often uncomfortably dressed in black tie, fidgeting with their collars and trying to talk shop while their wives shush them up. The courtyard is a delightful setting for the acts, usually up-and-coming stateside string quartets or chamber orchestras. Even more unusual is St. Croix's **Estate Whim Plantation Museum** concert series, held by candlelight in the charming 18th-century great house. The audience—again mostly locals—tends to dress more casually, but the musicians (often the same folks you heard the other night at Tillett) still wear evening clothes, keeping up the elegant tone of the proceedings.

The play's the thing... Broadway or the West End it ain't, mon. Live theater is restricted mostly to community players doing cabaret revues or *Nunsense*, which describes the fare at the surprisingly decent **Pistarckle Theater** (St. Thomas). There are few venues for local writers, but St. John's **Purple Door** holds an eclectic range of events from poetry readings to local plays—most of them speaking to the African-American experience—on a postage-stamp-sized stage. **Seabreeze Cafe** specializes in evenings that are charitably described as performance art. Often they're neither artistic nor well-performed, but they're always enthusiastic.

Concerts and dance performances... The gleaming, contemporary **Reichhold Center for the Arts** on St. Thomas and the **Island Center for the Performing Arts** on St. Croix are the venues for most major touring acts, from symphony orchestras to dance companies. Every Monday **Jackie's Courtyard** hosts the St. Croix Heritage Dancers, who perform quadrilles in traditional dress (including elaborate turbans and bandannas), then invite the audience up for an impromptu lesson.

The sporting life... Cricket, believe it or not, is the name of the game on the U.S.V.I. It's wildly popular throughout the West Indies; cabbies usually have the latest West Indian test matches on their radios. There's no professional team or venue here, but spirited pick-up games crop up on university playing fields, in high school yards, even on the beach. The Sport of Kings has its moment in the sweltering sun at **Clinton Phipps Racetrack**. For other sports details, see Diversions.

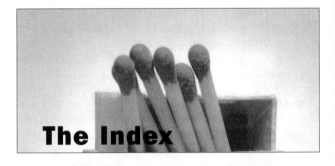

The Index

St. Thomas

Agavé Terrace. Hot jazz or steel bands, warm ambience, and cool sea breezes make this seafood institution with smashing water views a perennial choice for romantics, mostly over 35.... *Tel 809/775–4142. 4 Smith Bay. Live music nightly.*

The Atrium at Windward Passage. This is a cool, classy oasis in an otherwise pedestrian hotel, where jazz musicians often gig during happy hour.... *Tel 809/774–5200. Veterans Dr., Charlotte Amalie. Live music Wed–Sun.*

Bar at Paradise Point. A one-man steel band serenades sunset watchers who feel no pain after their second Painkiller (the house specialty).... *Tel 809/777–4540. Paradise Point. Live music nightly.*

Barnacle Bill's. Low- to medium-watt celebrities like Spyro Gyra and Dave Mason have performed at this popular barn, whose owners help organize the local jazz festivals. Live Mike

Madness Mondays pack them in for karaoke.... *Tel 809/ 744–7444. 16 Sub Base, Charlotte Amalie. Cover varies according to acts.*

Blackbeard's Castle. This restaurant/piano bar appeals to a quietly, elegantly gay crowd and older straight couples who want to appear worldly. Top jazz groups also perform in high season.... *Tel 809/776–1234. Blackbeard's Hill, Charlotte Amalie.*

The Bounce. The interior is far more restrained than the brilliant aqua facade of this downtown hotspot, where a very mixed clientele grooves to a great mix of reggae to techno from the DJ. It's discreetly gay after 1am, when no one really cares anymore.... *Tel 809/777–9237. 2A Commandant Gade. Thur–Sat. Cover $5.*

Cafesito. Tapas are an inspired idea in the tropics; the tidbits here are both tasty and inexpensive. The live music is usually Latino-themed, from torchy flamenco to sizzling samba combos.... *Tel 809/774–9574. 21 Dronnigens Gade, Charlotte Amalie. Live music several nights a week, no cover.*

Calico Jack's Courtyard Inne. This charming courtyard pub is named for the infamous Jack Rackham, a vain 18th-century dandy known as the Beau Brummel of Pirates.... *Tel 809/774–7555. Garden St., Charlotte Amalie. Live music weekends.*

Caribbean Disco Club. Dominican and Puerto Rican immigrants party down at this loud, brightly lit nightspot that specializes in merengue and salsa.... *No telephone. Sub Base. Weekends only. Cover $5.*

Chocolate Singles. It's actually more Latino at this small, dark, very local nightspot, with music to match.... *Tel 809/ 777–3782. Rte. 38 W. Cover varies. Wed–Sun.*

Clinton Phipps Racetrack. Like a Damon Runyon tale transported to the Caribbean. It's almost more fun eavesdropping and people-watching here than betting on the horses (hardly Derby-caliber).... *Tel 809/775–4555. Nadir, off Rte 30.*

Coconuts. The brick- and stone-work and wood beams of this beautiful 18th-century building contrast incongruously with the touristy crowd who do beers and shots and listen to endless strains of "Margaritaville" and "Lay Down Sally".... *Tel 809/774–0099. Back St.*

Copacabana. This throwback to the *Saturday Night Fever* days of mirror balls and pulsating colored lights attracts a mix of locals, gawking tourists, and very pretty people of all sexual persuasions.... *Tel 809/776–4655. 8353 Estate Contant. Cover $5.*

Epernay. Sleek black tables, sexy spot lighting, and a fabulous list of champagnes entice equally sleek, sexy, fabulous locals and yachties hoping to negotiate affairs of business or the heart.... *Tel 809/774–5348. 24A Honduras, Frenchtown.*

Eunice's Terrace. Arnold Caines serenades diners with Calypso ditties at this superlative West Indian eatery. Steel bands also entertain several nights weekly.... *Tel 809/774–4262. Rte. 38, Smith Bay.*

Fat Tuesday. Over 25 flavors of frozen daiquiris are served here to tourists decked out in the same tropical colors. The interior looks like a psychedelic deco diner, with the likes of Banana Banshee, 190 Octane, and Tropical Itch rotating in slush machines almost as big as laundromat dryers.... *Tel 809/777–8740. 27B Dronningens Gade, Charlotte Amalie.*

Frenchman's Reef Pool Bar. The big cruise ships seem to cruise right by the Marriott's pool; energetic steel bands keep things lively for the hotel crowd in between sightings.... *Tel 809/776–8500. Estate Bakkeroe, Flamboyant Point.*

Greenhouse. Canned and live rock music plays throughout the week at this classic meet market. Two-for-one happy hours (with free buffet) every evening but Sunday.... *Tel 809/774–7998. Veteran's Dr., Charlotte Amalie. Cover $5 when live bands perform.*

Hard Rock Cafe. It only rocks weekend nights, but the rest of the week it's a turista jungle out there at the bar.... *Tel 809/*

777–5555. *International Plaza, Charlotte Amalie. Live music weekends.*

Hotel 1829. The cool stone, brick, and wood bar is a delightful place to play backgammon while sipping a single malt and puffing on a stogie (there's a humidor in back).... *Tel 809/776–1829. Government Hill, Charlotte Amalie.*

Iggie's. This beach bar has long been a hot spot for Hawaiian-shirt types. Karaoke and insistent conviviality are the lure.... *Tel 809/775–1800. Bolongo Bay Beach Club, 50 Bolongo Estate.*

Larry's Hideaway. Hull Bay is the place to be Sunday afternoons, with locals and tourists getting down to a funky reggae/soca/calypso beat.... *Tel 809/777–1898. 10–1 Hull Bay.*

Latitude 18. This is a classic yachtie hangout, providing the necessities for the boating crowd: cheap beer and loud bands.... *Tel 809/775–9964. Vessup Point. Live music weekends.*

Mackenzie's Harbour Pub and Tap Room. The pubby ambience—brass lamps, hokey pirate's-head chandeliers, nautical prints, and pennants lure the kind of people who wear a captain's cap on their boat. Soft-rock guitarists play bland tunes several nights a week.... *Tel 809/779–2261. American Yacht Harbor, Red Hook. Music Wed–Sat.*

Mountain Top. All right, so it's a tourist trap, a zoo come sunset, and the daiquiris it claims to have invented aren't the best on island. But the views and drinks are equally mind-blowing.... *Tel 809/777–4707. Mountain Top, Rte. 38.*

Ocean Club. This faux–art deco club is decked out in Caribbean colors with murals depicting cavorting 1920s socialites. Check ahead, though, as the hotel was considering turning it into a meeting room after the hurricanes.... *Tel 809/777–7100. Wyndham Sugar Bay Plantation Resort, 6500 Estate Smith Bay.*

The Old Mill. Yes, an old sugar mill is the setting for good local food and color, especially Tuesday nights when it becomes the disco for those in the know, playing the latest techno/house/industrial/hip hop.... *Tel 809/776–3004. 193 Contant Hill.*

The Old Stone Farm House. The piano bar at this ultra-romantic restaurant with two-foot-thick stone walls and hardwood floors is a discreet gathering place for stylish gays.... *Tel 809/775–1377. Mahogany Run.*

Palm Terrace. Another piano bar, this one playing classical rather than pop music. It attracts corporate CEOs and their trophy wives, before or after one of the most expensive, pretentious—and superlative—dinners in the Caribbean.... *Tel 809/775–3333. Grand Palazzo Hotel, Great Bay Estate, Nazareth.*

Paradise. Another '70s disco revisited, replete with mirror balls and strobe lights.... *Tel 809/775–1800. Bolongo Bay Beach Club, 50 Bolongo Estate.*

Pistarckle Theater. This seasoned local troupe imports some of its talent from New York for revues and broad, slapsticky musical shows. They lost their handsome cabaret space in Frenchman's Reef in 1995; new quarters had not been found by press time, so call for information.... *Tel 809/777–1500. Box 1500, St. Thomas, VI 00801. Ticket prices vary.*

Positive Action. The closest thing the U.S.V.I. have to a strip club: the definition of topless usually includes pasties, but the girls always ask for a bottle of champagne.... *Tel 809/774–9422. 64 Kronprindsens Gade, Charlotte Amalie.*

Randy's Wine Bar and Bistro. This hip, dimly lit foodie hangout offers a phenomenal wine selection at unbeatable prices.... *Tel 809/777–3199. 4002 Raphune Hill, Al Cohen's Plaza, Charlotte Amalie.*

Reichhold Center for the Arts. State-of-the-art acoustics and lighting at this amphitheater provide the backdrop for name-brand international acts like Alvin Ailey and Nancy Wilson. The attractive office next door usually doubles as a gallery showcasing leading local artists.... *Tel 809/774–*

8475. *University of the Virgin Islands, Brewer's Bay. Tickets $15 and up.*

Shark Room. The way coolest hangout on St. Thomas, this fashionably black hole (yes, there are a few sharks mounted on the walls) offers everything from blues brothers to the occasional stand-up comedian, as well as an open mike on Mondays and Tuesdays.... *Tel 809/775–1919. American Yacht Harbor, Red Hook. Cover varies according to act; entrance free with dinner. Closed Sun.*

Sib's Mountain Bar and Restaurant. The bar section at Sib's attracts a younger-than-spring-break crowd year-round.... *Tel 809/774–8967. 33 Estate Elizabeth.*

Tasha's Place. Dreadlocks, colorful knit caps, and a good buzz are all that's needed for admission to this Rasta hangout.... *Tel 809/774–5826. 3A Gamble Gade, Charlotte Amalie.*

Tavern on the Beach. Crashing surf and pop standards on the piano form the background for civilized dining.... *Tel 809/776–8500. Marriott Morningstar Resort, Estate Bakkeroe, Flamboyant Point. Closed Sun, Mon.*

Tickles Dockside Pub. These two meet markets are always jammed with singles on the make. Each is dominated by a bar decked out in nautical paraphernalia like oars and old buoys.... *Tel 809/775–9425, American Yacht Harbor, Red Hook; tel 809/776–1595, Crown Bay Marina, Charlotte Amalie.*

Tillett Gardens. One of the most civilized evenings out in the U.S.V.I., for various al fresco concert series.... *Tel 809/775–1929. Rte. 38. Admission varies; call for schedule.*

Wahoo Saloon. Sports fanatics hang out at this large, open space hung with several giganto screens.... *Tel 809/776–8500. Marriott Frenchman's Reef, Estate Bakkeroe, Flamboyant Point.*

Walter's Living Room. This discreetly lit gay bar filled with potted palms (and potted customers) appeals mostly to locals, with more Americans in season.... *Tel 809/776–3880. 7B Crystal Gade, Charlotte Amalie.*

Wet Willy's. Where lots of young hotel staffers go to wet their whistles; earlier in the evening it draws the older local crowd. The vivid aqua-and-periwinkle exterior alone is worth a look.... *Tel 809/774–8769. 7 Bjerge Gade, Charlotte Amalie.*

St. Croix

Aqualounge. It could almost have been a set for the budget version of *Waterworld*: a scruffy wood shack draped with fishing nets, scuba gear, painted wooden fish, and steering wheels from yachts. Of course, it attracts the dive set in droves.... *Tel 809/773–0263. 58A King St., Christiansted.*

Attitudes. This new club serves up an odd West Indian/Italian hybrid cuisine, and a menu of jazz, rock, and reggae to a younger crowds of locals and tourists. When the folks strike an attitude, the attitude strikes back.... *Tel 809/773–3075. 54B Company St., Christiansted. Live music Wed–Sun. No cover with dinner, $5 otherwise.*

Blue Moon. This waterfront bistro is the hippest spot on St. Croix come weekends, when live jazz wafts through the dimly lit space.... *Tel 809/772–2222. 17 Strand St., Frederiksted. Weekends, except summer, when closed.*

Bombay Club. The lovely 18th-century bar, all weathered stone and exposed brick, sees a lot of quiet deal-making over gin and tonics.... *Tel 809/773–1838. 5A King St., Christiansted.*

Cheeseburgers in Paradise. Rock, reggae, burgers, tanned hardbody jock gods and goddesses, draft beer, and margaritas make this feel like a U.S.C. Phi Delt reunion.... *Tel 809/773–1119. 67 Estate Southgate. East of Christiansted. Live music weekends.*

Club Comanche. You'd almost expect the pianist to break into Noel Coward's "Mad About the Boy" at this gloriously '40s South Seas B-movie set, replete with an outrigger canoe and wicker peacock chairs. Forty- and fiftysomething patrons.... *Tel 809/773–2665. Strand St., Christiansted.*

Duggan's Reef. The "You're not getting older, you're getting better" wild bunch hangs out at this glorified sports bar set on a beautiful sliver of beach.... *Tel 809/773–9800. Rte 82, Reef Beach.*

Eeez's Specialty Cafe. This Caribbean coffee shop jumps with live reggae on weekends, attracting a mix of dreadlocked locals and twentysomethings.... *Tel 809/773–9765. 8AB Company St., Christiansted. Cover $3. Live music weekends.*

Emergency Room. The barkeeps call the bar the Operating Room (cordials drip from IVs); the dance floor sees more than its share of operators, too. You'll find everything from karaoke evenings to dancing lessons (line, ballroom, even the twist and frug).... *No telephone. Gallows Bay Marina.*

Estate Whim Plantation Museum. The strains of Chopin or Joplin waft through this elegant, candlelit space.... *Tel 809/772–0598. Centerline Rd. near Frederiksted and Airport. Admission varies; call for schedule.*

Footprints Lounge. Some of the dancers (even the male strippers) at this club are so bad, you wonder if management shouldn't paint footprints on the floor to help them out. The clientele is heavily local—island wives out on the town, as well as couples on non-ship nights... *Tel 809/773–4650. 18 La Grande Princesse, Christiansted.*

The Galleon. Intimate piano bar with lovely marina views; despite the pianist's show-tune repertoire, the clientele is very straight—and often off-key.... *Tel 809/773–9949. Green Cay Marina.*

Hondo's Backyard. There's an upstairs disco that attracts the teenybopper crowd, as well as a delightful courtyard that caters to a better-heeled post-college group.... *Tel 809/773–8187. 1114 King St., Christiansted.*

Indies. Live jazz or calypso acts play in this 250-year-old arched brick-and-stone courtyard crawling with bougainvillea, hibiscus, and oleander.... *Tel 809/692–9440. 55-56 Company St., Christiansted. Live music weekends.*

Island Center for the Performing Arts. The largest venue on St. Croix, this open-air amphitheater hosts top international performers in several media, music to dance, especially during high season.... *Tel 809/778–5272. Peppertree Hill. East of Fredericksted. Tickets $15 and up.*

Jackie's Courtyard. The St. Croix Heritage Dancers perform quadrilles in full period costume Monday evenings in the handsome 18th-century fieldstone courtyard of this fine local restaurant.... *Tel 809/773–1955. 46 King St., Christiansted. $25 show and dinner.*

La Grange Beach Club. Barefoot dancing in the sand to terrific live rock bands draws crowds Sundays. Sunsets find looped and loopy drinkers arguing over whether they saw the "green flash".... *Tel 809/772–5566. 72 Estate La Grange. Live music weekends.*

Lizard's. Everyone from local high schoolers to survivors of midlife crises ends up at Lizard's eventually for 2-for-1 happy hours, excellent black bean soup and conch chowder, and bluesy bands.... *Tel 809/773–4485. Strand St., Christiansted.*

Lost Dog Pub. This is a favorite spot for a casual drink, a game of darts, and occasional live rock and roll on Sunday nights. Decor runs toward extravagantly colored decals, lifeguard shirts, and surfboards.... *Tel 809/772–3526. King St., Frederiksted.*

Luncheria. Nachos and notches on the bedpost at this Mexican joint with el cheapo slurpy drinks and snacks (free during "Fiesta Time") in a historic courtyard.... *Tel 809/773–4247. Apothecary Hall Courtyard, Company St., Christiansted.*

Mango Grove. It's easy listening under the stars and the Cinzano umbrellas in this breezy courtyard.... *Tel 809/778–8103. 53 King St., Christiansted.*

Midland Night Club. This large pit with surprisingly good acoustics in the middle of the island can blast on weekends with throbbing merengue and reggae acts imported from the D.R. and Jamaica.... *Tel 809/778–0979. Kingshill.*

Moonraker Lounge. The acoustic guitar sets here seem frozen in the '70s, with favorites running toward Beatles covers and the like.... *Tel 809/773–1535. 43A Queen Cross St., Christiansted.*

Mt. Pellier Hut Domino Club. Piro, the one-man band, plays on Sunday, when there's a great BBQ. Miss Piggy, the beer-swilling sow, entertains daily for the price of a Sharp's or Kaliber.... *Tel 809/772–9914. 50 Montpellier.*

On the Beach Bar and Cafe. As the name suggests, it's just a few tables on the beach at a casual resort that caters to the settled "guppie dink" crowd.... *Tel 809/772–4242. On the Beach Resort, Frederiksted.*

Pier 69. Another watering hole famed for its rum concoctions and live steel bands in the courtyard. The intriguing bar is shaped like a boat, and there's a great mural of musicians behind the stage.... *Tel 809/774–0069. 69 King St., Frederiksted.*

Planet Q. This floating party is organized by St. Croix's leading gay citizens; it's usually structured around a theme (Disco Divas, Carnival, etc.).... *For info call Virgin Islands AIDS Community Research Organization, tel 809/692–9111.*

Pleasure Spot. Roast chicken on a spit, pool table, sports pennants, video games, beer ads, and sports on the tube hit the spot for locals and cruise shippers alike.... *Tel 809/772–2100. 66 King Street, Christiansted.*

Sandbar. Another laid-back beach disco, just a shack with an awning and a couple of picnic tables, known for its reggae evenings.... *No telephone. Coast Rd., just south of Frederiksted. Live music weekends.*

Serendipity Inn. Saturdays pack regulars in for great, reasonably priced lobster and manager Lynda Early's cabaret stylings. Sarah Vaughn she ain't, but.... *Tel 809/773–5762. Mill Harbour, Concordia.*

Stars in the Night. The island's top calypso band, Blinky and the Roadmasters, performs weekends in this large, spartan restaurant.... *Tel 809/772–9914. 14 Strand St., Frederiksted. Music weekends only.*

Top Hat. The cozy bar is decorated with stylish photos of regulars in top hats, captured by chef/owner Bent Rasmussen. The crowd runs to slightly overdressed fortysomethings.... *Tel 809/773-2346. 52 Company St., Christiansted.*

2 Plus 2 Disco. The DJ spins calypso, soca, diva disco, house, ska, and reggae, with live acts on weekend. Guests from the big hotels gravitate here.... *Tel 809/773-3710. 17 La Grande Princesse, Christiansted. Cover $5.*

Wreck Bar. Everything from live reggae to crab races (they actually play the "Star Spangled Banner") at this usually jam-packed hole-in-the-wall where crowds spill over into the courtyard.... *Tel 809/773-6092. 5AB Hospital St., Christiansted.*

St. John

Asolare. By far the most sophisticated restaurant in the U.S.V.I., with an intimate bar ideal for sipping single malt scotch and pretending to be oh so adult.... *Tel 809/779-4747. Cruz Bay.*

The Backyard. This rickety wooden structure with a corrugated tin roof is the sports bar of choice on St. John. (No, wait—it's the only one).... *No telephone. Frangipani Square, Cruz Bay.*

Bad Art Bar. The name is no exaggeration, with busts and velvet paintings of Elvis, 'toon pillows, tables painted in day-glo colors, and National Lampoon posters. Frozen drinks bear names like Busted Nut and Witches Tit; a stand-up comic leads limbo contests while pouring high-test drinks down competitors' gullets. It's the grooviest hangout in the U.S.V.I., maybe in the entire Caribbean.... *No telephone. 1F Cruz Bay, (above The Purple Door restaurant).*

Cap's Place. A dive, pure and simple, but with great conch fritters and potent drinks.... *No telephone. Waterfront. Cruz Bay.*

Don Carlos. This Mexican cantina rocks with great bands from mariachis to steel pan. Cheap Coronas and canapés help fuel the evening.... *Tel 809/776-6866. Estate Carolina, Coral Bay.*

Etta's. This overgrown courtyard eatery makes scrumptious, spicy island food. Happy hours are always jammed with locals, who jam to reggae and soca on weekends.... *Tel 809/776–6378. 34E Enighed, Cruz Bay. Music weekends only.*

Fred's. This hole-in-the-wall courtyard serves up some of the best steel bands on St. John.... *Tel 809/776–6363. Across from Lime Inn, in the heart of Cruz Bay. Music weekends only.*

Mongoose Restaurant. This open-air hangout in the Mongoose Junction mall corrals excellent jazz (Fridays), blues (Saturdays), and reggae (Sundays).... *Tel 809/693–8627. Mongoose Junction, Cruz Bay.*

Morgan's Mango. A riot in pastel colors, from the interlocking gazebos to the seemingly endless list of frozen drinks. Live soft classical guitar or a samba combo contribute refinement to the ambience.... *Tel 809/693–8141. Across from National Park dock, Cruz Bay.*

Paradiso. This gleaming space (with parquet floors, champagne posters, wood beams) is the haunt of choice for trendy Martha's Vineyard/Nantucket types.... *Tel 809/693–8899. Mongoose Junction, Cruz Bay.*

The Purple Door. The space is a virtual shrine to Africa, with batiks and gourd instruments providing the decor. Live acts run toward local plays and book readings with African-American themes.... *Tel 809/693–8666. 1F Cruz Bay.*

Pusser's. The specialty drinks at this faux-tropical pub, whose decorative theme is "The sun never sets on the British Empire," pack quite a wallop.... *Tel 809/693–8489. Wharfside Village, Cruz Bay.*

Saychelles. This is where they take the Eurotrash out in Cruz Bay, the inimitable scent of galettes, Gauloises, and hibiscus hanging in the sea breeze.... *Tel 809/693–7030. 4 Cruz Bay, Wharfside Village, Cruz Bay.*

Seabreeze Cafe. "Naked Poets Dressed in Khaki" and other (oxy)moronic performance artists overwhelm the tiny stage at this mellow spot where it seems Judy Collins is always playing on a tape loop.... *Tel 809/693–5824. 4F Little Plantation.*

Skinny Legs. Impoverished boat people (all right, middle-class yachties) hang out at this glorified tin-and-wood shack day and night.... *Tel 809/779–4982. Emmaus, Coral Bay.*

Woody's Seafood Saloon. It's "Happy hour, dude!" at this ultra-casual eatery with passable food; Courtney Love would be mobbed and Madonna ignored.... *Tel 809/779–4625. Across from Chase Manhattan Bank, Cruz Bay.*

hotlines & other basics

Airports... Cyril E. King Airport (tel 809/774–8100) on St. Thomas is one of the Caribbean's busiest. You know that this is no laid-back island backwater as soon as you hit the terminal: the walls are plastered with ads, especially for duty-free shops, while rotating racks brandish brochures, menus, and flyers offering discounts on anything and everything. On the other hand, the baggage handling is as slow as molasses and the cabbies don't circle like hawks as they do in town, but instead lounge outside chatting. St. Croix's **Alexander Hamilton Airport** (tel 809/778–1012) is quiet and unhurried by contrast.

American (tel 800/433–7300), **Continental** (tel 800/231–0856), **Delta** (tel 800/221–1212), and **USAir** (tel 800/428–4322) are the major domestic carriers offering direct flights into St. Thomas. Between St. Thomas and St. Croix, you can fly on **American Eagle** (tel 800/433–7300), **Sunaire Express** (tel 809/778–9300), and **Leeward Islands Air Transport** (tel 809/774–2313), or LIAT, nicknamed, "Leave Island Any Time" or "Luggage in Any Terminal" for its lackadaisical attitude. But the best way to fly between the two islands (especially if you're spending a few days on each) is via **Seabourne Seaplanes** (tel 809/

777–4502), a delightful 20-minute glide from Charlotte Amalie harbor to King's Wharf in Christiansted.

Buses... VITRAN (St. Thomas: tel 809/776–4844 or 809/774–5678 for schedule information; St. Croix tel 809/773–1290 office, 809/773–7746 for schedule information) buses slowly wend their way between Charlotte Amalie and Red Hook on St. Thomas and Christiansted and Frederiksted on St. Croix daily, from 5:30am to 9:30pm. The fare is $1, except for in-town trips on St. Thomas, which cost 75 cents. Vitran buses have all the charm of the New York City subway at rush hour: inadequate or nonexistent air-conditioning, jostling crowds toting the day's shopping, and capricious scheduling. If you have the time to spare, however, they *are* the cheapest way to see the countryside, and you could meet some intriguing locals.

Car rentals... The big national companies are all here: **Avis** (tel 800/331–1084, or 809/774–1468 on St. Thomas, 809/778–9355 on St. Croix, 809/776–6374 on St. John); **Budget** (tel 800/527–0700, 809/776—5774 on St. Thomas, 809/778–9636 on St. Croix); **Hertz** (tel 800/654–3131, or 809/774–1879 on St. Thomas, 809/778–1402 on St. Croix, 809/776–6412 on St. John); **National** (tel 809/776–3616 on St. Thomas); **Thrifty** (tel 809/775–7282 on St. Thomas, 809/773–7200 on St. Croix). The majors have both airport and town locations. Smaller local operations on **St. Thomas** include: **ABC Rentals** (tel 809/776–1222 or 800/524–2080); **Anchorage E-Z Car** (tel 809/775–6255); **Cowpet Car Rental** (tel 809/775–7376 or 800/524–2072); **Dependable** (tel 809/774–2253 or 800/522–3076); **Discount** (tel 809/776–4858); **Sea Breeze** (tel 809/774–7200); **Sun Island** (tel 809/774–3333). On **St. Croix**, try: **Atlas** (tel 809/773–2886); **Caribbean Jeep & Car** (tel 809/773–4399); or **Olympic** (tel 809/773–2208). On **St. John**, call **Best** (tel 809/693–8177); **Cool Breeze** (tel 809/776–6588); **O'Connor Jeep** (tel 809/776–6343); **St. John Car Rental** (tel 809/776–6103); or **Spencer's Jeep** (tel 809/776–6628). The various companies are comparable in rates and selection of vehicles, all with air-conditioning and radio; choices range from automatic to stick to four-wheel-drive (sorry, no convertibles). You must be 25 and be a creditable credit-card user.

Dentists... The **Virgin Islands Dental Association** (tel 809/775–9110) is a member of the American Dental Association and represents a large number of practitioners throughout St. Thomas and St. John, including various specialists. On St. Croix, visit the **Sunny Isle Medical Center** (tel 809/778–0069, Sunny Isle Shopping Center).

Doctors... Call **Doctors on Duty** (tel 809/776–7966, Vitraco Park) for referrals on St. Thomas. **St. John Community Health Clinic** (tel 809/776–6400, 3B Susannaberg, Cruz Bay) offers several specialists, as does the **St. Croix Hospital and Community Health Center** (tel 809/778–6311, 6 Diamond Bay, Christiansted, north of Sunny Isle Shopping Center, on Rte. 79). Call ahead regarding your stateside health insurance; some places will honor major companies.

Driving around... An American driver's license is valid in the U.S.V.I. for 90 days. The minimum age for drivers is 18. Driving is on the left side of the road, even though the steering wheel is on the left side of the car. Most of the locals screech around the hairpin turns, and goats, chickens, and cattle amble lazily about the more bucolic sections of St. John, making driving, um, picturesque.

Drugstores... On St. Thomas, try **Sunrise Pharmacy** (tel 809/775–6600, American Yacht Harbor, Red Hook; tel 809/774–5333, Wheatley Shopping Center). The **Drug Farm Pharmacy** main store (tel 809/776–7098, 2–4 Ninth St. Estate Thomas) is located across from the General Post Office. On St. Croix, the best choices are **People's Drug Store, Inc.** (tel 809/778–7355, 1–1A King St., Christiansted; tel 809/778–5537, Sunny Isle Shopping Center, Christiansted) or **D & D Apothecary Hall** (tel 809/772–1890, 50 Queen St., Frederiksted). On St. John, stop by the **St. John Drug Center** (tel 809/776–6353, Boulon Shopping Center, Cruz Bay). Most of these are open 8–8 (none 24 hours).

Emergencies... Dial **911** for police, fire department, and ambulance service. The emergency room of **St. Thomas Hospital** (tel 809/776–8311, Sugar Estate, Charlotte Amalie), is open 24 hours a day, as is the **St. Croix Hospital and Community Health Center** (tel 809/778–6311, 6 Diamond Bay, Christiansted, north of Sunny Isle Shopping Center, on Rte. 79). On St. John you can call the **St. John Community Health Clinic** (3B Susannaberg, Cruz Bay, tel 809/776–6400) or call an **emergency**

medical technician directly (tel 809/776–6222). **Bohlke International Airways** (tel 809/778–9177) operates the only air ambulance based in the U.S.V.I., with EMTs available around the clock.

In case of boating accidents, call the **U.S. Coast Guard** (tel 809/772–2943, or channel 16 by radio). For scuba diving mishaps, call the **Recompression Chamber** (tel 809/776–2686).

Ferries... Ferries run between Cruz Bay (St. John) and both Red Hook and Charlotte Amalie on St. Thomas; there are also departures for Tortola, Jost van Dyke, and Virgin Gorda in the B.V.I. from Charlotte Amalie. Call 809/776–6111 for schedule and fare information. The **Virgin Island Hydrofoil** (tel 809/776–7416) makes three daily trips between Charlotte Amalie and Christiansted for $32 one way or $60 round trip. The ride takes 75 minutes. A new catamaran, the plush **Fast Cat** (tel 809/778–1004), also makes three daily round trips between the two towns, for $25 each way. Fast indeed, she takes a mere 45 minutes.

Festivals and special events... The biggest deal in the islands is the **St. Thomas Carnival**, held every April just after Easter; among Caribbean carnivals, this is second only to Trinidad's for color and spectacle. Wild processions of *mocko jumbies* (20-foot-high spirits on stilts) and steel bands swarm through the streets of Charlotte Amalie during the 48 hours of nonstop carousing; clubs vie in heated competitions for best costumes and themes. The nude and drag scenes certainly rival the Big Easy's Mardi Gras (as do the opportunities to score). Just hang out anywhere in Charlotte Amalie; there are crowds wherever you go. The **St. John Carnival** (held the first week in July) and **St. Croix Christmas**, celebrating the traditional 12 days between Christmas Eve and January 6 (the Feast of the Three Kings) are also boisterous and flamboyant.

Guided tours... The **V.I. Taxi Association City-Island Tour** (tel 809/774–4550) is geared toward cruise-ship passengers, providing a whirlwind 3-hour tour of St. Thomas's photo ops, including Drake's Seat and Mountain Top. The **St. Croix Environmental Association** (tel 809/773–1989, Box 3839, Christiansted, St. Croix 00822) runs a variety of hikes concentrating on the island's natural history, from sampling bush teas in the rain forest to bird-watching on the desolate East End beaches. Sweeney Toussaint, raconteur extraordinaire, keeps up a running narrative of local lore, much of it unprintable, during his **St. Croix Safari Tours** (tel 809/773–6700, pickup at your hotel), expounding on history, botany, politics, and culture during a 5-hour excursion by safari-van. The **National Park Service** leads a variety of nature- and bird-watching hikes, as well as snorkeling expeditions. Their snorkeling trips are cheaper than commercial ones (no free drinks and boat ride thrown in), and certainly far more instructive (perhaps too much so for some). For more information contact the **St. John National Park Visitor Center** (tel 809/776–6201, wharfside, Cruz Bay).

Newspapers... The main paper is the *Virgin Island Daily News*, which trumpets having won a Pulitzer Prize, though it more often than not resembles the Podunk Press, especially with its salacious bits of gossip and wonderfully cranky letters to the editor. It's best for a quick scan of the day's major headlines, items of strictly island interest, and for keeping up with your local sports teams (don't expect box scores). The *St. Croix Avis* has a completely local bias, but is good for clipping coupons for shops and restaurants.

By far the most intriguing publication is a scurrilous little newsletter called *Island Melee*, published by Nom D. Plume and Shirley U. Jest. A front-page box warns you to expect "some of the truth" either "none of the time" or "once in a while." The *Melee* is a mélange of barbed political jabs, satire, gripe columns, Letterman-style top-five lists, "unclassifieds," and soap-opera parodies. A typical headline: "Motorist Uses Turn Signal, Confusion Breaks Out, Traffic Stalls." The advice in the delightfully misanthropic "Horrorscope" column runs toward "Keep St. Croix beautiful. Don't come out of your house this week," "When opportunity knocks, you'll be in the bathroom," and "This week your complexion will look like a pizza with toppings."

You'll find complete listings of current happenings in the *Virgin Island Daily News* weekend section, and in free tourist handouts such as *St. Thomas This Week*, *St. Croix This Week*, *Virgin Islands Playground*, *Quittin' Time*, and *What To Do St. Thomas/St. John*. Except for *Quittin' Time*, all of these freebies might as well be government (or chamber of commerce) mouthpieces.

Opening and closing times... Shops throughout the U.S.V.I. are open 9–5 Monday through Saturday. Havensight Mall shops (predictably adjacent to the cruise-ship dock) occasionally stay open until 9pm on those nights when several cruise ships linger late. Some shops worship the god Mammon on Sunday if a lot of cruise ships are in port.

Parking... There is free parking in the square by Fort Christiansvaern in Charlotte Amalie, and by the Visitors' Bureau in Christiansted. Otherwise, there are several parking lots, all cheap (no more than $2 per hour). Although the attendants look like they just flew in from Times Square, they're usually reliable.

Radio stations... Try **WIYC (104 FM)** and **WVGN (105 FM)** for the best mix of news, chat, and music, from soft pop to hard rock. You can hear weather reports daily at 7:30 and 8:30am on **99.5 FM**.

Restrooms... You won't find many public lavatories, except at the airports and a few major beaches. Restaurants and gas stations generally aren't finicky about the "for customers only" credo (unlike many of their urban stateside counterparts), but you should order a cup of coffee for form's sake. You can always duck into a hotel lobby bathroom or ask at the tourist offices (but be sure to pluck a brochure from the rack to be polite).

Smoking... Although there are no official smoking laws in the U.S.V.I., many restaurants have created "No Smoking" sections. The high percentage of European travelers (especially in recent years, thanks to the plummeting dollar) means a potent haze wafts through many of the more lah-di-dah restaurants and bars.

Taxes... Hotels add a 7.5 percent surcharge to bills, which may not be quoted in their rates; there is no departure tax at the airport. Miraculously, there's also no sales tax, so have a ball courtesy of the government.

Taxis... Taxis here are actually communal minivans, whose prices are fixed on all three islands, and usually based on at least two passengers. The rates are reasonable, though, and cabbies will usually take a single passenger at the same fare. But there is often a maddening wait while they gossip and try to load up their vans (especially at the airports), so you might be making several stops along the way to your destination. Fares are posted at the airports and hotels. On St. John, cabbies tear about in brightly painted, open-air safari vans that ply a regular route between the Hyatt Regency, Cruz Bay, Maho Bay, Cinnamon Bay, Trunk Bay, and Caneel Bay. Hailing a cab doesn't work. Period. There are taxi stands in every major town, and, of course, most hotels usually have a taxi or two lurking in the parking lot.

Telephones... The area code in the U.S. Virgin Islands is 809, which can be dialed direct from the U.S. mainland. **Sprint** and **MCI** calling cards can be used to access any number. Pay phones cost 25 cents for each five minutes. To make overseas calls on a public phone, try **East End Secretarial Services** (tel 809/775–5262, Red Hook Plaza, St. Thomas); the **Business Bureau** (tel 809/773–7601, 42–43 Strand St., Christiansted, St. Croix); **St. Croix Communications Centre** (tel 809/772–5800, 61 King St., Frederiksted, St. Croix); or **Connections** (tel 809/776–6922, Rte. 10 W. at Vesta Gade, Cruz Bay, St. John).

Tipping... The usual American tipping customs prevail. Fifteen percent is the norm in restaurants and taxis, though St. Thomas has its share of actor/model types spending a season in the sun who are accustomed to larger tips. Maitre d's and captains in the fancier non-hotel restaurants still linger at the end of the meal, hoping for a handout. Many hotels tack on a 10–15 percent service charge.

Travel documents... American and Canadian citizens must present proof of citizenship when they enter the U.S.V.I., whether by plane or by boat. A passport is best, but a birth certificate or voter-registration card with a valid driver's license or photo ID will do. Britons require a valid 10-year passport to enter the U.S.V.I. A visa is not necessary if you stay fewer than 90 days, have a return or onward ticket on a cruise ship or major airline (any airline that flies from the U.K. to the U.S.), and complete visa waiver I-94W, which is supplied either at the airport of departure or on the plane.

Visitor information... From the U.S., you can call the **U.S.V.I. Division of Tourism**'s toll-free number (800/USVI–INFO). The Division of Tourism has offices in St. Thomas (tel 809/774–8784, fax 809/774–4390, Box 6400, Charlotte Amalie 00804), St. Croix (tel 809/773–

0495, Box 4538, Christiansted 00822; tel 809/772–0357, Strand St., Frederiksted 00840, located on the pier), and on St. John (tel 809/776–6450, Box 200, Cruz Bay 00830). There are two **Visitor Centers** in Charlotte Amalie: one across from Emancipation Square and one at Havensight Mall. In St. Croix, go to the Old Scale House, across from Fort Christiansvaern at the waterfront in Christiansted. The **National Park Service** also has visitor centers at the ferry docks on St. Thomas (Red Hook) and St. John (Cruz Bay).

FROMMER'S COMPLETE TRAVEL GUIDES

(Comprehensive guides to sightseeing, dining and accommodations, with selections in all price ranges—from deluxe to budget)

Acapulco/Ixtapa/Taxco, 2nd Ed.	C157	Italy '96 (avail. 11/95)	C183
Alaska '94-'95	C131	Jamaica/Barbados, 2nd Ed.	C149
Arizona '95	C166	Japan '94-'95	C144
Australia '94-'95	C147	Maui, 1st Ed.	C153
Austria, 6th Ed.	C162	Nepal, 3rd Ed. (avail. 11/95)	C184
Bahamas '96 (avail. 8/95)	C172	New England '95	C165
Belgium/Holland/Luxembourg, 4th Ed.	C170	New Mexico, 3rd Ed.	C167
Bermuda '96 (avail. 8/95)	C174	New York State, 4th Ed.	C133
California '95	C164	Northwest, 5th Ed.	C140
Canada '94-'95	C145	Portugal '94-'95	C141
Caribbean '96 (avail. 9/95)	C173	Puerto Rico '95-'96	C151
Carolinas/Georgia, 2nd Ed.	C128	Puerto Vallarta/Manzanillo/Guadalajara, 2nd Ed.	C135
Colorado '96 (avail. 11/95)	C179	Scandinavia, 16th Ed.	C169
Costa Rica, 1st Ed.	C161	Scotland '94-'95	C146
Cruises '95-'96	C150	South Pacific '94-'95	C138
Delaware/Maryland '94-'95	C136	Spain, 16th Ed.	C163
England '96 (avail. 10/95)	C180	Switzerland, 7th Ed. (avail. 9/95)	C177
Florida '96 (avail. 9/95)	C181	Thailand, 2nd Ed.	C154
France '96 (avail. 11/95)	C182	U.S.A., 4th Ed.	C156
Germany '96 (avail. 9/95)	C176	Virgin Islands, 3rd Ed. (avail. 8/95)	C175
Honolulu/Waikiki/Oahu, 4th Ed. (avail. 10/95)	C178	Virginia '94-'95	C142
Ireland, 1st Ed.	C168	Yucatán '95-'96	C155

FROMMER'S $-A-DAY GUIDES

(Dream Vacations at Down-to-Earth Prices)

Australia on $45 '95-'96	D122	Ireland on $45 '94-'95	D118
Berlin from $50, 3rd Ed. (avail. 10/95)	D137	Israel on $45, 15th Ed.	D130
Caribbean from $60, 1st Ed. (avail. 9/95)	D133	London from $55 '96 (avail. 11/95)	D136
Costa Rica/Guatemala/Belize on $35, 3rd Ed.	D126	Madrid on $50 '94-'95	D119
Eastern Europe on $30, 5th Ed.	D129	Mexico from $35 '96 (avail. 10/95)	D135
England from $50 '96 (avail. 11/95)	D138	New York on $70 '94-'95	D121
Europe from $50 '96 (avail. 10/95)	D139	New Zealand from $45, 6th Ed.	D132
Greece from $45, 6th Ed.	D131	Paris on $45 '94-'95	D117
Hawaii from $60 '96 (avail. 9/95)	D134	South America on $40, 16th Ed.	D123
		Washington, D.C. on $50 '94-'95	D120

FROMMER'S COMPLETE CITY GUIDES

(Comprehensive guides to sightseeing, dining, and accommodations in all price ranges)

Amsterdam, 8th Ed.	S176	Miami '95-'96	S149
Athens, 10th Ed.	S174	Minneapolis/St. Paul, 4th Ed.	S159
Atlanta & the Summer Olympic Games '96 (avail. 11/95)	S181	Montréal/Québec City '95	S166
		Nashville/Memphis, 1st Ed.	S141
Atlantic City/Cape May, 5th Ed.	S130	New Orleans '96 (avail. 10/95)	S182
		New York City '96 (avail. 11/95)	S183
Bangkok, 2nd Ed.	S147	Paris '96 (avail. 9/95)	S180
Barcelona '93-'94	S115	Philadelphia, 8th Ed.	S167
Berlin, 3rd Ed.	S162	Prague, 1st Ed.	S143
Boston '95	S160	Rome, 10th Ed.	S168
Budapest, 1st Ed.	S139	St. Louis/Kansas City, 2nd Ed.	S127
Chicago '95	S169	San Antonio/Austin, 1st Ed.	S177
Denver/Boulder/ Colorado Springs, 3rd Ed.	S154	San Diego '95	S158
		San Francisco '96 (avail. 10/95)	S184
Disney World/Orlando '96 (avail. 9/95)	S178	Santa Fe/Taos/ Albuquerque '95	S172
Dublin, 2nd Ed.	S157	Seattle/Portland '94-'95	S137
Hong Kong '94-'95	S140	Sydney, 4th Ed.	S171
Las Vegas '95	S163	Tampa/St. Petersburg, 3rd Ed.	S146
London '96 (avail. 9/95)	S179	Tokyo '94-'95	S144
Los Angeles '95	S164	Toronto, 3rd Ed.	S173
Madrid/Costa del Sol, 2nd Ed.	S165	Vancouver/Victoria '94-'95	S142
Mexico City, 1st Ed.	S175	Washington, D.C. '95	S153

FROMMER'S FAMILY GUIDES

(Guides to family-friendly hotels, restaurants, activities, and attractions)

California with Kids	F105	San Francisco with Kids	F104
Los Angeles with Kids	F103	Washington, D.C. with Kids	F102
New York City with Kids	F101		

FROMMER'S WALKING TOURS

(Memorable strolls through colorful and historic neighborhoods, accompanied by detailed directions and maps)

Berlin	W100	San Francisco, 2nd Ed.	W115
Chicago	W107	Spain's Favorite Cities (avail. 9/95)	W116
England's Favorite Cities	W108		
London, 2nd Ed.	W111	Tokyo	W109
Montréal/Québec City	W106	Venice	W110
New York, 2nd Ed.	W113	Washington, D.C., 2nd Ed.	W114
Paris, 2nd Ed.	W112		

FROMMER'S AMERICA ON WHEELS

(Guides for travelers who are exploring the U.S.A. by car, featuring a brand-new rating system for accommodations and full-color road maps)

Arizona/New Mexico	A100	Florida	A102
California/Nevada	A101	Mid-Atlantic	A103

FROMMER'S SPECIAL-INTEREST TITLES

Arthur Frommer's Branson!	P107	Frommer's Where to Stay U.S.A., 11th Ed.	P102
Arthur Frommer's New World of Travel (avail. 11/95)	P112	National Park Guide, 29th Ed.	P106
Frommer's Caribbean Hideaways (avail. 9/95)	P110	USA Today Golf Tournament Guide	P113
Frommer's America's 100 Best-Loved State Parks	P109	USA Today Minor League Baseball Book	P111

FROMMER'S BEST BEACH VACATIONS

(The top places to sun, stroll, shop, stay, play, party, and swim—with each beach rated for beauty, swimming, sand, and amenities)

California (avail. 10/95)	G100	Hawaii (avail. 10/95)	G102
Florida (avail. 10/95)	G101		

FROMMER'S BED & BREAKFAST GUIDES

(Selective guides with four-color photos and full descriptions of the best inns in each region)

California	B100	Hawaii	B105
Caribbean	B101	Pacific Northwest	B106
East Coast	B102	Rockies	B107
Eastern United States	B103	Southwest	B108
Great American Cities	B104		

FROMMER'S IRREVERENT GUIDES

(Wickedly honest guides for sophisticated travelers and those who want to be)

Chicago (avail. 11/95)	I100	New Orleans (avail. 11/95)	I103
London (avail. 11/95)	I101	San Francisco (avail. 11/95)	I104
Manhattan (avail. 11/95)	I102	Virgin Islands (avail. 11/95)	I105

FROMMER'S DRIVING TOURS

(Four-color photos and detailed maps outlining spectacular scenic driving routes)

Australia	Y100	Italy	Y108
Austria	Y101	Mexico	Y109
Britain	Y102	Scandinavia	Y110
Canada	Y103	Scotland	Y111
Florida	Y104	Spain	Y112
France	Y105	Switzerland	Y113
Germany	Y106	U.S.A.	Y114
Ireland	Y107		

FROMMER'S BORN TO SHOP

(The ultimate travel guides for discriminating shoppers—from cut-rate to couture)

Hong Kong (avail. 11/95)	Z100	London (avail. 11/95)	Z101

irreverent notes